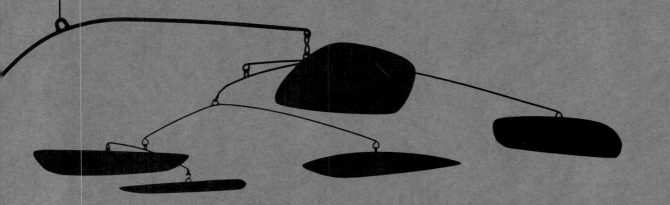

CALDER, *an Autobiography with Pictures*

London 1967

CALDER an Autobiography with Pictures

Allen Lane The Penguin Press

My thanks to Jean Davidson, my son-in-law
for his enduring patience in taking down these notes.

FOREWORD

Life is always increased when one is with the Calders. No matter where they go . . . with them goes *much* pleasure . . . and great delight.

And laughter, for Calder vastly enjoys the comic spirit and more than most men can turn a wry, clipped joke at any time of night or day—and make it from the simplest means. Even better, he enjoys the wit and humor of others.

Things can be deadly serious too, and often are . . . for whole evenings when the talk turns to wars or peace or the political facts of life. He is just as acute in these areas, and as highly perceptive, as he is in the fields of art.

The Calder households, in France and in America, are absolutely devoid of any sham. There is not a false note in any place they live. One feels only the simplicity and directness of their lives . . . and to be in a Calder house is to bask in an unanalyzable beauty which seems more like a living form than an arranged set of contrived objects and walls.

Calder is a man of tremendous integrity. Right from the start he has understood—with intensity—who HE is, what *he* feels, and what *he* can imagine. He has never once diluted any of these things.

Of course, what distinguishes him most of all is that a full generation before this present space-seeking age began he was intuitively perceiving—as the great artist always does—what the future was to be and he forsook the earthly SOLIDS, the laborious, heavy masses, and tackled *space*. He began to define and encompass SPACE by slicing it up. And this tremendous inventive effort happened in the span of ONE man's lifetime.

Up until Calder's time sculptors had for 32,000 consecutive years belabored the massy object—with varying degrees of success.

Calder, a generation before our time, was in full orbit. Long before atoms were ruptured into flying particles or rockets ricocheted from planet to planet, this weighty man had blasted off.

And today even his monumental stabiles rest their enormous size and weight LIGHTLY on elegant fins and flanges and reach outward from the earth.

This book reveals Calder and one is blessed to know this "ton of a man" . . . this agreeable genius.

—ROBERT OSBORN

CALDER, *an Autobiography with Pictures*

"Lawnton is where I was born . . ."
Alexander Calder's home in 1898

January 15, 1965

11:30 a.m. Without notes, Calder begins dictating his auto-biography, recapturing his first childhood souvenirs while talking.

Lawnton is where I was born and that has been swallowed up by Philadelphia. My birth . . . I don't know anything about that, but we were living in one end of a double stone house. I think it was very handsome.

My uncle Ron, one of father's brothers, came to see us there once. It had snowed so much that Uncle Ron had to spread out his overcoat and creep over it to reach the house.

We probably lived at some distance from any bus or train station, but it must have been fairly near Oak Lane, where Doctor George Stewart lived. He assisted in my birth—quite a package—I weighed eleven pounds. I always thought I was born—at least my mother always told me so—on August 22, 1898. But my grandfather Milne's birthday was on August 23, so there might have been a little confusion.

In 1942, when I wrote the Philadelphia City Hall for a birth certificate, I sent them a dollar and they told me I was born on the twenty-second of July, 1898. So I sent them another dollar and told them, "Look again." They corroborated the first statement.

11

Sandy at two and Peggy, four, in Lawnton

My sister Peggy was born two years before me, in Paris, during a stay of my parents. Her being born in Paris I found exciting. Mother used to call her "Peggy from Paris" and wished she had red hair and played the violin. Mother was disappointed on either count, but Peggy was a good girl. When Peggy was born she weighed nine pounds, and my mother was badly torn. I suppose she was torn again when I was born, since I weighed eleven pounds; so there might have been some delay in registering me.

All this I could not remember, so I must have overheard or deducted it.

The first thing I really remember——I must have been three——we no longer lived in the Lawnton stone house, but in a small Philadelphia apartment. The back view was a railroad yard, a great field of tracks, and I found passenger trains and freight cars quite fascinating.

12

About that time we used to have our meals sent in, probably from a nearby boarding house which provided such food ready cooked. Colored women would bring the meals on a tray. One night a new woman brought our tray. Mother must have made some remark, because the woman answered:

"I am not a servant, I am just a boarder."

This became a traditional family joke.

Somewhere around the age of three, I seem to remember Christmas. I think I remember people putting lead soldiers in my stocking, but I may well have seen them only the next morning upon opening my eyes.

About this time or later there was a great furor against slot machines in Philadelphia. We lived near an empty lot; the police brought the slot machines there, piled them up, then destroyed them. This caused great excitement among grownups, kids, Negroes, and whites alike; they were all looking among the debris for coins. I knew it was money but attached no particular significance to that fact. The movement fascinated me, the activity.

In Philadelphia we lived in a very poor neighborhood. Some of the Negro kids used to wear their older sisters' high-up buttoned shoes, that went halfway up their shins. They'd run and race around in high heels—it was uncanny.

I remember the New Year's Day Mummers' Parade up Broad Street in Philadelphia—a spectacular procession, like masses of circus clowns.

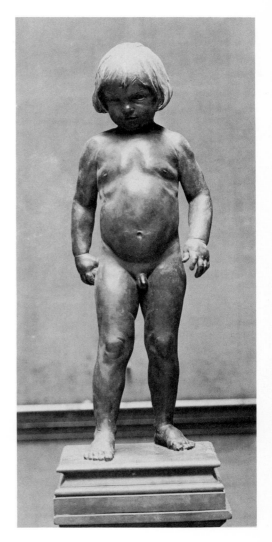

In Philadelphia, when I was four, father made the "Man Cub," for which I posed. I remember his studio over an old livery stable, two flights up. I liked it because the door opened with a long chain. Father used to sweep the floor out into the air over an empty pot. At that time I believe I did a clay elephant. I also pissed in the pants of a wool suit. Mother washed them and hung them near a potbellied stove, and they got a bit singed. While I posed for the "Man Cub," I held an orange in my hand. Later in San Francisco I posed for my mother too; she painted several portraits, and it was sort of a bore.

One evening—it was dark at any rate—it must have been when we lived in the small Philadelphia apartment near the railroad yard, Peggy and I were raising a stink. And mother did not seem able to calm us, so she put on her cape and said she was leaving. This put the fear of God into us, or of some other beastie. There are few things in your life with another person that do something deep to you, and this was one. It could have shaken my love for her.

My mother knew some relatively wealthy sisters, somewhere in Philadelphia, and when I was five or six we went and visited one for lunch, once. As I did not like meat, I was to be given a

"While I posed for 'Man Cub,' I held an orange in my hand"

13

"... my grandfather Milne's birthday was on August 23, so there might have been a little confusion"

boiled egg, and I was asked how I liked it cooked. I said:

"Hard, with a little juice in the middle."

The egg arrived—hard, with a little gravy. I was disappointed by that egg; in spite of which I think my description is a good one.

During the summer of 1903 or 1904—I think it was 1904, I must have been six—we were lent the beautiful house of Dr. Richard Hart in Stafford, on the Main Line outside Philadelphia. Dr. Hart had taken care of father and become a friend of the family. He probably loaned us the house while traveling abroad. This was the largest house we had ever lived in. I don't know whether I would approve of its furnishings and style now, but then I was overjoyed. A big house in the country, two fine horses, a well-kept carriage, and a large icehouse. Slabs of ice one foot thick were stacked in a large cellar, with sawdust between the slabs and straw over them. The ice would keep during the whole summer. You'd climb down a ladder and walk over the straw in the darkness. It was mysterious and cool on the warmest summer days.

There was also a swing with two opposed seats, onto which Peggy and I used to climb and play. I was excited by the new sense of ease, space, and comfort.

We also had wonderful rides in the carriage; the stableman might have been a Negro. Dr. Hart was wealthy and he just lent sick father his house with his servants. It was while riding in the carriage with the stableman that I saw for the first time the sphincter of a horse.

I remember a storm. Mother and father were on the porch and a bolt of lightning seemed almost to touch them.

Somewhere around that time I remember going to see the doctor who had delivered me years ago, Dr. Stewart, his wife Zaidee—a name which stuck in my memory—and their three kids. They had a car, a rare event then, and we all went down to ride with them. The machine broke down, which made it an even more thrilling experience.

At the end of the summer of 1904 we moved to a place on the Philadelphia Main Line again, about twenty or thirty miles away from the wonderful house Dr. Hart had loaned to us. I was six then, and I started going to school. I remember weeping. Also there was some confusion about my being given a buckboard (a coaster wagon with slats) and/or a velocipede. I always thought I ought to get both and I only got one—so I don't distinctly recollect which one I actually got.

At that time a cook came in to work for us—a white woman, I think—and there was some question of getting her to bake homemade bread. My sister Peggy took me aside:

"Did you see her nails?"

They were black.

John Lambert was a painter of means. In 1905 he gave father $10,000 to go recover out West from his heart disease. Lambert was a nice-looking guy with a mustache. Some years later in Switzerland, I was told, during a walk in the mountains a friend of Lambert's pointed at a chamois, asking him if he saw it. Lambert did not; he was going blind, and died a few years afterward.

In the spring of 1905, mother took father out to Arizona. My sister Peggy and I were left with some friends, Dr. Charles P. Shoemaker, a dentist, and his wife Nan. They had a daughter named Margaret, a bit younger than I. I think they lived on Regent Street, in Philadelphia, in one of the houses of those great rows of similar buildings. Shoemaker must have had some sense of humor: he enjoyed drawing and gluing elaborate valentines around the photos of friends and family members. Mrs. Shoemaker had a sister named Jane Harley and a brother named Todd. I think Todd lived in New Hope and was also a sculptor like father.

It seems to me that Jane Harley was capable of placing newspapers on carpets and upholstery to protect them from bleaching in the sun. To this day, I hate such expedients, or anything that is just temporarily so—trees tied with gunny sacks, seat covers, traveling salesmen's suits blocking the view of rear windows.

I took my parents' departure and our new surroundings as a natural course of events. Mother wrote to us about being able to see the locomotive when the train ran around a curve. There was a mechanical element in this picture which interested me, I suppose. She also wrote about the Harvey Company—it held the place of the diner in those days—which gave them a tray of food at one station and took it out at the next.

We seemed to be living on trays in those days—tray *bien!*

January 16, 1965

11:05 a.m. Calder dictated till 12:25 p.m.

In the spring of 1906, mother returned to take us out to Arizona where the climate suited father. I do not remember being uncomfortable in any way at the Shoemakers', but mother must have been upset by our separation, because she later claimed we had "wasted away." I guess she had kept us too fat.

Mother decided to make some khaki pants for me. It was very funny—the army cloth was so tough that the needles broke all the time. We also went to a large store and she bought high walking shoes for Peggy and me "on account of the snakes."

I think we were on the train on our way from Philadelphia to Arizona during the San Francisco earthquake, of which, however, I was not aware.

Hour after hour, I stood on the observation platform. I loved it. The *tick-tick* of the wheels made me feel at home. I would come back covered with soot. I remember getting to Needles, Arizona—it was very hot, terribly hot. I also enjoyed looking out of the train window, especially at night when we stopped at a station. Several times since, I have crossed the continent on a train and I have enjoyed it. Even now, I enjoy it.

We got into Tucson, at the end of our track, around eleven in the evening. It was an unprecedented hour for me to be up and I still remember it. We did spend the night in Tucson. Father must have met us at the station. The next day we took a twenty-mile ride in an open vehicle pulled by two horses—the four of us and our few belongings and a young man who was ill. His name was Wayne. We were bound for Oracle, Arizona. It took a full day.

At one moment Wayne saw a jack rabbit and grabbed for his gun.

"An antelope!" he yelled. We all laughed.

Oracle consisted chiefly of the ranch house run by a Negro named Neal. We stayed opposite in a little cottage belonging to the ranch. Wayne slept in the ranch house with other sick people —about ten of them. I remember seeing them walk with a small paper-lined tin box in their hand. While walking, from time to time they opened the lid and spat in the box. To be separate from the other ill people and to get plenty of air, some of the boarders of the ranch lived in tents about eight feet long with a wooden floor. They often slept with their heads sticking out in the open for air, and it was not uncommon in the morning to see a cow licking a man's face.

In the ranch house there was an inmate named Riley, an elderly man, who became a friend of mine. He showed me how to make a wigwam out of burlap bags pinned together with nails. Riley used to worry over my picking Mariposa lilies—he was afraid of the snakes.

There was an old Negro named Smith who did the dirty work around the place. He would make soap out of bacon fat and ashes and boil the laundry with the mixture in a big cauldron. He had a piano and used to sing to himself. Mother asked him one day:

"What can I get for you when I go East?"

"A piece of plush."

She gave him a piece of velvet, which he put over his piano. That word "plush" amused us for a long time.

There were two English cowboy brothers. The sanatorium was

a real ranch with a cattle roundup every fall; the calves were also branded. It was most spectacular.

Later, when we got to Pasadena, my toy horses were sent out to me. They were eight or ten inches high (made in Germany, probably)—cowhide and sawdust. In Pasadena, to emulate the cowboys, we branded all the horses and the sawdust came out.

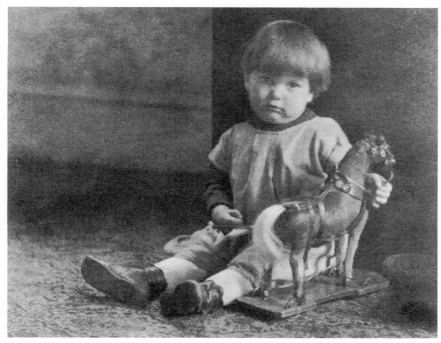

Another inmate, Ladd, an architect, had made himself a brand, though I don't know exactly what he branded. It was in the form of a triangle, symbol of his trade, with an L squeezed into it. I guess that is what inspired me later, in Pasadena, to make mine, out of a piece of wire which had held a roll of toilet paper.

The eight or ten house inmates of Oracle Ranch would have their meals at the same time. The butter squares were kept in a bowl filled with water, on account of the heat. Riley used to spear butter over his shoulder with his fork. People protested because of his using his fork—they did not find this hygienic. He said he never used his fork to eat with.

I think there was an elderly man named Field and his wife. Father later saw him in California.

Some distance away from the ranch there was a little store where one could buy chewing gum or candies. Near the store there lived some people named Crouse. Somehow, it seems to me that I stole one day a package of chewing gum; then my mother paid it back. But I don't recall whether she actually was aware of my stealing it or whether I was scolded or not.

17

Young Sandy, here aged seven, in shirt and trousers "crudely cut" by his mother, grew up amid such sculptures as these by his father, Alexander Stirling Calder

I remember the time when Apache Indians came around. They ate live-oak acorns. I used to also, but I have tried them since and they don't seem too delectable. There were Apache Indians all around the ranch. In one instance two Apache women came by on a horse and mother wanted to take their picture. It was against their faith to have a graven image of themselves, so they rode at mother brandishing a stick. Mother snapped the picture from behind a tree.

For our arrival in Oracle, father had a surprise for us: a little black dog which he had bought for forty-nine cents—all he had in his pocket. He called the dog Kohinoor. So we called him Kohie. We cherished him till late fall, till we moved to Pasadena, northeast of Los Angeles, when we abandoned him to the ranch.

Peddlers carrying merchandise—suits, hats, cloth—would run two wagons hitched to each other and pulled by as many as ten mules. It was very exciting.

The ranch had a big dog with a big voice. One day he went after one of those mule trains. The driver was going to shoot him, and Neal the Negro ranch owner came out, and he was going to shoot the driver.

I remember Peggy rushing into the cottage, yelling, "A snake, a snake!" Somebody rushed out and shot it. I am not sure that it was not a gopher; but there were really rattlers around, although I don't seem to have seen any.

Along with Kohie, we had a donkey named Jacko, and we used to ride him. Peggy would ride one morning and I would ride in the afternoon, and then we'd reverse the procedure. Peggy would really ride, but I'd always stop and play with some kids. Father's horse was called Pico (I think it means "spot" in Spanish). To ride with him, mother must have hired another horse. There were plenty of horses around. At that time father did not work or sculpt; he was resting.

On Decoration Day father arranged cowhorns on Jacko's head so I could ride him in the parade. Jacko was rather old and stubborn. The parade rode off and left me behind. One of the English cowboys came back and whipped him. Jacko became more lively and spurted along, probably the only time I went into a gallop, holding on to the pommel.

Father was very fond of a breakfast food called Malted Something or Other, and mother sent for it to Los Angeles. When it was served to father, the other inmates wanted to try it too; they called it "Calder's Mush."

I don't remember much about the departure from Oracle; when we left Kohie we probably cried—Peggy was also sentimental.

We arrived in Los Angeles, at a hotel called Eastlake or Westlake. We just marked time while father and mother looked for a place to live in. They finally found one in Pasadena, nine miles by the electric trolley, an exciting trip. The house was a sort of two-floor bungalow, very modest and small, on a corner lot. There was a winding cement path leading to it from the sidewalk. On both sides of the path the geraniums were so thick that we found them marvelous. Yet six months later, we attacked them with a switch. This was on Euclid Avenue, very near California Street.

We found ourselves next to a numerous family, with at least six kids, the Horrells. I believe they came from Tennessee. Later on, the one younger than I—the last one, I guess—became a big football star at the University of California. I think one of his brothers became chief of police and got into some difficulty. Another one became a well-known automobile racer. At any rate, we all went to a school called McKinley. I was in the second grade.

On our way home from school one day, Peggy and I got into a running stone fight with Kam Horrell. Somehow, nobody seemed to get hit. Mother went to protest to Mr. Horrell, who answered, "You can horsewhip him if you want, but I can't do anything with him."

The Horrells were a picturesque and tough outfit. I can still remember the names of most of them. There was Mattie, the older girl, then another girl whose name I don't recall, then the four boys, Jum, Kam, Steve, and Chilian. They lived next door, except for a vacant lot, where somebody was piling loads of fresh earth. That somebody intended to make a garden out of it, but dropped the project.

The neighborhood gang also included Albert Blockmacher; his father owned our house and they lived near by. Peggy had a friend a block away, Louise Brown. She dragged Peggy to Sunday school and Peggy got involved in the competition for new members, so she bribed me to go too by giving me a tin-foil ball and some United Cigar coupons. (You traded these coupons to get certain minor objects; I remember getting a humidor for father once with a whole batch of them.) My buddy at Sunday school was Willis Holstead. He used to tell the teacher he'd lost his nickel for the collection, and would buy chewing gum with it.

One time, father went to see some painter friends. Upon his return from their studios he said:

"The oil smells so good."

He was probably referring to the mixture of turpentine and linseed oil. I never forgot his remark.

Mother came from Milwaukee and she had brothers and friends there who were better off than we were, some of whom had boys who had engines and trains. A mechanical train running on a 1¼-inch track was sent to me. All the neighborhood kids, the Horrells, the Blockmachers, and people whose names I forget, came to play with these things in the fresh-earth lot where I'd set the tracks. The trains were several inches long. My old hide-and-sawdust horses (I had not branded them yet) were about eight inches tall. It dismayed me to see the other kids playing with the trains and horses without any discrimination for size and color.

Most of the time we were very good friends, but it also dismayed me when the Horrells would yell:

"Wee-ou . . . Wee-ou . . . Wee-ou . . ."

as the trains went by, when I wanted them to say with me:

"Too-oot . . . Too-oot . . . Too-oot . . ."

I guess this happened because we came from different sections of the country, they from Tennessee and I from Philadelphia, but I did not realize it then.

At that time, on Euclid Avenue in Pasadena, I got my first tools and was given the cellar with its window as a workshop. Mother and father were all for my efforts to build things myself—they approved of the homemade. I used to make all sorts of things, little seats, or a tonneau cover for my coaster wagon.

My uncle Ron, one of father's five brothers, was clever manually and mechanically. (He was always invited, on account of that, to help us pack before we moved.) He visited us once in Pasadena and bought me a wagon in a store, with iron wheels and tires; then he bought an eight-foot plank, had a steering wheel turned at the carpenter's, rigged up a steering with pulleys and some rope, and made me a coaster. With all the cement sidewalks of a real-estate boom and the gently rolling hills of Pasadena, I enjoyed this thing very much.

My workshop became some sort of a center of attraction; everybody came in. Peggy once gave me a very nice pair of pliers at Christmas. I made her a little Christmas tree, completely decorated, out of a fallen branch. So she wept because my gift was homemade.

Peggy had, among many others, a doll named Thomasine. We decided to build her a backyard castle with a moat. I picked up in the streets the bits of copper wire left from other people's spliced cables and made jewelry with little beads for Thomasine and other ladies. This is about the time I branded the horses, and Peg made series of cow paper-dolls—she had a roundup of these on the walls of her room.

As the season of the Tournament of Roses drew near, in December, the Horrells and all the other kids had broomsticks with a big nail at the end for a lance. They were also making chariots. I remember one chariot made of a rather tall box, big enough for a boy to stand in. This particular chariot went so violently around the corner that it hit the pavement. I don't think the kid was hurt—they were tough boys.

On January 1, 1907—I was nine—mother, Peggy, and I actually went to the Tournament of Roses. In those days they just had four-horse chariot races and tent-pegging. (The men would come galloping on horseback at a deeply driven tent post and try to root it out with a blow of their lance.) There was a parade of floats through the arena (where the Rose Bowl takes place now), and then the four-horse-chariot tournament. [The final and most spectacular attraction of Calder's circus, completed in the thirties, is a chariot race.] I also remember well some other races with lighter chariots pulled by four donkeys. In one of these, the guy who was trailing pulled out a piece of tin tied on the end of a big stick and banged it on the donkeys' asses—he finally won and that touched me very deeply.

Sometime after the Tournament of Roses, we were playing hide-and-seek with the neighborhood gang. While running, I tripped on a board and skidded hard on my cheek. For several months father called me "Moldy Pippin." I must have torn some muscle in my cheek, which makes me smile upside down—or at least lopsided. It never bothered me, but I did not share my father's humor.

In 1908, Mother, Peggy, and I left the Los Angeles port of San Pedro to travel to San Francisco by boat. We were met by Jessica Westphal, a friend of a friend of ours in Pasadena. When we docked in San Francisco, it was frightening and exciting to hear the hacks working for the different hotels screaming competitively at the top of their voices and inviting guests to come to the particular hotel they were working for.

We stayed in a little hotel where I was delighted at the opportunity to run the elevator. Once we were invited to a Bohemian restaurant, whose walls were embellished with paintings. I still remember one particular painting, outlining a stomach to the left—I don't remember exactly how this was done—and to the right a cannon, composed of a bottle of champagne representing the barrel and two dishes representing the wheels. The inscription was:

HERE SHE COMES, OLD STOMACH!

We also went around the city, but all I remember is the City Hall with its finial figure slanted over the twisted walls and torn dome. I heard so many things about the 1906 earthquake that this memory is quite confused with tales of twisted buildings and fires.

Sometime after our settling in Pasadena father had built a

studio from a barn close to our house. He had put a skylight in it—that's what he was always doing. He also rented a studio on Figueroa Street in Los Angeles. Between Los Angeles and Pasadena there was an Indian ranch where there lived Sioux from Dakota, and various other tribes, maybe Arapaho, and father got some to pose for him while my mother painted them. I remember well the name of one of the Indians who posed for father—Nazhionketi.

Alexander Stirling Calder at fifty

23

"I took these activities as a matter of fact."
Statues by Alexander Stirling Calder

I took this activity as a matter of fact, since the barn close to our house on Euclid Avenue and the Figueroa Street studio were somewhat removed from my daily life.

At the McKinley School, the boys used to indulge in severe strap fights. They'd use the straps which held their books together and slap each other around the legs, keeping it up while weeping, sometimes. I don't think I ever undertook any such fights.

I remember that I used to wear homemade short-sleeved shirts, crudely cut by my mother—straight on either side, with a slot at the neck and an opening that was closed by a shoelace. I never recall worrying over it. But later, Sandra and Mary, my daughters, and Peggy's kids needed the run-of-the-mill things when they went to school.

Sandy, at eleven, in 1909 in Pasadena. His sister Peggy, thirteen, is seated behind him and his mother is at his right. Gwladys Sills, the actress, is at the upper left

Close to Euclid where we lived, on the other side of California Street, lived Arthur Jerome Eddy, a well-to-do Chicago lawyer, who had built himself a Spanish-type house. Abroad, he frequented the modern Paris Group. He knew Marcel Duchamp. I don't think father or mother could ever understand why Eddy did not like and buy father's stuff. He never bought anything of father's, but he was very friendly. It is funny too that father had books on Picasso and Matisse, but that he never seemed to be influenced by either.

Eddy came from a fat family and he did not want to become too fat himself, so he went to Mahoney's gymnasium; he even subscribed a course for me. I used to go and undress and put on a bathing suit. I did not care much for the exercise and seem to remember that I was always struggling in and out of a bathing suit. The following year Eddy told me to choose between more physical-fitness courses and a bicycle. I was delighted to choose the bicycle.

25

I forgot to tell about another black dog. While father was out at the Indian ranch, looking for models probably, he saw a little black dog being badly mauled by an Indian boy. So he bought it, for fifty cents this time. She was a female and we called her Ursa Minor—Ursa for short. We had Ursa several years and she used to run after cars. I remember once on California Street, near our house, she ran after an electric brougham. The driver stopped the car, opened the door, and spat at her. He was well dressed. He missed the dog.

Ursa went with us when we moved to Linda Vista, on the Arroyo Seco. Later, when we moved East, she was sent to my grandfather Milne in Philadelphia, who was to keep her till we became settled again.

We spent two or three years on Euclid Avenue, then moved to the northwest of Pasadena, to a side street called Linda Vista (Beautiful View) overlooking the Arroyo Seco. The house was very amusing. It was made out of a barn with vertical siding and vertical strips nailed over adjoining planks. It belonged to a cultured woman whose name was Mrs. Masters. The character of the house was attractive, while our old Euclid Avenue house, for all we liked it, was nothing much more than a roof. We developed new friends, and went to a different school called Garfield. The school was about ten blocks away. A trolley ran by it, which we took sometimes. At Garfield School I was in the fourth grade. I remember distinctly making a blotting pad out of wood, with a blotter tacked on the bottom and a wire hook to hang it on the side of the desk. I was even flattered once when an older boy looked at it, displaying some interest.

In the fourth grade there were two boys much older and bigger than the rest of the class. I always found their presence strange and uncanny: Eddie Rochelle, a Mexican, and a Negro called A-G—his name might have been Agee. He was a tall Negro.

I had been read in school the stories of King Arthur, and became very enthusiastic. So I made myself a helmet out of a piece of galvanized iron with a piece of screen over the face. I made some gauntlets out of a pair of gloves that my mother gave me, using wire rings and metal on the outside. Chuck Hunt, the son of an architect with whom father worked once or twice, was Sir Lancelot; I was Sir Tristram. Chuck Hunt was very agile—he rode his bicycle without handlebars through Pasadena. He made a helmet out of a lard can. I did not approve of its shape. So one day we did battle. He hit me on the ass with the flat of his sword. That day I gave up the lists forever.

We used to go down in the Arroyo Seco and pick holly. A cement bridge was being built there which still exists now. I was very much interested in the construction activity. There was also poison oak, and I got a frightful dose of it and had to spend three weeks in bed. Mother read me *A Child's History of England* and to this day it is about all I know of history.

Father met a Frenchman named Hector Alliot. He and his wife lived in Los Angeles, where he was a librarian. He was very friendly, and told me of the Suez Canal and de Lesseps, which interested me very much.

My father needed a lot of fresh air and slept on a porch. As far back as I can remember he always had to set up some rig there for his mattress. Our Linda Vista barn-house had a fine porch that suited him.

I had a workshop there too. But this time it was a tent with a wooden floor, like the boarders' tents at Oracle. I remember coming home and enjoying eating the peaches in a little garden by the tent.

It was about this time that I received the bike from Eddy. I was at a loss how to ride it. A family named Mason undertook to teach me by putting me in the saddle and pushing me as fast as they could run.

I liked the bike, but I was still faithful to the old coaster which Uncle Ron had built for me and to which I had added the tonneau cover.

January 17, 1965

11:10 a.m. Calder dictated till 12:30 p.m.

So we were to move East in the fall of 1910. Father felt better; he had met with some success. He had done three spandrels in Pasadena, with his friend Myron Hunt the architect, the father of Sir Lancelot. He did these spandrels for the Throop Polytechnic Institute, now called California Tech. Now he felt the need for getting back to the "Metropolis of Art," New York.

The mover was named Orth, and on the side of his van was painted the globe and across it: "The world moves, so does Orth."

I guess I learned a bit about packing as I watched very closely while the movers took off the wheels of my coaster, crated it, and crated my bicycle. This is probably what makes me so difficult with other people when we are packing.

When we left Pasadena, Peggy, taking leave of her friends.

27

These eagles "hatched" the mobiles. Above is one of the four bronze eagles sculpted by Sandy's grandfather, Alexander Milne Calder (the bearded man at the left), and now in place on the Philadelphia City Hall Tower. Below is "Son of the Eagle," done in the 1900s by Calder's father

wept. I did not seem so moved. Somebody gave me a stupid little book called *A Dog's Day*. I read it to Peggy on the train and it cheered her up.

Before we could get to New York we had to stop for a while in Philadelphia, where father had kept his studio rented in his absence. For two to three months I went to Germantown Academy. It was a good school, and it was rather fine for me. It gave me a little bit of an edge when later I went to a less advanced school in New York State at Croton-on-Hudson.

Being a newcomer to the Germantown Academy, I was hazed at first by two kids who were trying to suppress or depress me. This took place in the yard garden, by the steps leading to the classroom, during a recess. I got the idea of running up a fire escape to report this, but they cut me off. I was twelve then. I don't think I cried.

Our athletic rival was Penn Charter. Their colors were red, blue, and black, which I always found an amusing combination of colors. I still like it today.

In the meantime, father and mother were rushing around the countryside looking for a place to live, as near New York as possible. Finally they decided on "The Old Gate House," on the estate of a Mr. and Mrs. Stevenson at Croton-on-Hudson. On the estate, seven acres were encircled by a wall which in parts was thirty-five feet high. The Stevensons lived in the southwest corner, overlooking the Hudson. We, in a northeast corner house, originally a small square building, to which another square construction had been added later, at some distance, with a long passageway connecting the two. Unfortunately Mrs. Stevenson did not want any dogs on the property, so Ursa Minor was consigned to grandfather Milne for good.

There was a very bright pink paper on the walls of the room mother occupied. This paper was so recherché and expensive that Mrs. Stevenson would not let mother cover it up, so she had to hang gray curtains over the walls. This made it possible for her to use her room as a studio and get back to painting, at times. There was also a chandelier made of lead and tinted glass—most lugubrious—which we were not allowed to get rid of either. So we attacked it with water colors and bits of Chinese paper.

One feature of these new surroundings was extremely nice for me: a big artificial pond, eighty or a hundred feet square. It was two feet deep and was used for ice-cutting. We learned to skate on this in the winter. And in the summer we used a snub-nosed boat that belonged to the Stevensons. I used it all the time. I speared frogs from it, caught newts, studied water life. Also, somebody had given me somewhere along the line an *Outdoor Handy*

Book, which interested me very much. I was about the proper age for a Boy Scout and had somewhat the tendencies. Again, I was given a cellar room as a workshop.

I remember the life in Croton as very agreeable. Peggy went to school at Ossining, three miles south of us, at a Miss Bentley's and took the train every morning, while I went to the Croton Public School. I began in the fifth grade. Alongside the classroom there was a corridor, used as a cloakroom. The fifth-grade teacher used to sneak out to the cloakroom and peer in the door to see whether she could catch anybody doing something wrong. But I was soon moved to the sixth grade, where I had a teacher named Miss Cahill; she was full of pizazz—that is, energy. Miss Cahill seemed to appreciate me a bit more. These were kids of workmen, plumbers, carpenters, and I was a bit more advanced, particularly thanks to the Germantown Academy.

Somehow, the following year, the whole class of the seventh grade was given a chance at the eighth grade. I don't know how it happened—the school must have been quite liberal.

I had a few fights around this time—not very serious, but I never knew how to fight. When I was smaller it was quite hopeless, and when I was bigger I sat on the smaller one, but was at a loss what to do next. Luckily, on the whole we all got along pretty well. I guess living on the Stevenson estate—they were wealthy people—gave me some sort of prestige, which I really did not rate.

It never occurred to me before, but my schoolmates were rather aloof and did not come and play with me the way the Horrells and the gang had in Pasadena, probably for fear of being chased by Mrs. Stevenson, who preferred peace and quiet to dogs and boisterous boys.

There was a Stevenson boy—he is still in existence—named Harvey, a bit older than Peggy. He was very nice and taught us how to skate. He went to a private school down the river. Behind his back we called him "The Squire."

Harvey was quite athletic and used to try to get me to play catch with him; this I would do somewhat reluctantly, but then I would ask him to sit down in the shade of a tree.

Mrs. Stevenson had an architectural mania. She built stone houses all around the area. There was plenty of stone in the neighborhood quarries and the workers in those quarries knew how to dig holes, place sticks of dynamite, and blast. There was one very ambitious house with a subterranean garage, due to the slope of the street it was on. As practically all the workmen were Italian, she would wheel out her victrola and play Italian records during the lunch hour.

Croton-on-Hudson. Sandy, aged twelve, and Peggy, aged fourteen

29

I think it is due to her influence that Harvey Stevenson took up architecture at Yale. It must also have been because she fancied having a sculptor on the premises that she lent the house to father. Here again, there was a large garage that he converted into a studio by putting a skylight in it——one more!

Upon entering high school, the year after the eighth grade, Peggy and I used to go to Ossining together in the morning, with lunch in paper bag.

The year before, Peggy had made friends with some of the Acker girls in her school. We visited them often in their house on top of a long steep hill with a view of the Hudson, through gardens. On the intermediate floor, I still remember a tower room. As I vaguely remember things, it is one of the fine houses I have known. I think there were five Acker children: Ernest, Wilhelm, Eleanor, Marjorie, and Marie-Louise.

Mr. Acker owned and operated a small chemical plant down by the river. He handled sodium, nitrate, and things of that nature. Ernest amazed me one day by telling me he had thrown bits of sodium on the snow, whereupon they exploded.

We had a cook named Anna Tuceling; she was of German origin, gay, good-natured, lively——she was rather fun. I don't quite remember whether she originated the remark about "The Squire." I played cards with her. The kitchen was the lower level of the long passage between the two square houses.

It was while at Croton that my uncles Ron, Ralph, and sometimes Norman used to come out bearing gifts of candy and at times toys. Ron, the athlete, was head of the gym of the Parish House of the St. Thomas Church, somewhere on the New York East Side. He was powerful, with big muscles, and used to play tag with us. Ralph was an architect with Carrère and Hastings. He had a roommate, Jerry Holmes, who worked for McKim, Mead, and White. Norman was a painter, though the only thing I ever saw of his was a naked lady on a beach with a lot of soap bubbles.

Sometimes after lunch on Sunday, Ralph and Norman would show us how, as boys in Philadelphia, they imitated cat and dog fights on the fence of the lady next door. On such occasions, I was always sent to the kitchen to invite Ann Tuceling to see the fun.

I also used to ride my bike around in Croton, the one Mr. Eddy had given me in Pasadena. There was a supply shop——pumps, bells, horns. I was about to buy a horn for my bike, like the other kids, when I discovered it cost forty cents. I don't know now whether I did not have the money or did not think it wise to invest so much in a mere horn. But, I was treated to "cheapskate" by my erstwhile companions.

January 18, 1965

11:10 a.m. to 12:15 p.m.

We had our first real contact with the snow in Croton. Harvey Stevenson had an eight-foot-long "Flexible Flyer." With him we used to go down the post road right into the village of Croton.

His father, Mr. Stevenson, was connected with the American Telephone and Telegraph Company. One time they imported lots of cement poles from France and Belgium. They compared these poles with their own by putting a cable attached to a winch on the end of the pole and breaking it under pressure. That was a very interesting spectacle. This was done on Mr. Stevenson's property. I don't know what conclusion they reached.

Just as in Arizona and in Pasadena, father was always sleeping in the open. I remember he used to crawl out of my window at night to a bed he had established on the roof. He had rigged up his mattress on several two-by-fours, with a canvas overhead for protection. He also took cold baths every morning, plunging into a cold tub of water. I somewhat developed the same habit too and always needed plenty of fresh air.

While we were at Croton, Everett Shinn, the painter, came to see us several times. He took an interest in my mechanical trains and we even built a gravity system down the yard wall. We ran the train on wooden rails held by spikes; a chunk of iron racing down the incline speeded the cars. We even lit up some cars with candle lights. One day I was delighted to get a letter from him in this envelope:

31

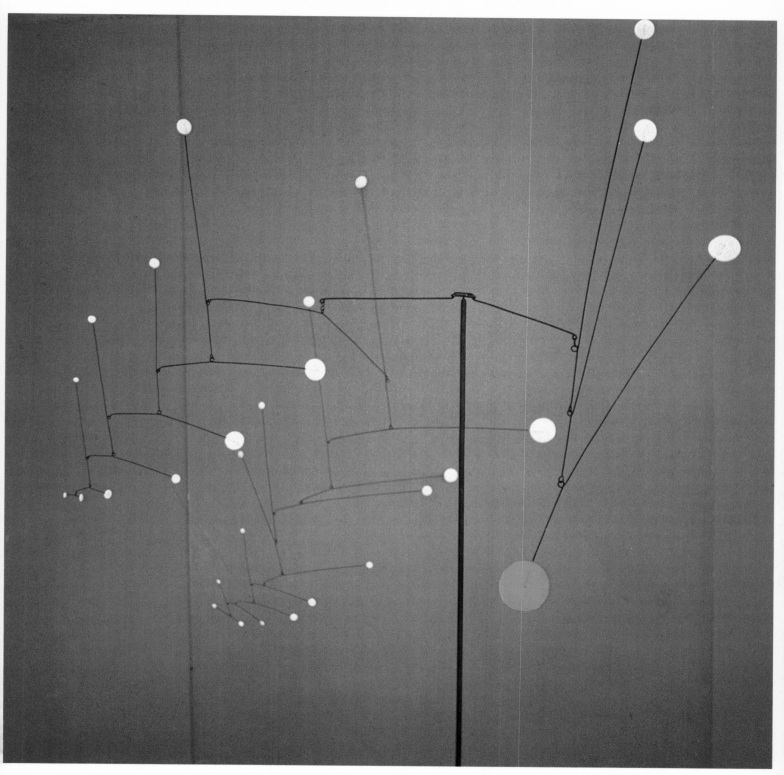

"Red Disc and White Dots," 1956

"The Mantis," 1936

"Bull in Sheet Brass," 1929

"Stabile in Curves," 1936 Abbott Laboratories

Soon, father felt the need of being really in New York. So he rented a place at 51 West Tenth Street. He had the main studio of a very old building, with a flat skylight in the middle of it. It was terrible, because the top of everything bleached with the light while the vertical surfaces were in shadow. I did not like it at all, but I suppose he finally got used to it, though I don't quite see how he could work there.

After he secured that studio, father, who commuted every day, wanted to get closer to it. So we moved down the river to Spuyten Duyvil—a name of Dutch origin supposed to mean "in spite of the devil," or "spitting devil." A stream there connects the Hudson to the East River.

From Spuyten Duyvil, Peggy and I went to high school at Yonkers High. The school must have been built without a lavatory for the boys, because there was a U-shaped protuberance on one side, made of the same brick and lined with slabs of slate. And above the slates there was written all over the walls: "All bulls with short horns please stand close."

Once more we used to take our lunch in a paper bag. I guess mother avoided cooking. We had a new cook from Czechoslovakia or somewhere else in Central Europe, and one day we were surprised to find a slice of chocolate cake in the middle of our sandwich. However, she made Bavarian cream deliciously, so I forgave her.

This time there lived next door a family of eight kids, the Heuers. Between our house and theirs was a very narrow cement path and a fence that we used to hop over with ease. Our house belonged to an old Scotch spinster and she had cut herself out on the third floor of her house, leaving us the two floors below. She had built a separate outdoor staircase of quartered oak—it was sawed in some way so it had a fancy bunch of knots. The Heuer kids used to whistle up her speaking tube and ask her if she would not come down and play . . . we never dared.

The cherry tree in our backyard got drastic attention—we ate all the cherries.

In an empty lot across the street we played baseball with neighborhood kids. Our house became a depository for bats and gloves. The kids used to bang the door as they came tearing in and out. Miss Stewart once came down and protested to father, "You are disintegrating my house!"

I tried to play baseball with the others and did not make out very well. Neither could I play tennis too well. Peggy was rather good at both and she even won a prize in a local tennis tournament.

There were five rich Johnson brothers, descendants of the owners of a steel foundry on the little river. They owned a lot of

Spuyten Duyvil. They were God-fearing people and sponsored a local club with five tennis courts. But the people who really enjoyed playing on Sunday were the office clerks, who had few other opportunities. So these God-fearing guys closed the club on Sundays and the poor clerks could only play if they were free on Saturday afternoons. While the wealthy Johnson kids could rush somewhere else in their cars to play even on Sundays if they fancied.

There was quite a crowd of kids around. One boy named Schramme was very athletic and a good pitcher. Peggy played with us and she was much better than I. She had had some training playing indoor baseball at the Garfield School in Pasadena.

Somehow, I seemed to be the one they ganged up against more or less—that is, the athletic boys. Sometimes during our evening gatherings under a street lamp they'd shove me around and make nasty remarks. My uncle Ron, who knew a lot about boys, told me, "Pick the biggest and go after him."

So, I picked Schramme. For all his physical prowess, I seemed to be holding my own and rather enjoying it, when mother and Peggy came out of the house. Mother ordered me back in. Thus the outcome of the fight was never known, but it seemed to do the job. The kids no longer bothered me.

Here too, I had a cellar workshop. I think I was respected by my playmates for what I could make out of wood and leather with my tools and hands. One time I even made an electric light plug out of a cork, a nail, and a piece of copper wire. But after drawing an enormous spark from this apparatus, I quit bothering electricity.

It was about this time that Uncle Ron was placed in charge of the St. Thomas Summer Home (for East Side boys) at East Marion, on the Sound at the east end of Long Island. It was quite a place. He took me along with him on two successive summers. The choir consisted of thirty or forty boys who were "selected for their voices." They were rascals and made rough remarks when they were given beans for dinner.

We were given a prize for the one who consistently—during fifteen days—made his bed the best. The first summer I won the prize: a big box with about eighty lollipops. So I did my best to convey the booty home. I had to fight against all the wiles of the choir, who finally got rather annoyed with my selfishness.

The second year, I won the prize again and tried to improve matters by placing one lollipop on each plate at dinner. But this too proved rather catastrophic. Some guys thought they should get several lollipops and others did not want any at all. Fortunately Uncle Ron did not take me a third time.

Then along came the San Francisco Fair of 1915.

In 1913 Karl Bitter, an Austrian sculptor, was appointed director of sculpture for the fair. Gutzon Borglum, another sculptor, objected that Bitter was a foreigner. Some bystander retorted, "Who the hell is *Borg-lum*? It sounds like a fart in a bathtub." This amused me a lot. Bitter really did not want to go to San Francisco, and he finally got father appointed Acting Chief of Sculpture.

So, off to California we went!

In San Francisco we got settled in Broderick Street. Well, once more father had the skylight and I the workshop in the cellar.

January 19, 1965

11:15 a.m. to 12:45 p.m.

But this time father's skylight was located in some very large iron workshop erected on the fair grounds. I often went to visit him and was very much interested in the pointing machine for enlarging small sculpture.

This consisted of two parallel needles, one longer than the other, according to the enlargement. It worked with a parallelogram. The small sculpture and the framework for the large sculpture were placed on two turntables which turned together through sprockets and a bicycle chain. The sculptor would put a cross on the small plaster figure and drive a nail into the wood framework where the other needle came. Rotating all about the high and the low spots, these would be represented by nailheads in the enlarged structure. The gaps between nails would be filled in according to the taste of the sculptor at work. I'd be particularly fascinated by the mechanics, the rotating motions and the parallel needles of the process.

This reminds me that once at Croton-on-Hudson where we lived before moving to Spuyten Duyvil and to San Francisco, father received by river boat a seated female figure which had been enlarged in New York. She was full of nails as usual, and Anna Tuceling baptized her "Lady Prickles."

In San Francisco I went to Lowell High School, out near Golden Gate Park, and Peggy became a freshman at the University of California. It was here that my short athletic career commenced. I tried to play rugby, which was then played in preference to football by the whole West Coast. We used to go out to Golden Gate Park and practice.

Then we moved to the house of Mrs. Westphal at the corner of

Sandy, at sixteen, with his mother and father

Taylor and Green Streets, on Russian Hill. The grounds were so steep that the house had three levels. People there could live on different levels without any awareness of each other. The wood out of which the house was made was supposed to have been shipped from the East and around the Horn.

The man who lived above us was fond of displaying flags; he had a flagpole. At the time of the quake and fire he had run Old Glory at the top of his pole. And during the fire, marines who did not quite know what to do decided to save that house.

It was a very pretty house. Its windows looked across the bay toward Berkeley. There was an old pianola in one of the rooms, and Peggy and I pumped it so hard that we used to "rise in our stirrups" while playing "Black Diamond."

In the winter of 1914–1915 my family moved to Berkeley, and as I continued to study at Lowell High School, I stayed with Walter Bliss and his wife at Vallejo Street, near the Presidio. Bliss was an architect and he had built his own house—it was quite elegant. From the gold-walled dining room we could watch the fireworks of the exposition. The Blisses, who had no kids, were very kind to me.

"In San Francisco I went to Lowell High School." Class picture. Sandy seated second from right

37

Walter Bliss loved flowers and waged a never-ending war against slugs. So, I made him a two-pronged fork out of wire with a trigger ejector with which he could demolish the slugs at his ease. Later on, Peggy and I discovered another way to treat slugs —that was to pile them all up and pour salt on them, which made them dissolve. A friend of ours had still a third system: to throw them over the wall into your neighbor's yard.

When I lived with the family in the Taylor Street house and went to Lowell High School, I had to take a cable car and change to an electric car on Market Street. There was a turntable at the end of the street where we'd change to the other car. The cable car would take corners fast and you'd have to hang on at the corners. On a flat street you could catch up with it if you ran, but on a hill it would beat you.

I was always delighted by the cable car on Pacific Avenue, which consisted of the merest platform with four posts and a roof over it, trailing behind it a very small Toonerville Trolley, a sort of closed trailer. When they got to the end of the run there was always a short incline in the street, one way or the other, and they always arranged for the trailer to coast down to the car with the grip.

The machinery and the movement interested me and the spasmodic yanking was rather reposeful. Some of the cable cars on California Street were gaily painted, basically white with gold trickles and spots of color like a circus wagon.

I think we had moved to Berkeley because father had a job on the Oakland City Hall, near by. Here, we lived at the bottom of Strawberry Canyon, at the foot of some steep hills. Higher up was a fire reservoir for the campus of the University of California. It also served as a swimming pool for the men of the university.

For some reason or other I had to take a chemistry course at the university during the summer of 1915, so I had the privilege of using the pool, where we spent hours sunbathing. I learned to swim and to dive under the coaching of an old Norwegian. He was rather funny because he always wore a white gob's hat and turned the brim down. Spending all day in the sun, the lower half of his face was dark brown and the upper part pink.

My sister joined a sorority and became very fond of a noisy athlete named Hayes, whom she eventually married and who belonged to a fraternity. Between the fraternity and the sorority, they all seemed to have a very gay time. This led me to the belief that I too must go to college. But my father said:

"What do you want to study?"

And here, I was a bit nonplussed. But a fellow at Lowell High School, Hyde Lewis, told me he was going to be a mechanical engineer. I was not very sure what this term meant, but I thought I'd better adopt it.

Father was still connected with the fair. He asked the chief engineer for the name of a school in New York. The result was the Stevens Institute of Technology in Hoboken, New Jersey, right across the river.

So we moved to New York, on Claremont Place, Manhattan, opposite Barnard College, where Peggy was to go for her junior college year. The dean of Barnard tried to make her wear a hat to walk a mere half block to college. After the freedom of California campuses, this was insufferable.

In our Claremont Place home, I distinctly remember father trying to sleep and getting angry at some noisy people playing cards across the yard. He finally yelled at them, "Swine, shut up!"

Father set up his shop in an old movie studio he discovered at 11 East Fourteenth Street. For the first time he built a vertical window instead of a skylight. The place had been frequented by Mary Pickford and others. The bottom cellar under the studio had been a movie darkroom. During father's regime this cellar was stacked with old newspapers that he used from time to time to pack sculpture. Father had an assistant, Duane Champlain, another sculptor. He'd ask Champlain to get some papers to pack something. The other would leave for the cellar and never come back—he'd start browsing among the old papers. After waiting patiently, father would finally call him.

Mother delivered me to Hoboken. She inspected closely the dormitory where I was to live during my first college year. It was called Castle Stevens and was located in an old summer house of the Stevens family. I had a room on the third floor with two other fellows. It had been the drafting room of the engineer Stevens who founded the institute. It was a beautiful room in a square tower, really a wonderful room, with windows looking up and down the river and across—it was all windows.

While inspecting the room where I was to live, mother went to the bathroom. A few minutes later one of the boys burst in on her and backed out with an exclamation. However, mother was satisfied that the toilet was clean enough for me.

The first day in college felt like racing cars starting from a standstill. People were selling drafting instruments, comparatively expensive and of which I knew nothing. Others were inviting you to join a fraternity, and there even was a football coach whose theory was:

"Anybody who can walk is an athlete."

The first day we had a machine-shop course. By the time I cleaned up to go to the fraternity, the fellow who had invited me there had disappeared——that's the last I saw of that outfit for some years.

The lack of knowledge of drawing instruments led me to buy an inferior set, forced down my throat the first day by an older student. This annoyed me for a long time. I kept this set till graduation.

As to the football coach, I believed him and tried to play football all the time I was in college, without actually getting into a single game. He had four teams and I remained on the lowest. Maybe I should have quit trying to play football and found some other sport that would have been more beneficial to me.

Later on the coach said something that stuck. He was telling the players to make up their minds on what they were going to

"I tried to play football all the time I was in college, without actually getting into a single game." However, Sandy made the lacrosse team. He is in the front, second from right

do and only then start wondering what the other fellows were going to do. This piece of advice stuck. The coach had been a graduate in architecture of Penn State, and I have often wondered since what became of him.

President Humphreys did not allow any fooling and there was no hazing at Stevens. The year before I arrived there had been another football coach whose best player was put on the sidelines for foul play. That coach had taped him up and put him back into the game, claiming he was somebody else. For this, Humphreys had sacked the coach.

At Stevens they had the honor system. One signed a pledge before every exam not to cheat or copy and infractions were ruled on by the Honor Board. I once was on the Honor Board and we had a case where some ten students were accused of misdemeanor. We ruled very strictly on the case—we were all doing our duty—and we were very much surprised to have Prexy Humphreys reverse our decision to throw every one of these students out. He was a good man; his idea was to educate people, not expel them. He too was doing his duty.

Later in his lectures there was one phrase that stayed with me, the idea that "good enough is best." But while this might hold for engineering, it is not for artists.

During my freshman year, two of my best friends were a Chinese, Chor Hing Ou, a colorful student always good at joking, and Mariano Juncadella, a Cuban. But they dropped out about the second year. Before graduation, close to 75 per cent of the original enrollees dropped out. I still remember vividly, when I was a freshman in college, hearing a fellow who had flunked out. He was turning in his tools to the instructor of the machine-shop course. And he said, "First they puke all over you, then they kick you out because you stink." I am afraid his language was even stronger! He was going back home to Brooklyn or Jersey. A few dropped out on account of financial reasons and many others because they were unable to keep up. I don't know what became of Chor Hing Ou or Juncadella and have often thought about them. Years later, in 1922, when I took a ship that went through the Canal and stopped in Havana, I wrote Juncadella. He came on board, but I was sleeping on a pile of rope and could not be found.

One of the freshmen, Rube Ford, was a wonderful athlete and a delightful guy, but not too good a student. Later, when he flunked out, he was the proud possessor of a little car. I overheard the local Hoboken cop, who had the Stevens beat, say:

"Gee, I wish something would happen to Rube, so I could help him out . . . he's such a swell guy!"

In our freshman year we learned that a "colored ringer" had come to Rutgers College, our deadly rival. Of course, he was to play football. Our coach urged the men to ask him what fraternity he belonged to, to get his goat and upset his playing. We did not get the "ringer's" goat and Rutgers beat us 39 to 3. The man was Paul Robeson and later he could have replied, "My fraternity is Phi Beta Kappa." In 1924, I went with a fraternity friend to see Paul Robeson play Emperor Jones, in Greenwich Village. I was so enthusiastic when the play was over that I insisted on going backstage to say hello, despite my companion's remonstrances. I did not begrudge him the old score.

A fellow stood out in our freshman class. He was Reginald Philippe Deghuee, known as Rex and often called De-ghooey by the professors. Short and very stocky, I don't know how he did it, but he ran very fast and had been a football star in high school and continued to be one throughout college. He was immediately elected class president, a job which he held for three years. He was also good in his studies; after enlisting in the war he came back to Stevens later and graduated. His expressions when declaiming or electioneering were very amusing. He pleaded his case with great solicitude. He later went to Pittsburgh, where he disappeared in the soot.

My best friend was Bill Drew, William Benedict Francis Drew. I met him in Castle Stevens. Drew was also a baseball and football star—for Stevens at any rate. We passed many nights consulting over mathematics and other things. I guess I was a bit the better student. It was he who introduced me to the fraternity. Now he is a very big plumber in New York and lives on Park Avenue. There were three of us in the class of 1919 in our fraternity. The third was Bob Trube. Bob came from a family of people who had not much chin, so he used to walk between classes with his chin high up in the air, chewing his cud. Bob had been brought up in France, where his father, also a Stevens man, was an engineer. As a result Bob spoke French. Soon after graduation he started working abroad. He worked later for quite a while for Solvay chemicals in Syracuse, New York. When I went over to England on my way to France, he greeted me in London. Then his father greeted me in Paris and introduced me to some terrific meals. Bob died in 1932 in Paris of an infected tooth.

After my freshman year, sacrificing the tower room with the beautiful light and views on the river—this meant a lot to me— I elected to move to another room with three other roommates who had become friends. Two were my classmates and our beds were right together, side by side. I had the center bed. The great fun in roughhousing was to shove me down between the beds. My two classmates were Kenneth Plimpton and Buz Philips. The third was in his junior year, Walter Baggaley.

January 24, 1965

11 a.m. to 12:30 p.m.

I took every course as it came. I had some facility in mathematics —won a hundred once or twice in exams. In high school, I had been trained to be studious, working every night at home, seldom going out. On top of it all, I liked mathematics.

In addition to football, I decided to try to play lacrosse. The first time out, we ran through Hoboken and back; I tried to catch up with another fellow—the captain of the track team. I went to bed very uncomfortable that night, not only sore in every muscle but sick to my stomach through exertion. I don't think anything like this happened again. With the lacrosse team we ran a quarter mile twice, every day or so. One day I won. I don't know how it happened. I was congratulated by everybody. It was during the junior year.

During our sophomore year, we had a math professor, a graduate of Stevens, who used to make all the students take their rubbers off as soon as they entered the class. He argued that our hair would fall out if we did not comply.

Later, the electricity course was a bit vague for me because it was carried out in a badly lit room in an old prep school building inherited by the institute. This inheriting of old buildings can be very bad for many places. It would be good if one could modify them, but in most cases they were designed for something else. Some World War I buildings were good for dormitories, but with their extensive black spaces between windows, they later made very poor classrooms. These buildings I saw later, when I was already through college.

In spite of being a fraternity member, I must have been rather democratic at heart. Once, when we were considering the membership of a man in my class, I was asked for an opinion:

"I like him, he says hello to me."

Thereafter, I was addressed by the fraternity with whistle and hello!

The fraternity was Delta Tau Delta. I won't bother to explain why the letters were selected—it is an old story and secret stuff. There were twenty to twenty-five of us. I was very fond of my fraternity brothers and enjoyed their company.

Members were chiefly athletes—and the sons of well-to-do businessmen or engineers. I was not much of an athlete, neither well to do, so I joined later. They invited me because I was a fairly good student and played lacrosse, I guess.

Peggy had decided to teach me how to dance when we lived

Bud
Seiler

"I was very fond of my fraternity brothers"

The House

Bemy wood

Larry Martin + Ladies

Hartmann

Hartmann + Sig Johnson

Lord + Koch

Walter Baggaley

Bob Trube, Bill Drew + myself

on Taylor Street in San Francisco. I first danced with her and some friends. I guess I was rather slow. But in Stevens we perfected our dancing and became a fine bunch of finale hoppers. Once the lacrosse team went to play at Swarthmore. We lost the game 6 to 1. But we were invited to stay for a ball they were having and were able to show them some new steps.

Jada—Jada—Jada-jada-jing-jing-gee! or something like that. This consisted in taking a run and three steps very fast sideways.

In spite of my enthusiasm for lacrosse, I was not very agile. Father came to watch a game one day and he heard some boys say, when I got a ball on my stick:

"Go it, Sandy, don't fall down now."

In the fraternity house, I was often consulted about mathematics. We had a little Japanese named Matsui as a major-domo. He claimed to be related to one of the big Japanese houses, and to have been involved in Tokyo riots. He then had lived two years in Paris before taking a boat to New York. He landed in Hoboken and in Hoboken he stayed. His initials were N. J. As I was always interested in foreign languages and knew his initials stood for Neogi Joseph, I asked him where did he get the Joseph. He replied:

"I beg your pardon, sir, I Christian gentleman!"

He had a big Irish wife and was very nice. He also had a sewing machine. When we joined the naval reserve as students in the fall of 1918, we borrowed it to improve the sloppy clothing issued to us, in order to make it look seagoing. This involved cutting down collar width and sewing the seams tighter around the ribs. Having reduced the collar we needed a bigger hat, but that we could not manage and we had to buy it. The fellow who inspired this undertaking was a fraternity brother from Chicago. He was training on a boat and told us what was seagoing and what was not. I was the main seamstress.

Before joining the naval reserve, however, in the summer of 1916 I had spent five weeks at the Plattsburg Civilian Military Training Camp, quite enjoyably pretending to be a soldier. A year later, in the spring of 1917, we entered the war and military training was decreed for Stevens. All people with experience were asked to step forward. I did so and was made guide of the battalion. That's the guy who walks out front. As I had a way of arching my back, throwing my chest and belly forward, I soon got nicknamed "the man of 400 degrees."

This embarrassed me quite a bit. So I used to take home my breeches on Sunday and try to sew in the seat of the pants on mother's sewing machine. It was good sewing training for later achievements, but it did not work. I simply had to become hardened to the compliments of my onlookers.

Our military training consisted mostly in lining up, counting off, close-order drill, and marching on the athletic field. I learned to talk out of the side of my mouth and have never been quite able to correct it since.

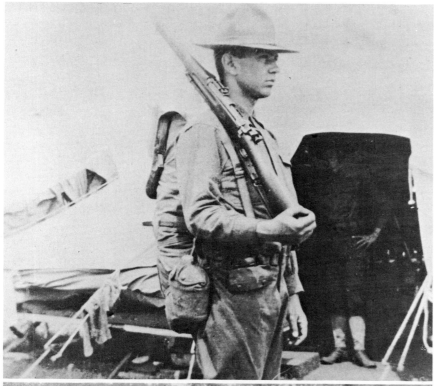

"The man of 400 degrees"—standing up and . . . on his belly

The most amusing feature of the drill was the number of dogs who drilled with us and seemed to understand the maneuvers of the file closer. They seemed to grasp everything, and when we came up to company front they would be standing at the head of the line. They were not K-9, but plain ordinary mutts.

In the fall of 1918, this time we had joined the Student's Army Training Corps, Naval Section, and we discovered that all the canteens were open to us, especially the one at Brooklyn where there were charming girls to dance with. Thereafter we spent most of our time organizing our weekends, and it was rather a disappointment to have our corps disbanded at the end of the war.

Incidentally, during our college life there were two letters, KB —Konstant of Buggeration—which were very important in our lives. They represented the number by which the result one got must be multiplied or divided to get the true answer. KB was a fictitious and variable coefficient out of which one could get the true answer from a mistaken conclusion.

Finally came the big day of graduation, and next the getting of a job.

January 25, 1965

10:15 a.m. to 11:45 a.m.

My first job. In 1919 I went to work in Rutherford, New Jersey, for an automotive engineer named Tracy. He had been a racing-car driver. There were two other employees, one older, the other younger than I. My first misfortune was to tell them that I was a college graduate, and that "I thought I could learn it, if I did not know it" or something like that. They just eased me out after two weeks. So I learned that the first problem was to get along with fellow workers.

Then I consulted an old Scots mining engineer, a friend of father's. He sent me to a friend in the New York Edison Company on Fifteenth Street. I was given a job as draftsman. Work was at a very low ebb, so much so that the draftsmen played chess in the afternoon and nobody was doing much. Apart from a few explorations of various power plants such as the Waterside one at Fortieth Street, where big generators were housed with a large system for handling coal overhead, I found the occupation quite dull.

This went on till the late fall of 1920, when Fritz Murray, another fraternity brother, invited me to join a journal called *Lumber,* in St. Louis. I guess I was not greatly inspired—I had only one suggestion to make in the nine months I stayed there. Murray made lots of photos of logging installations and collected data about them. I suggested they glue the information on the back of the photos. At the end of a year or so, Murray believed this sug-

48

gestion was worthy of a raise and he asked one for me, but the boss was adamant and I left.

I guess my next job was with Nicholas Hill, a hydraulics engineer; he was also a fraternity brother, but did not remember it, being much older than I. He had designed a water-supply project for Bridgeport, Connecticut, and there were a lot of maps to color —my job. I once asked the boss a question or two regarding engineering operations and was rebuffed: "Get along with your maps!"

In the meantime, another draftsman there landed a job with some "efficiency engineers." He took me along to Miller, Franklyn, Bassett. By the way, there was no Miller and no Franklyn, but merely a Mr. Bassett whose book on efficiency I had to buy. Therein I learned that if you have a nightclub doing well—don't enlarge it, because people like to bump their rumps. (Sometime later, I met a big handsome girl named Fischbine, the daughter of an electric company called Miller and Fischbine. I asked her, "Where is Mr. Miller?" "He does not exist. Fischbine does not sound well by itself," she modestly explained.) The outfit decided to send me to Youngstown, Ohio, to the Truscon Company, who made window sashes. I resolved to start this third job with a new face, a more mature one. So before going to Ohio, I raised a mustache to look more like a seasoned engineer. It did not help much in Ohio, but I kept it for nine years more, in various states of wax, no wax, trailing and droopy.

During my college years, and till I went out to Ohio to work for the Truscon Company, my idea of a pleasant evening was to go to a Stevens dance at my fraternity. I wore mainly suits that my parents bought from a friend who was in "the clothing business." Maybe he was not in the clothing business at all, or maybe he was not a friend. At any rate, before leaving for Ohio, I went over to the old fraternity one evening in a Brooks Brothers suit. I was congratulated all around and those who did not believe it had to touch the label. I guess the fraternity was somewhat snobbish. The girls came from nearby colleges or well-to-do families. One time I took a girl and nobody looked at us or bothered to cut in. But on one occasion I barely managed to get a dance from another girl I had invited—my fraternity brothers were all cutting in. I did not quite grasp why then, but understood later it was because she danced "very close."

After college, I mostly supported myself with the jobs as they came, $30 a week in some cases and $165 a month with the efficiency engineers Miller, Franklyn, Bassett, the best salary I obtained. I received a little help here and there from father and mother, but I distinctly remember trying hard to borrow three dollars from mother to go to a dance at Webster Hall and being

Alexander Calder at twenty-two. ". . . I raised a mustache to look more like a seasoned engineer"

49

refused. I was very peeved. Later on, however, when I left for Paris, mother gave me seventy-five dollars a month for quite a while.

In Ohio, my immediate boss came for two weeks each month.

Above him was a man who came twice a month.

Then another man who came only once a month. I saw him twice because I stayed two months. He showed me how to eat a piece of pie in four bites: that was efficiency.

As I did not smoke and was surrounded by tobacco fumes of others, I'd leave the office and go for a breath of fresh air in the yard. One day the plant efficiency engineer (their own) warned me, and then had me fired because I was not being efficient.

None of these experiences meant too much to me or discouraged me greatly, because I had never been too enthusiastic over the jobs in the first place. In this last one, I was just counting labor tickets. So Miller, Franklyn, Bassett demoted me to assistant accountant. I took it as a matter of course. I had a six-month contract and—who could tell?—I might turn out to be a fine accountant.

In the process, I read books (one or two) by Alexander Hamilton and enrolled at Pace and Pace—here the two names were on equal terms—Business College in downtown New York. Soon, I was quite confounded by all the machinations for pretending you had kept your books honestly. So I left after some months of desultory attendance.

One time, I had a job with the department store Abraham & Straus, in their "systems" department. There were four or five of us under one director, way up in the attic of the building. There was some dispute with a salesman about which system for making change for the customers was the faster: the Lamson Conveyor or the cash register. So, I was stationed on the main floor with a stop watch, counting the time it took customers to pay and get their change with either method. I was bareheaded and was often interrupted by people asking for their way out or for the nighties department. To stop this, I took to wearing a bowler. This mystified everybody, including the house detective. I guess I left before concluding on the Lamson Conveyor or the cash register, but after a discussion with the boss—a rather heated one. He had become crabby after being flooded with inquiries:

"Who is this man with a bowler, a gray herringbone suit, a mustache, and a stop watch?"

Next I had a rather sordid job, working for an insurance company investigator. I had to make lists of burnt knitting machines in a place which had had a fire and in which arson was suspected. I went back to the office to draft my report. There were a lot of figures and the crude electric bulb hurt my eyes. I complained to the boss and was told, "To hell with your eyes."

So I said, "To hell with you."

Upon which I took my coat and left.

The next job took me to a little town in West Virginia to demonstrate a motorized garden cultivator. I had gone through a few days of instruction with the mechanic. I soon discovered that although the machine cost only twenty-five dollars originally, the replacements were very dear. In other words, they made their money through servicing. The mechanic had advised me, "If anybody asks what the price of a part is, estimate it low."

In West Virginia, I was shown a garden patch to demonstrate the ability of the machine and merely succeeded in ripping up a perfect row of cucumbers that I had singled out inadvertently. Next, I was taken to the country club with some mower attachment; here the machine refused to budge. So again I came back to New York.

In New York, the next job I had was with a Mr. Williams and his father; they were machinery designers, inventors of sorts, and I was supposed to do their lettering. They were both very nice.

In Pasadena, as before, my parents had gathered musicians and singers around occasionally. One of these was Clinton Balmer, a painter who liked to sing. He came to New York and in 1922 he taught drawing at a public school on East Forty-second Street. He gave night classes. I guess it was father who suggested that I try to join his course and draw under him. I became very enthusiastic —more so than in any other of my post-college ventures so far— and attended consistently.

There was a nude model we drew in charcoal—which I find a sloppy medium now. But then I enjoyed it. I don't remember much of Clinton Balmer's instructions; he was a pleasant and mild man. But I remember that when you wanted to draw a new line, he asked you to draw a shadow over the old line—we crosshatched it. I still do that now when working on a stabile or other model. It was a real pleasure for me to find myself in a group that shared the same interest. Ben Shahn thinks that we were perhaps in the same class, but I don't remember . . . I don't seem to remember any particular student in that class. There were no playboys, and I guess we all concentrated on what we were doing.

It is about at this point that I lost my enthusiasm for the fraternity parties and dances I used to enjoy so much. I went to the fraternity one evening and was hailed by a brother who eventually held an important chemical engineering job:

"Sandy, have you been painting any naked women lately?"

This was the last time I went to the fraternity.

Anyhow, a graduate who gives up engineering is regarded as

"Special characteristics: none"

Act, May 28, 1796
Sec. 4588, R.S.

58069

SEAMAN'S CERTIFICATE OF AMERICAN CITIZENSHIP
(To be retained by seaman)

I, GEORGE W. ALDRIDGE, Collector of Customs, District of NEW YORK, do hereby certify that Alexander Calder; an American seaman, Aged, 23 years or thereabouts; of the height of 5 ft. 10 in., Color, of eyes Hazel, of hair Dk Brown, Complexion Ruddy, Special characteristics None.

has, this day produced to me proof and I do hereby certify that said

Alexander Calder;

is a CITIZEN OF THE UNITED STATES OF AMERICA.

In Witness Whereof I have hereunto set my hand and seal of office this MAY 20 1922 day of ______ 19__.

GEORGE W. ALDRIDGE, Collector of Customs
By L.W. Reinhard
Acting Deputy Collector.

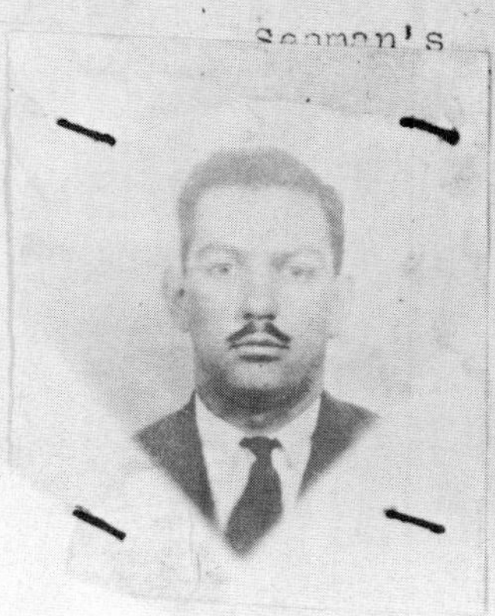

Seaman's Signature — Alexander Calder

Seal

Seaman's Left Thumbprint

somewhat of a screwball by the rest of the engineers, and they are apt to consider that he's "gone wrong." Three such cases come to my mind: myself, Stevens class of 1919; Leslie Glenn, Stevens class of 1920, who became a preacher; then there was Fritz Breitenfeld, Stevens class of 1920, who became a chiropractor, I believe.

January 28, 1965

4:00 p.m. to 5:50 p.m.

In the spring of 1922, the steamship *Great Northern* had its name changed to *H. F. Alexander*. It was in overhaul at Chester, Pennsylvania. They wanted men for the crew. The company scheduled a one-way trip to New York, then from New York to San Francisco, taking in Hawaii, and returning to San Francisco. Applicants were asked to write the engineer at Chester, Pennsylvania. I did so, mentioning that I had a degree as a mechanical engineer—and never had an answer. The stepfather of Peggy's husband, of my brother-in-law, was a banker in Aberdeen, Washington. I advised him by postcard that I would like to sign up as a fireman—it was an oil burner. I got a wire back telling me to look up somebody in downtown New York for the job I wanted. Thus, I entered the boiler room through the "big door," and sometime in June 1922 we shoved off down the Hudson.

The *H. F. Alexander* was quite a large ship. It carried over seven hundred passengers and a crew of about a thousand, counting the waiters. When I proudly showed father my seaman's certificate before leaving, he remarked on the fact that at "Special Characteristics" there was inscribed *"None."* My mustache must have been too short at the time. It was strange to be faced with the four hours on duty and eight hours off schedule. Once or twice I had worked somewhat similarly at Stevens, before exams, and found it rather amusing, though one would get very sleepy. At any rate, work in the boiler room and leisure on deck were two distinct compartments.

There seemed to be two or three lightweight boxers on the crew. One of them was an Irishman of whom I was rather fond, so I called him "limey." This did not please him and he replied:

"If you call me limey again, I'll sock you."

There were some giants too. One morning we had an unusual breakfast with hard-boiled eggs. An enormous Italian ate seventeen. The crew, though well fed, were always hungry. When the waiters were serving the passengers, the giants or the lightweights would block the passageways and swipe food off the trays. One guy got a box of caviar and when he got it opened he said, "Jesus Christ, what's that stuff?"

It was on board the *H. F. Alexander* that I made my knee-patches. I had short drawers and overalls. Grease and dirt got into my knees, raising pimples. I took two squares of wiper's rags and prolonged the drawers over the knees. So I got the name "Kneepad Boy."

Down in the boiler room we were supposed to turn a valve, remove a strap of metal, remove a U-shaped tube about two feet long, and clean the filter at one end and the nozzle at the other —then put it all back. As a measure of economy the ship had filled its tanks with Cuban oil. It turned out to be full of sawdust. Many times boiler pressure went off due to stoppage of these burners, and as there was only one little penknife for five or six firemen, the officers would show off by pulling as many tubes out as possible at one time and throwing them on a table, as if the firemen and not the inferior fuel were responsible for the stoppages; thereupon you could not find the penknife. This did not seem rational to me.

I made one or two inventions during this trip. I rigged up a baffle where the breeze came down in the boiler room and directed it toward me. I am not quite sure whether or not I deprived others of any fresh air in the process, or whether this device was beneficial to all.

The other invention was to spew a mouthful of drinking water up into the air—it would come down with a shower effect.

I guess I also hammered out a scraper in the ship's workshop, to alleviate the penknife shortage.

There were great coils of hawser on the deck and when off duty, I used to like to sleep on them. That's how I missed my Stevens friend Juncadella in Havana, though what I saw of the Havana stop was exciting: bumboats bringing fruit and drink, trying to sell them to the passengers and sailors; sailors on shore leave, leaving in these bumboats—there were all kinds of happenings and even some that I did not quite understand at the time.

In Panama, I had two hours of shore leave. I hopped a cab and went to the native city at around midnight. It was very spectacular—no traffic laws, the buildings with open fronts, curtains between pillars instead of walls. I guess I found all this more spectacular than my other crewmates because I did not drink at all at the time.

It was early one morning on a calm sea, off Guatemala, when over my couch—a coil of rope—I saw the beginning of a fiery red sunrise on one side and the moon looking like a silver coin on the other. Of the whole trip this impressed me most of all; it left me with a lasting sensation of the solar system.

When we entered San Pedro, off Los Angeles, I was sent to get some waste (wiper's rags) in a locker on one side of the ship. There was a porthole giving on the dock. I tarried to watch the boarding operations. So, I was hailed by imprecations upon delivering the stuff in the boiler room.

Many of the crew were hoping we would not get to Hawaii too soon so they'd have more money to spend—they must have been paid by the day. By the time we reached San Francisco, I had had enough of the boiler room, so I decided to stay ashore. My good friends the Blisses were there to meet me. We had not met for five years. They took me home to dinner and then to the City Hall to watch the Shriner's Parade. The Shriners march this way, they meet, they march that way; then they separate, and repeat the motions. I have always regretted missing this human mobile because I fell asleep in our reserved spot in the stands. I just naturally fell asleep.

After two or three days in San Francisco, I managed to catch an empty lumber schooner returning to Willapa Harbor in Washington. They sent lots of lumber from Washington and the empty boats went back with some passengers. I intended to visit my sister Peggy and her husband, Kenneth Hayes.

The boat left at about five in the evening. They immediately served supper. It seemed to open and close on onions with a square meal in between. There was a ground swell and a rough sea. The boat was much smaller than the *Alexander,* and my previous experience and my seaman's certificate were not of much use. I suffered quite a lot till I got rid of the onions. There was a lady and two young things on board, and their Ford too. If I had not got rid of my seasickness before I saw them, I would have on the spot. They wore pink fluffy ruffles as waists, high-heeled slippers, and khaki breeches.

We made Willapa Harbor in two days and I continued by bus to Aberdeen.

January 29, 1965

5:00 p.m. to 6:00 p.m.

Aberdeen in those days, with its sawmills, logging trains, and logging ponds, was very spectacular. Every mill had a burner, a sort of metal silo—with a hemispherical gauze top, a spark arrester—

in which they burned the sawdust. In the day you heard the whine of saws; at night you could see the glow of the burners. They burned all day and night—otherwise the mills would have been snowed under with sawdust.

Peggy and Ken came down to meet me from American Lake, near Tacoma, a several hours' drive. They took me back there with them. Their two boys, Calder and Kenneth, were four and two at the time. Pine-covered slopes surrounded the lake. They were misty at times. The lake was big and uncontaminated, and there were few boats on it. It was fine swimming water. Playing with the kids on the water's edge was good fun. I even swam with the smaller one on my back. We used to go dancing at a nearby lodge, "The Shingle Weaver's Crawl." I spent two carefree summer months there.

Then, I don't know who thought of it, but there was some question of my working in the bank of my brother-in-law's stepfather, the Hayes and Hayes Bank. There was also some question of my working in a shingle mill at Markham. But Kenneth finally chose that job, while I got another one as timekeeper in a logging camp at Independence, Washington.

Here, I lived in a shack built on skids and yanked off a flatcar at the proper spot on the camp. My camp's foreman was Cranky Jack Moore and his wife was Bertha the Cook. I was supposed to make out pay checks for people. I also had to scale the logs as they were loaded on the flatcars.

They would fell the logs up the mountains, then bring them in by means of a high lead and a high line. The lead consisted of a topped tree. There was a very special man called the high-climber. He'd climb up a tall tree as it stood, and cut off the top. With a belt and a rope, an ax and a saw, he would climb up there. When he got through, the tree would be guyed with six or eight cables, and an enormous block pulley on top, weighing about two hundred pounds, with a cable running through it would drag the logs, with the help of a donkey steam-engine, to the foot of the tree or its vicinity. If a ravine had to be crossed, two trees would be topped, one on either side. Then a high-lead cable would be strung from one tree to the other and a carriage pulley would drag the trees across by means of a cable pulled by a donkey engine.

The donkeys were set on heavy skids and could pull themselves by siwashing from stump to stump—they'd attach a cable to a stump and pull themselves toward it. Logs were held by short lines with hooks called chokers. I was fascinated by this cable, pulley, donkey, and log world, and above all by the crews of small men handling these huge trees so much bigger than themselves.

The ground was very mountainous and uneven, and there were

many stumps. The men made the trees fall where they wanted. This was done by felling the tree with a very definite cut and boosting it behind that cut with wedges. The men would saw halfway through the trunk of the tree, and chop a wedge-shaped opening on that side. Then they would saw from the opposite side and drive a wedge in behind the saw. Finally, the remaining wood became so reduced that the tree would fall away from the wedge. The idea was to hang the tree up on its stump horizontally.

The most dangerous job of all was that of the sawyer, called the "bucker-up." He was the man who cut the felled trees into logs. When the bucker-up cut the logs, he was sometimes uncertain as to which way they were going to swing. Sometimes he was even caught by the sudden movement of the log as it separated from the rest of the tree. There could be real trouble. A guy was killed in the process, right in our camp; he left his upper teeth in a log.

However, the most highly paid jobs were those of the high-climber and of the saw filer—they got ten dollars a day. In our camp there was a story about a high-climber who started to notch the top of a tree, but as he did not saw it deep enough, the tree started splitting down, threatening to tear off his sustaining rope. When he saw this he planted his ax through the rope, cutting it and burying the ax in the solid wood with the same blow. He then hung on to the ax till he found a way to reach the ground safely. Maybe the story is merely a legend, but it could well be true.

I had a few verbal fights with Bertha the Cook—once because I forgot to order some supplies that she felt she needed badly. Once I even had a row with Cranky Jack Moore, her husband. He might have been jealous of my having gotten the job through the boss and of my being a college graduate.

The language was as tough, rough, and spectacular as were the jobs involved. It would complete the circle from "f———ing the dog," which meant that a particular person was stalling on the job, to "dirty old bald-headed Christ and all the f———ing angels," when anything went wrong. And plenty of things did go wrong, despite the over-all achievement. The cables frayed and presented sharp points called "jaggers." All wore thick hide gloves of the best quality, but on occasion these jaggers would run through a hand when a cable was seized inadvertently.

The logs, when on the ground, were sawed off in one-yard lengths, then split up with soft steel wedges. The steel was soft so that the wedges would not break, but they would after a while when badly mushroomed. A chunk of metal would fly off horizontally, like shrapnel, inflicting severe wounds in many cases.

I had not drawn or painted much since night class in New York, but somehow the desire to paint the logging-camp landscape made me write home and ask for paints and brushes. I remember painting on wood three snow-covered peaks that must have covered quite an arc, thus re-creating somehow or other on a flat surface a circular field of vision. The effort might not have been too successful, since mother used this painting later to place a fishbowl on.

The food was pretty good and at any rate plentiful. Anything that could come out of a can did. They opened the cans with a cleaver. The toast was painted with melted butter. The butter remained in a dish on the stove and a special varnish brush was dipped into that. There were pies, jam, bacon, eggs galore. The idea was to feed the men as much as possible with no waiting periods in between, so that they could not argue and talk themselves into a fight.

Once, I remember getting a ride in somebody's car on our way down fifty miles to Aberdeen and being placed in charge of a fellow who had lost a finger. He was lifting a cable off a stump and the donkey driver tightened up the cable inadvertently—he was probably a long way off. They got the man tight on applejack to ease his sufferings.

In those days there was a young boy called the "whistle-punk." His duty was to pull a rope which came by straight runs and right-angle take-offs from the donkey whistle. He'd send in a message to the donkey operator. The message meant take up the cable, or slack off, etc. One little mistake, or error in interpretation, could cost a man a finger or a hand. Nowadays this job is done electronically.

There was also a handy man named Jim Watson who used to split firewood for the cookhouse. One of his chief preoccupations was how to relieve his bladder without getting out of bed.

Bertha Moore's kitchen assistants were called "cookhouse flunkies." And one day Watson came out with this:

"These cookhouse flunkies don't wear enough to flag a handcar."

January 30, 1965

4:00 p.m. to 5:50 p.m.

I guess I had a definite row with Cranky Jack Moore which broke up our relations. My relatives in the bank seemed to find it amusing that I could get along with him at all, but it ceased to amuse me, so we parted company.

I got another job in a nearby camp, building a railroad, getting ready to do the logging. I stayed there close to three months. The boss here was a very nice Irishman, Pat Murphy. He'd only annoy me—I always loved a lot of fresh air, like my father—by closing all the windows when shaving, because it dried up his soap.

This time my job was a drafting job that took a certain amount of engineering. We were drafting the cuts and the fills for the railroad. I even devised some short-cut method of calculating all this. It worked very well, but I don't quite remember the exact procedure now. This job was more satisfactory to me than all those I had held so far, because I was at least using some of my engineering knowledge.

But there was another draftsman who insisted on closing the windows and building a fire. I found it too hot and opened the windows and poured water on his fire. I don't know if I left on account of that or not. I guess I really wanted to get back to art school in New York. Also, I was getting fed up with all these miscellaneous jobs. I remember the dullest of all, some interim job which consisted in opening cases of six cans of applesauce and gluing some label on each can—to pretend the applesauce came from somewhere else—and then closing the case again. That is certainly about the dullest thing I ever had to do. I also remember working in another Aberdeen lumber yard, belonging to some Englishman. I forget what I did precisely, but it was not much. So I asked the owner if there was a chance of becoming part of the business. He said no. He was an old-timer who had built his business by fighting tooth and nail with local competitors.

Through some business connection, father had known a certain Canadian engineer. Father saw him in 1923 and told him I was looking for a job as an engineer. He said he could not import me, but if I came to Canada to seek a job, he could take me on. I went to Vancouver and called on him, and we had quite a talk about what career I should follow. He advised me to do what I really wanted to do—he himself often wished he had been an architect. So, I decided to become a painter.

I guess it was in September–October 1923, at twenty-five, that I entered the Art Students League, in New York at Fifty-seventh Street near Columbus Circle. I had piled up a few thousand dollars in the logging camps, in spite of which I came back to live at home with my parents at 111 East Tenth Street, east of Third Avenue. Mother was certainly pleased to see me and father was too, though later on he might have had some misgivings about my early failure to earn money as an artist and about my having quit engineering, which guaranteed my earning a decent living.

Mother seemed to think I should go to the class of George Luks at the Students League, but I had some difficulty in getting in and spent some days in the class of Kenneth Hayes Miller.

59

This class seemed rather funny to me, because Miller's technique was to have his students draw a life-class figure which could be a nude sitting on a stool; then the student, to show his imagination, was supposed to invent the drapes, the shelves, little windows, fruits and flowers, and an assortment of shadows, as background.

Miller only came in once or twice a week, and during my short stay there, though informed of his technique, I did not have the pleasure of meeting him. I was behind a painter named Jan Matulka, of Czechoslovakian descent, whom I did not know then but got to know later. At any rate, I was fascinated by the funny creases in his trousers and did a rear-end view of him drawing. After three days' wait, one morning I got into Luks's class. Here, there were several old ladies with tortoise-shell hair. They were probably one-time schoolmistresses who had saved up for this grand occasion—to go to New York and paint. They lived on a

"I guess the center of my composition was usually a derrick or some such device . . ." Calder's early efforts at the Art Students League

very modest scale; I remember they used to save the paper napkins from the lunchroom as paint rags. There were also some young people, even some very young girls. I made friends with a fellow named Chadeayne. He lived up the Hudson River, knew a man who had taught painting at Vassar, and had studied with him. Chadeayne could paint beautiful sunsets and sunlight effects on walls, leaves, and so on, but his pictures were lacking in people; he did not know how to draw or paint them and hoped to learn this at the Art Students League. He was rather friendly, so he and I would go around New York where a building was going up, or by the elevated, and he would pour on the sunlight out of a tin can.

My chief delight was probably hanging up the canvas with a few nails and string. Thus I could attach it to a fence, a post, or anything. I guess the center of my composition was usually a derrick or some such device, and I tried to carve out its most potent features from the surrounding atmosphere. Later we used to go out painting in the evening, and I thought I was getting pretty good at painting artificial lights.

I also went in the evening to John Sloan's class, where my best friend was the monitor John Debrowsky. He died two years ago in London at the age of ninety. I never was conscious that he was much older than I when I knew him at the Art Students League. Sloan was a good instructor, not trying to make you do it his way but urging you to develop some capabilities of your own. But Debrowsky first attracted my attention by drawing a nude with two pencils, one red and one black, and starting with the feet and running right up. Later on, when trying to earn a living, at a time when we all would have liked to do fashion art, he turned out some drawings that looked impeccable to me, but he could not sell any.

We got to be an *équipe* of four or five of us; another was named Brodsky, a somewhat similar-sounding name to the monitor's. There were short pauses in the class. We would draw very rapidly and the first who finished would show off his drawing. We certainly were the most boisterous of the lot, which comprised many timid, meek and mild students.

They used to sell wrapping paper at the League and we found out that it was pretty good for drawing. You folded a sheet into eight rectangles and it would fit in your pocket. With this we used to pass our time drawing people in the subway on our way to and fro.

I seemed to have a knack for doing it with a single line. And once, in one of my job-hunting moments, I tried the *Police Gazette*. The editor, Robinson, was interested in this single-line drawing and gave me a modest job, doing half-pages of boxers training,

"I seemed to have a knack of doing it with a single line." Art Students League drawings

Calder's portrait of his father

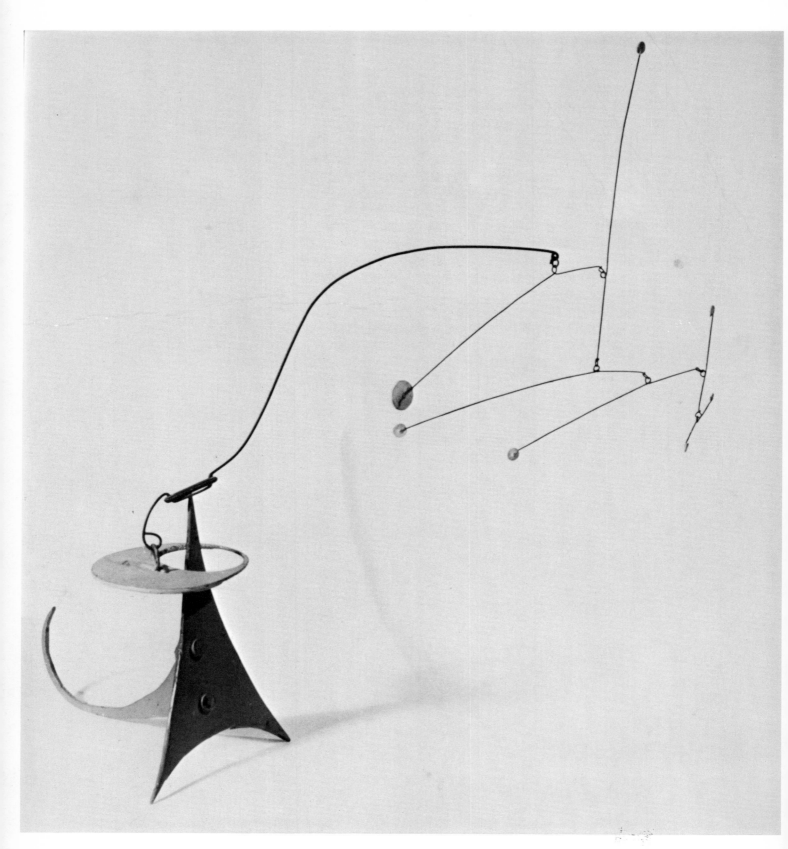

Little Pierced Disc

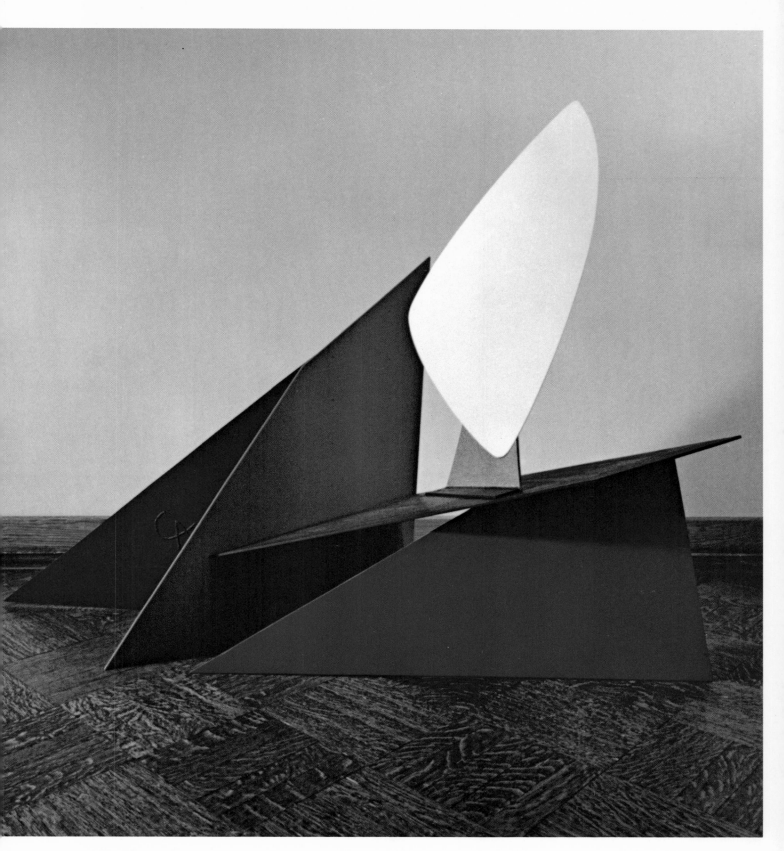

"Multicolore," 1958

"Birds"

"Pomegranate
1949

which developed into covering other sports as well. I got to be pretty good friends with Robinson and a year later we went out to paint on a Sunday. It was a rather dreary day and there was a Long Island farm in the distance. Robinson set up his canvas on an easel and started to paint the farm. I nailed my canvas to a tree behind him and started to paint him. As I did not buy new canvases but old ones from the League, there was a naked lady on mine who gradually retired as Robinson increased. He saw it about midway and was horrified.

I remember another time when I was out painting with Chadeayne on the Stevens campus overlooking the Hudson. This time I had an old canvas. I finally covered it with a penetrating Prussian blue, then proceeded to paint on it a red derrick on a barge that was passing before me. Due to the Prussian blue, the red derrick became pink.

One day there was a new model in Sloan's class, a small woman. I was startled to learn that she was Brodsky's wife.

Luks came in quite high sometimes and we used to have a rather good time in his class. He was even reputed at one point to have painted out the picture brought by a young lady who after painful labors was convinced she had achieved the acme of perfection. Luks was the son of a Pennsylvania miner; he sold quite a bit of his stuff and lived fairly well.

Sloan, on the other hand, was a careful, frugal man. Once a client bought from Sloan twenty pictures for twenty thousand dollars—which would keep him going a long time. Luks would have blown this in a few months.

In his class, Luks would take a large varnish brush and dip it in the probably brown or gray residue of yesterday to smear a whole new canvas with the mixture. Then with another brush he would put in a pink egg for a head, blue eye-dots, red lips, climaxing with the fine art of putting in the shadows and highlights— everybody else trying to do the same thing.

Sloan never touched anybody's work, but he could make a cutting remark if he felt like it. I once did the head of a girl and modeled the neck by using a lot of black. I thought it was quite exciting, but he said:

"Oh! The girl with the dirty neck!"

I guess I never quite forgave him.

At the same time, somehow, I took a liking to the painting of Guy Pène du Bois. I felt his girls looked like wood carvings, even somewhat like toys. He had a stunt of painting everything black with blue on one side and orange or red on the other. I was interested in what I thought was a certain solidity in the result, though others feel they look like candy-box designs. I stayed with him several months. I had been with Luks about three.

The fourth teacher I had at the League was Boardman Robinson. He was an excellent teacher. I guess it was he who taught me to draw with a pen and a single line. He was a real person, a big red-headed guy with a beard. I liked him very much. He'd had a job on a newspaper doing daily cartoons at which he was very able. One day they published something of his which did not please the editor and he got bounced forever. Maybe his teaching helped me a bit more than that of others to get my first job as an artist with the *National Police Gazette*. My first paid job. I'd get twenty dollars for a half-page layout.

Thomas Hart Benton, who specialized in horse-and-buggy scenes, was teaching in another class. I went to see the girl monitor and stopped to talk and draw a bit. Benton's motto was, "Even if it's wrong you make it definite"—it might have been his *malheur*; his paintings reminded one of plasteline figures.

My drawing of pugilists for the *Police Gazette* took me to the Madison Square Garden gymnasium, run by a Mr. MacLevy. It was a very exciting room where the men trained. The gym was set in the crop-end of what must have been at one time a theater, for there was a balcony dominating the happenings. There was a white wall for playing handball; in front of this men were shadowboxing, boxing the punching ball, then the heavy-bag, then shadowboxing again. Shadowboxing never ended and it's what finally got you. It was not long before I brought a canvas to this balcony.

Mr. MacLevy came to look at the canvas and swapped it with me for a year's tuition in boxing. I took the canvas home to my father's studio, where I spent the summer of 1924. I was going to complete the canvas and tighten up the drawing. Mr. MacLevy came down one Sunday morning to see how it was coming along. He liked the canvas, but he had a black eye and after looking at my work for a while he said, "Mr. Calder, could you fix this eye?"

There was some cream and lipstick lying around, but it was impossible to match the yellow color of MacLevy's skin. So I made an orange mixture, with red and orange *gouache*, and painted the bruised area quite satisfactorily. He went away happy, I wondering whether the *gouache* would stick on.

I continued for several months with my boxing training, but never got anywhere; it was not any better for me than football. The ex-pro, named Dany, used to say when urging me to put up my gloves and fight:

"You are like an old whore at a wedding."

Maybe he was right.

After my return from the logging camp, and while studying at the Art Students League, as I said before, I went to live with my

67

"Sandy" Calder Goes a-Sketching at Coney Island

LIKE THE JAZZ-MANIA IN "PROCESSIONAL" IS THE EVER-MOVING PICTURE OF LIFE SEEN AT CONEY ISLAND, NEW YORK CITY'S GREAT COSMOPOLITAN RESORT. Artist "Sandy" Calder Has Got Some of This Hurly-burly Into His Sketch, Showing the Side-shows, the "Hot-dog" Stands, the Merry-go-rounds, Games of Chance and the Tin-type Galleries. There's Something Doing Every Second of the Day.

AT THE HORSE SHOW WITH A SKETCHING PAD, BY SANDY CALDER

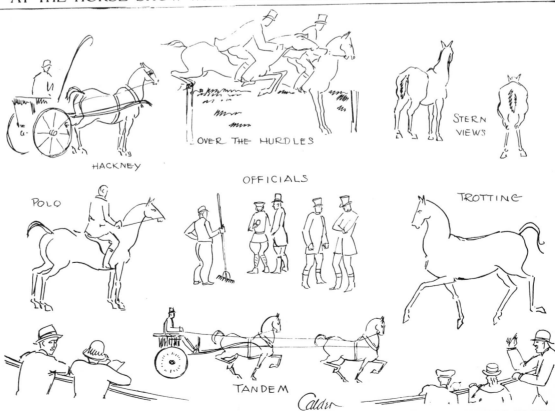

NEW YORK'S ANNUAL SOCIETY AND SPORTING EVENT, AS SEEN BY SANDY CALDER. DESPITE THE ENCROACHMENTS OF THE AUTOMOBILE AND OTHER Mechanical Means of Locomotion, King Horse Still Claims a Loyal Following. Calder Has Caught a Number of the Show's Incidents in "Action Sketches," Reproduced Above.

A SPANISH BEAUTY REHEARSES HER DANCES.

CASTANETS!

SPANISH

LOOSENING UP

ROUGH STUFF

APACHE

VAUDEVILLE STUNT

GETTING HER BREATH

Calder

Pen-and-ink Impressions of Finland's Wonder Runner

A START

SOME OF THE BOYS

"*Boardman Robinson . . . maybe his teachings helped me a bit more than that of others to get my first paid job with the Police Gazette. I'd get $20 for a half-page layout*"

A HIGH-JUMPER TAKES A RUN

THE GREAT PAAVO NURMI

—AFTER THINKING IT OVER

WARMING UP

THE ARENA

Calder

parents. I stayed with them about a year on East Tenth Street. While I was living here—in 1923, obviously—I was always crossing Third Avenue, and there were some very funny shops in that section. There was a "Fat Man's Store"; then there was a store that sold odd bits of clothing—dickies, waiter's aprons—the window was teeming with things and there was a sign:

IF YOU DON'T SEE IT IN THE WINDOW, COME IN AND ASK FOR IT.

And then there was the prize: opposite Cooper Union was a building with a staircase going down to the basement, and propped against the stair rail was a big painting six, seven feet wide by four high. It depicted an enormous room with a double bed in the middle of the far side and mama in bed and papa in a nightshirt, with bare legs, standing around, and a thousand cockroaches all over the place. This was the advertisement for:

HELLO DAD INSECT POWDER

I was so fond of this sign that I made a feeble attempt to purchase it from the owner—and he kicked me out very brusquely.

In the summer of 1924 my parents went to Europe for several months and I then lived in father's studio at 11 East Fourteenth Street. I returned to live with my parents afterward. Then in the fall of 1925, I moved from home again to a sort of sun parlor—an old Stevens fraternity meeting room—atop a five-story building at 259 Madison. It was built on I-beams over the roof, with plenty of glass all around, and was very hot. The sun reverberated strongly there. I had a cot and remember spending several nights in the place. But it was difficult to do any work on account of the glare. While living there, I got a job decorating a Fifth Avenue store for A. G. Spalding—I made drawings of athletes doing this and that. I must have gotten close to $150 for that. I think some of these drawings were good, and it is too bad I kept none—I guess there are none left.

I lived with my parents off and on and had a couple of other rooms in New York while at the Art Students League. When we lived on East Eighth Street, the light in my hall bedroom, where I worked a bit at night, annoyed my father, who was trying to sleep out on his roof-porch. He told me in no doubtful terms to turn the light off and voiced some regrets at my having abandoned engineering for the modest calling of an artist.

About this time, my mother had a carroty cat and I used to sit on the floor and wrestle with him in the evening. Whereupon, father would growl, "Get a book!"

I finally ended up in a second-floor hall bedroom—that is, at the end of the hall and no wider—on Fourteenth Street west of

Seventh Avenue. There were crimson incrustations which I white-washed, but they peeled off and fell on me. I could not work very well there, either—it was too contiguous. When I wanted to get up, I put everything on the bed, and when I wanted to go to bed, I put everything on the floor. I managed to do some bit of a tropical scene on one of the walls, though, with real bananas and oranges in wire rings sticking out of the painted plaster.

I had no clock and faced south, so I made a sundial with a piece of wire—a wire rooster on a vertical rod with radiating lines at the foot indicating the hours.

I'd made things out of wire before—jewelry, toys—but this was my first effort to represent an animal in wire. I don't know what became of it, so I have drawn it now, forty years later, as I remember it.

February 1, 1965

11:20 a.m. to 12:30 p.m.

An art dealer, Marie Sterner, had told me to paint athletic events; so with my *Police Gazette* pass in hand, I went to bicycle races

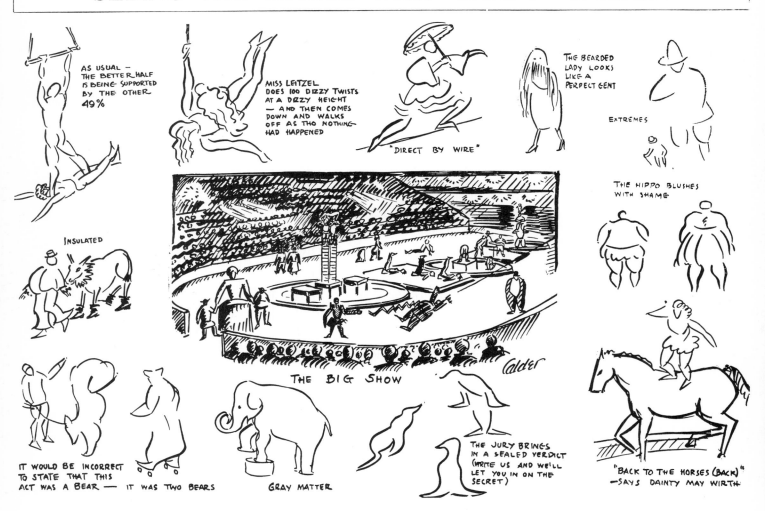

Circus drawing done on the spot by Calder in 1923, thanks to his Police Gazette *pass*

and fights. The bike races, the sprints especially, were very funny, with great big fellows trying to stand up motionless on their pedals to later speed by the opponent who had been forced into the lead.

I went to the circus, Ringling Brothers and Barnum & Bailey. I spent two full weeks there practically every day and night. I could tell by the music what act was getting on and used to rush to some vantage point. Some acts were better seen from above and others from below. At the end of these two weeks, I took a half-page layout to the *Police Gazette* and Robinson said, "We can't do anything with these people, the bastards never send us any tickets."

Circus drawn from memory nine years later

Circus drawings,
1932

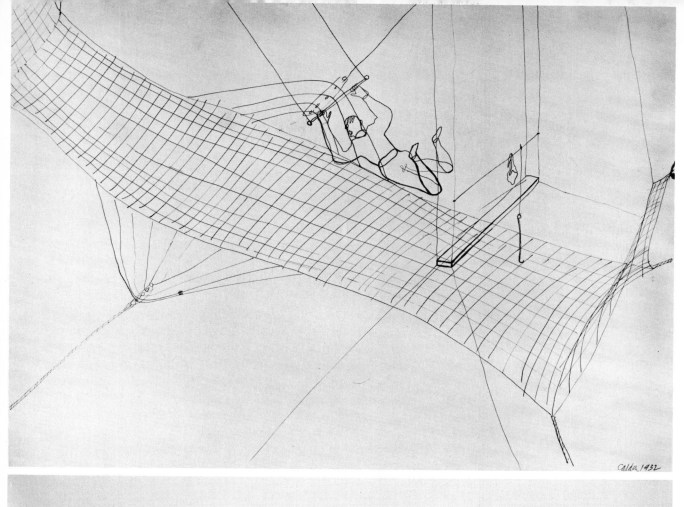

During all this time in New York, I tried to make a living as best I could. I answered many ads. One wanted a "modern and futuristic" design for an envelope. I did not know much about these two terms, but I cut up and organized some scraps of paper and presented that. I had made a more modest alternate drawing, interlaced tulips coming out of a bowl; this was the futuristic choice.

Another time, near Nassau Street, I was invited to paint bathing beauties on banjo-ukuleles. Somehow, my ladies bulged too much, bringing to an end this pleasant occupation.

Another employment offered me was to draw book-match covers, actual size, and then try to peddle them to buyers. I did not bite on this one—the minutiae, the lack of pay, and the improbability of selling any were too much.

As I rode in the subway a lot, I had many ideas for car cards—the advertising overhead. I discovered these were controlled by Barron G. Collier. This tycoon was supposed to have overadvertised many businesses into the red, putting them in debt and thus being in a position to take them over at low cost. He was also supposed to be on so many directing boards that he could not spend more than one day a year with each of the businesses he thus controlled.

Well, I went to see him and was intercepted by a little squirt who admonished me that if I had any ideas about car cards I should keep them under my hat, "because otherwise somebody would steal them."

So Paris seemed the place to go, on all accounts of practically everyone who had been there, and I decided I would also like to go. My parents were favorable to this idea. I must have been seeing Clinton Balmer, my first teacher, occasionally, because he again came to my assistance. In June 1926—I was twenty-eight—he got me a job on a British freighter, the *Galileo* of the Ellerman's Wilson Line. My mother came to say goodbye in Hoboken, then she rushed to Manhattan, to the south ferry, and watched me go out to sea. She said the boat looked awfully small.

This boat ran from Hoboken to Hull. We took seventeen days. It was fine June weather. I was a sort of day laborer, painting the ship. For if it had not been painted it probably would have burst asunder, having been built in 1908. At any rate, it was necessary to cover up the rust to reassure shippers when she docked.

I slept down forward in the forecastle, with all the others, and I opened my porthole. The second day out, however, I was told the water was rough and might come in and that I would have to close it. So eventually, I'd take my mattress into a housing over the steering mechanism in the stern. As there was a big chain moving over a quadrant there, to avoid skidding into it while sleeping I attached my body with a rope to a post.

One crew fellow addressed me as "Chavver." I was at some trouble to explain my name was Calder. Somehow, later I found out it was an expression in Hull for "buddy." They also called me "Hardbake," because I stripped to the waist.

The steward of the *Galileo* kept his job by being economical, and as a result curry would be lavishly used to disguise the poor food. Sometimes the man who arrived with a pan of food would look around inquiringly at our faces—and then scrape it overboard.

I had taken a few of my drawings with me. I showed them to the mate, who of course confided to me that he detested the captain. All the stories of Conrad were borne out in this instance.

As it was June, one fine day I had stripped down to my undershirt and was lying on the deck beneath a lifeboat, painting it. One little roll and I would have found myself overboard—I was greatly tempted by a nice swim.

When we got by the Straits of Dover, I was still in my undershirt, and while we were passing other ships, my shipmates urged me to put on my shirt so that I would not be arrested for "indecency" by some police launch. When we arrived in Hull, after seventeen days, we were "warped" into the dock with long cables. The docks in Hull were approached through a lock and the maneuver had to be accomplished with the proper tide. The ship was soon surrounded by sailors looking for work. I was even put in the charge of the second mate, who took me to a hotel after I had promised that I would not tarry and would leave Hull on the morrow. Thus, I would not augment the cloud of faces around the next ship. I had only gotten the job in New York because there was a sailor lacking from the quota. The skipper had taken me on when I signed a paper that I would be content with five pounds instead of nine, the customary rate (a month's pay).

Much later, I heard vaguely that the *Galileo* had been scuttled in New York Harbor when she caught fire while carrying explosives.

The next morning, I took the Hull-to-London train and met Bob Trube, my Stevens fraternity brother. He invited me to stay with him for a couple of days. I had a bath in a very deep long tub, very British, and was soon off to Paris by train and boat.

In Paris, I was received by Bob's father and taken to a wonderful dinner at Lavenue. Mr. Trube lived at the Hôtel de Versailles, so I stayed there too, for a while, 60 avenue de Montparnasse. I had a mansard room and could look all the way across the roofs of Paris. The second night Mr. Trube took me to a Scandinavian restaurant, the Stryx, rue Higgins, behind the Dôme. Here I encountered smorgasbord for the first time and knocked out fifteen out of seventeen dishes—I did not like anchovies.

February 2, 1965

4:00 p.m. to 6:00 p.m.

Mr. Trube and I walked along the sidewalks and passed by the Dôme. Though I did not understand much about the place, he sneered at "all the artists who don't do any work"—probably because he'd come up the hard way as an engineer.

Some twenty-five years later, I'd been through the Dôme, the Coupole, and all that. I had a show in Paris at the Galerie Maeght. Mr. Trube came and admired my work, this time.

I stayed on at the Hôtel de Versailles for several months. The first few days in Paris, I was at a loss what to do and did not understand much about café life. I sat on a cement bench outside the Dôme and looked at the seated and the passers-by. I guess that the first fellow I recognized was Arthur Frank. He had described Paris to me before I left New York. He had done this with a diagram of Montparnasse and Montmartre. Arthur Frank, a painter, was a quite pleasant and rather vague soul. He had separated from his wife; they had put their furniture in storage and he no longer knew where it was.

Gradually, I met other friends. In New York, six months before leaving, I had picked out some racy tweed cloth at Wanamaker's; one piece had a base of orange with a yellow stripe. I had enough of this for a two-pants suit, so I had it made in New York by a little tailor named Grand. I also had a straw hat with a fraternity ribbon on it. (I no longer went to the dances, but harbored the ribbon.) And I was told by Frank that his friends called me "the cantaloupe with the straw hat." I finally got the habit of going into cafés at will—ease came a bit later on.

Another person I met was Bill Hayter, who was at the time married to a girl I'd known at the League.

I don't think I wasted much time before I went to the Grande Chaumière to draw. Here there were no teachers, just a nude model, and everyone was drawing by himself; the atmosphere was more subdued than at the Art Students League. I was there once when two little American girls from a Southern state came in and one cried out:

"I don't know which it is, but I want to etch or sketch."

There I also met a little Russian who worked for a printer. We made an appointment to swim the next day in the Seine, opposite the Concorde, at the Bains Deligny. He was very late, and in the meantime I played water polo with some fellows and met an Englishman, George Thomson. I have seen him off and on ever since. George worked for the Bank of India and had literary tendencies. One day George and I went to the Musée Rodin. I did not think much of the shaving cream—the marble *mousse* out of which blossoms the kiss of love. He found the kiss more important; the *mousse* distracted my attention. George was rather shocked by my attitude.

I'd only been in Paris two months when I met a girl doing advertising for a travel agency working for the Holland-America Line. She got me a round-trip job to New York and back to Paris, making sketches of life on board from which an advertising brochure was compiled. I also got a couple of hundred dollars.

I finally took a room and studio at 22 rue Daguerre. I was walking along the street when I saw advertised at a hotel, "room for hire." It was a four-meter by five-meter room, one flight up in the rear, with a skylight. This place was heated by a little gas stove on top of which was balanced a receptacle of water. It would evaporate, condense on the skylight, and dribble down on my neck. There was also a radiator, heated by water, barely warm enough to dry a handkerchief, if you waited all day. I still considered myself a painter and was happy to be in my own workroom, in Paris.

I'd get up at seven or eight in the morning and often skip breakfast. Sometimes I went for a cup of coffee, avenue d'Orléans. I remember particularly, one time about ten, a laborer was having a

"... the marble mousse ..."

"... I met a girl doing advertising for a travel agency. ..." S.T.C.A. stands for "Student Third Cabin Association." Calder did these as well as a brochure

79

mixture of things half red and half white.

"The red wine makes you go to sleep, the white makes you jump —so this way you keep on an even keel," he said.

I soon was making small animals in wood and wire and articulating them. I had made myself a little workbench and bought a few tools, some steel wire, and some soft wire in a hardware store on the avenue d'Orléans.

There was also a curious guy from California, a painter of sorts; he was curious because he'd order one course at a restaurant and would wait to see if he was still hungry before he ordered a second one. If he found the fried eggs too juicy, he'd admonish the waiter:

"Take these eggs back and blow their noses."

This was Clay Spohn. I went to call on him once. He'd taken a bath in a zinc tub several days before and he was waiting for someone to appear and help him empty it. It had never occurred to him to use a bucket. When he visited my studio and saw the objects I made out of wood and wire—I had a cow, a four-horse chariot which was quite wonderful but some damn fool lost it—he said, "Why don't you make them completely out of wire?"

I accepted this suggestion, out of which was born the first Josephine Baker and a boxing Negro in a top hat.

In the meantime, through Hayter I got to know José de Creeft, a Spanish sculptor living in the rue Broca, near the Santé, eight or ten blocks from the rue Daguerre. He induced me to make some things for the Salon des Humoristes.

Also, some girls I knew introduced me to a Serb who was in the toy business. The Serb said that if I made some articulated toys I could earn a living at it, so I was interested, because I did not have many nickels. The base of my subsistence was still seventy-five dollars a month provided by mother, and my ingenuity. I made my own workbench, for instance, and whatever furniture was needed, with planks and old cases. So, I immediately set to work and made some articulated toys with wire, wood, tin, and leather. When I looked for my Serb, he had disappeared, but I continued making toys in this way.

Previously, I had embellished a humpty-dumpty circus made by a Philadelphia toy company. There was an elephant and a mule. They could be made to stand on their hind quarters, front quarters, or heads. Then there were clowns with slots in their feet and claws in their hands; they could balance on a ladder on one foot or one hand. I had once articulated these things with strings, so the clown would end up on the back of the elephant.

In my quest to earn a living, I also tried several American advertising agencies in Paris and did a few things for them. At one

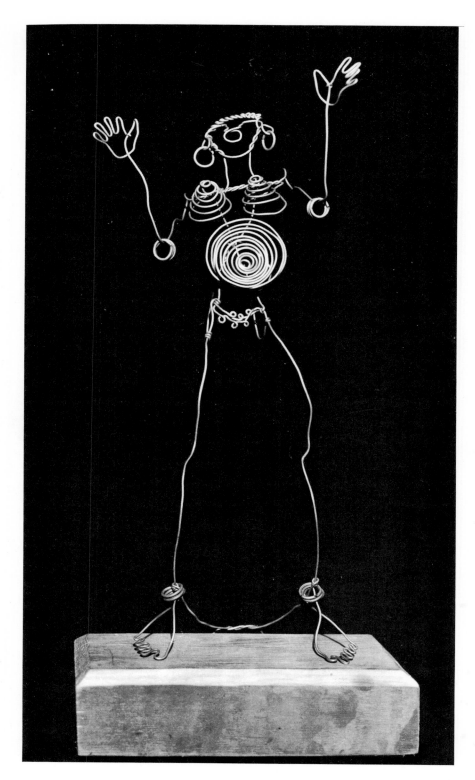

The first Josephine Baker was done by Calder in 1927, sometime after his arrival in France

81

PAUL VERDIER,
"CITY OF PARIS,"
SAN FRANCISCO, CALIFORNIA.

Mme. PRINCE,
FOREIGN REP. AND BUYER,
SAMUEL FLOERSHEIMER & BROS.

MR. DAVID SCHOLL,
BUYING for the SCHLESSINGER STORES
ON THE PACIFIC COAST.

"In my quest to earn a living
I also did the portraits of these buyers,
for the Paris-Herald Tribune in 1927"

of these agencies I met Lloyd Sloane, a California boy from Berkeley. He was married with two kids, and we got to be quite good friends. He had an artificial leg; I think it was the result of an early accident. So he liked to swim to keep fit, and he liked to go canoeing.

With a third pal, we once brought back a canoe from Corbeille to Paris. I had my straw hat on over a pair of trunks, and as I did not know where to put it, I kept it on my head and collected many compliments on our way down the river:

"It's called a *canotier*, after all."

Another time, Sloane had someone build him an outrigger canoe and we were going to go around Finisterre with this. Sloane had it shipped to Honfleur and we started out from a little ship-chandler shop. The canoe had a canvas top buttoned on the side. This was meant to prevent shipping water, but even in the relatively quiet waters of the mouth of the Seine, the waves would slap the side and work their way under the canvas. It was a fine day, sunny and windy. There was a beautiful broad beach on our left. . . . I don't know how much sailing Sloane had done, but I had done very little. We thought we were on our way to Trouville, when the socket which held the bottom of the mast tore out the two ¾-inch screws. The mast heeled over, we lost headway, and had to beach the boat.

I liked this sort of trouble and rigged the mast with a rope so that we could limp back. By that time the sea had withdrawn and we had to drag the canoe several hundred yards over the sand. Sloane, who had a watertight bag for his artificial leg, was always at a loss as to whether he should put it on or take it off.

We reached the chandler's and by the next morning he had anchored the mast properly. Prudently, we decided to head upriver for Rouen, turning our back on Finisterre.

February 3, 1965

5:00 p.m. to 6:00 p.m.

We spent three pleasant days on the river on our way to Rouen, not bothering to go very fast. We passed a place named Clères on the Seine which was full of flags—because, I was told, the river pilots came from there.

Years later, with some other people, I visited a wonderful private zoo belonging to a wealthy man at Clères. There were acrobatic monkeys at liberty on a little island located in a pond or a stream off the Seine, and also birds with long slender tails and a red disc about two inches in diameter on the end—this was right up my alley.

At one place on our way to Rouen, Sloane and I stopped to swim in the Seine. There were some farmers who ran very fast to see what we were up to. They wondered if the water got into me when I dove under the canoe. Then they gave us some Calvados and we went along.

Through Sloane, I met a fellow who ran a weekly called *Le Boulevardier,* somewhat similar to *The New Yorker.* He gave me some things to do and their artistic adviser, Marc Réal, became quite a friend because when I said I had a small circus, his face brightened up and he said, "Let's see it."

So he used to come with a gang and we'd play "Ramona" (*Belle brune de Barcelonne, tes baisers me donnent des frissons d'amour*) over and over again on the gramophone. He brought several friends, among them Guy Selz and Legrand-Chabrier, who was a circus critic and who insisted I have a net under my trapeze act. I promptly devised one.

One time Réal brought in Paul Fratellini and he took a fancy to the dog in my circus show. It was made of rubber tubing and he got me to enlarge it for his brother Albert, who always dragged a dog around with him. Before that he had had a stuffed dog. Mine trotted and its tail wagged around. However, they just ignored the fact that I had made it and never announced it in their act—it remained a gift.

I called on the Fratellinis three or four times during the years after that, and noticed the trouble they had with the beastie disintegrating—it had a hard dog's life in the circus, and it was welded and patched many times over.

One mild summer day of 1927, we were seated at the Dôme and somebody said:

"Lindbergh is due at Le Bourget."

So we took a taxi and on our way we overtook Leon Kroll, the painter, who was going there too. As we were supplied with peanuts in the shell, we bombarded him. I hit him on the nose.

We arrived and joined the crowd, very large but well ordered. It was not long before Lindbergh had apparently landed. I did not see the landing; I guess he came down behind us. Myron Herrick, the United States ambassador, appeared on a balcony somewhere. People wanted Lindbergh, so they cried, *"L'aviateur!"*

I tried to cry *"L'aviateur!"* too, and drew quite a laugh.

Finally, Lindbergh appeared.

Also through Sloane, I met the man who introduced me even-

Drawing for Le Boulevardier

*Calder in his late twenties,
with Albert Fratellini's mobile dog*

83

tually to the Gould Manufacturing Company of Oshkosh, Wisconsin. We all had lunch together. He was a banker; I said I made toys. Being from Oshkosh, he looked up the companies there. Later, in the fall of 1927, when I went back to America, I went to see Gould. They were door manufacturers, using plywood and thicker chunks of wood. I took their scraps and made various toys —a rowboat, a kangaroo, a bucking cow, ducks, a skating bear. I was given a very modest royalty, which was augmented much later when there was a notice about me in *The New Yorker*, mentioning the Oshkosh toys. It was by the *New Yorker* art critic, Murdock Pemberton, who has remained a friend to this day. Before that he had once said:

One of Calder's most successful action toys: the Kangaroo

"A. Calder is a good bet."

Before my return to New York, in the early fall of 1927, I wanted to take my circus with me, and I had to submit the two suitcases which held the show then—it has grown to five since—to the Douane Centrale in Paris. All the artists were stamped with a rubber stamp on the buttocks. Some still carry traces of this branding.

My return was marked by some unpleasantness. I had done a series of drawings which were incorporated in a publicity brochure for the Holland-America Line. Later on, the same girl got me to do some more drawings for what they called "Europe on Wheels" —a forerunner of the rent-a-car system. I did the drawings and

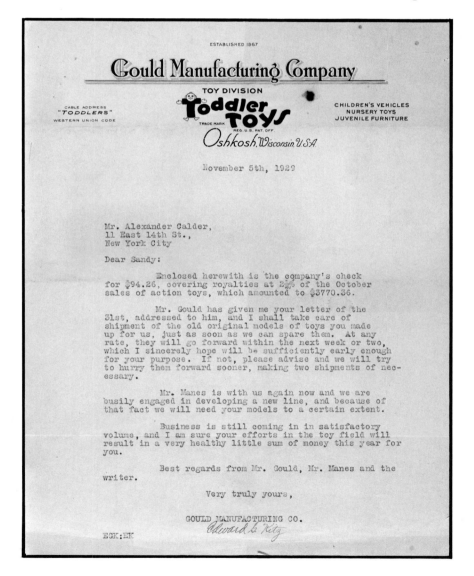

A check for $94.26 was enclosed

85

assumed I was going to be paid for these as I had been before.

When I returned to America, I still had a credit of fifty dollars with this outfit that had some connection with the steamship company. My ticket to America cost $150, so I paid $100, which was all I had, and told them to chalk off the rest against the $50 owed me by their promotions people.

When I got to New York, I stayed with my parents, and one day a man came and started counting all the furniture. I did not understand, but finally realized my father's apartment was being seized because I had not paid the fifty dollars. I had one lawyer friend, J. Weber App. He got me off the hook with the greatest of ease. But I remember especially a final appeal of the Yale promotions boy of "Europe on Wheels." He was also in New York at the time and he urged me:

"Come on, pay me back, be a white man!"

In New York in February of 1928, I showed wire animals and people to Carl Zigrosser of the Weyhe Gallery and bookshop and he decided forthwith to give me a show. My first show. There were about fifteen objects and we priced these things at ten and twenty dollars. Two or three were sold. Among those sold was the first Josephine Baker which I had made in Paris. I think it is about then that some lady critic said:

"Convoluting spirals and concentric entrails; the kid is clever, but what does papa think?"

"Convoluting spirals and concentric entrails; the kid is clever, but what does papa think?"

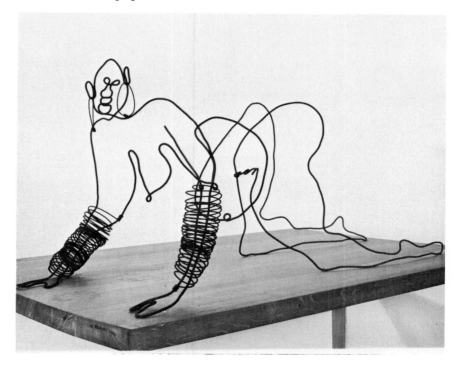

86

Father told me once that he was amused by the small wire things, but that my objects were too sharp to be caressed and fondled as one could do with small bronzes. However, I observed a few years later, with an object I had just painted black and placed on a mantelpiece, that somebody took the trouble to caress it and got full of paint.

That winter, I rented a gold-leafed triangular room on the third floor at Charles Street and Seventh Avenue. There was a fireplace in one corner of the triangle and I'd burn bits of wood I'd found in the street. But one day I dragged in a piece of wood over ten feet long and nearly ten inches square. Horrified, the proprietor pleaded with me that I let him buy me some wood. That did not do much good either; I once invited Marya Mannes and Jo Mielziner to a cold lunch and they ended up weeping with the smoke.

I gave a few modest presentations of the circus that winter. And after the wire show at the Weyhe Gallery, I resumed carving wood in the triangular room. I found a nice store called Monteath, where I could buy fine chunks of tropical wood. Pepe de Creeft had come to New York and I sent him there too. He came back horrified at the waste—they were burning scraps in the hearth. Incidentally, the yard was piled up with big square logs, some thirty feet long and two-and-a-half to three feet thick. Of different sizes and lengths, they had been squared to save shipping space—it was quite a marvelous storeyard.

In the triangular gold-leafed room, I also remember making a seven-foot-tall lady, holding a green flower, whom I called "Spring" —it was in the spring of 1928. I also made, during the same period, an eleven-foot she-wolf, complete with Romulus and Remus. To embellish either sex, I used doorstops I had bought at the five-and-ten—wood and rubber. These two wire sculptures I exhibited in the New York Salon des Indépendants, at the old Waldorf Hotel on Thirty-fourth Street.

"Spring" was held upright by a box pedestal with a counterweight in it. But the she-wolf necessitated two tables arranged end to end. I went home and got a piece of blue denim to put under Romulus and Remus and the she-wolf, in order to unify the tables. Later, I went home and had dinner. Returning to the Waldorf, I discovered somebody had used the space beneath the wolf to display some yellow dishes.

I objected.

The dishes were removed.

After the show, I doubled these objects into a bale and, in the fall of 1928, took them to Paris, where I showed them in the French Salon des Indépendants the following spring. A friend who'd been to see the show on a Sunday told me they were pulling

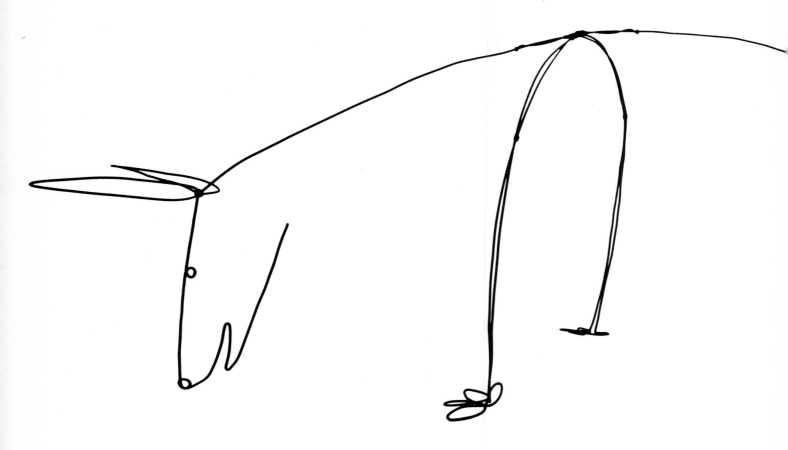

Romulus and Remus under the she-wolf

"Spring" to the side and letting her sway back and forth. Maybe I should not mention this, as it may well encourage others to do likewise with my objects.

When this show was over, I rolled them up again, all four of them, in the same bale and left them in the warehouse of my friend Maurice Lefebvre Foinet. Thus "Spring" and "Romulus and Remus" stayed there from 1929 to 1964——for thirty-five years!

When we undid them the next time, they had all the freshness of youth——of my youth. They were sent in private cases to New York to be exhibited at the Guggenheim for my November 1964 show, and have been acquired by the Guggenheim since.

While still working on wire sculptures, I bought a stock of material——chunks of wood at Monteath's——and took it all up to Bill Drew's uncle's farm near Peekskill, New York, eight miles from the Hudson. I spent all summer of 1928 there, most of the time alone, except for the farm hands, and on the weekends I would greet the Drews, the Murphys, the Ronans, and the Rileys, all of Irish descent and cousins.

88

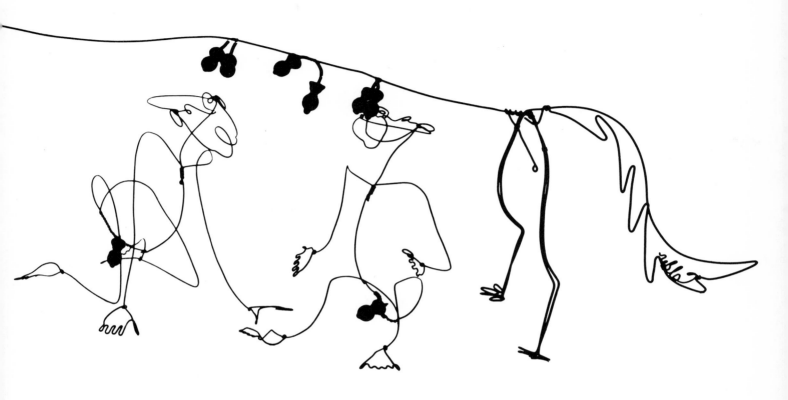

I worked outside on an upturned water trough and carved the
wooden horse bought later by the Museum of Modern Art, a cow,
a giraffe, a camel, an elephant, two elephants, another cat, several
circus figures, a man with a hollow chest, and an ebony lady bending over dangerously, whom I daringly called "Liquorice."

I did a lot of things that summer——enough to have a show of
wood sculpture the following year, in the spring of 1929, at the
Weyhe Gallery in New York. By this time I had returned to Paris,
where I was living modestly. Weyhe sold the cow for a fair price——
$350——that would have helped me for several months. But he did
not send me anything and only paid me later when I came to collect it.

Luckily, I had had a stroke of fortune. In the fall of 1928, somebody appreciated my wire portraits and ordered five objects in
wire to illustrate the strength of the frames they manufactured for
eyeglasses. Before leaving for Paris I completed this order. I did
wire athletes tugging at the lenses for the firm of Batten, Barton,
Durstine, and Osborn, and I got my first check for a thousand dol-

"Chunks of wood at Monteath's," out of which Sandy made among others a "Liquorice"—"an ebony lady bending over dangerously"

90

lars. I was about thirty and Hoover already had a million dollars by that time. Mine came much slower.

February 4, 1965

10:20 a.m. to 12:20 p.m.

In the fall of 1928, with the thousand dollars—after having laid plans for my later New York show—I decided to go abroad again and to pay myself the luxury of taking the *De Grasse* of the French Line as a passenger. I arrived in Paris and found quarters at 7 rue Cels—a ground-floor studio with a window. I used to open it at night, and the postman would stick his head through in the morning and marvel at my endurance.

I also had an orange bicycle with which I used to run around the *quatorzième arrondissement* to visit friends. I wore gray knickerbockers and red socks. At one point I had a cold and held a piece of camphor under my nose with a wire that looped and went behind my ears.

This trip, I lost no time in repairing to the Dôme. There I found Kuniyoshi, whom I knew slightly. He was with a small man in a bowler hat. The man in the bowler, looking at Kuniyoshi, said:

"Who's that?"

"That" was I; he was Pascin.

A week later some boys and girls I had met on the *De Grasse* came to my studio on the rue Cels for a "bottle party"—everybody brought what he liked best. I invited Pascin by letter, and the night before the party I saw him.

He said, "We're coming. We will be about forty because there is a *vernissage* of Hermine David." (Officially she was his wife.)

As the night was balmy, the window was open. People would pass in their bottles through it, like a *guichet* (box office), then walk to the door and come in. The bottles were the password. We wound up about fifty. The lack of glasses did not matter—we just rinsed them as they were needed.

The studio was rather nice, a square room with a Godin stove and walls sort of cobalt blue two-thirds of the way up and white above that—the way I had found it. There was a big door in the rear, in case you wanted to do a large sculpture, and I opened this and the balmy breeze scattered some chips of wood of my last carvings around the courtyard. Some passer-by yelled:

"Lots of chiseling!"

I was a bit embarrassed by the noise and the chips, but I did not really mind.

I had just made a female figure, fifteen inches high, out of bits of wood, scraps of metal, bits of chiffon . . . she was walking at quite a pace . . . I have no idea what became of her.

During the evening, Pascin tore up pieces of paper and made very amusing and indecent *ombres chinoises* of a man following my lady.

Someone in New York, a girl named Elizabeth Hawes, had told me to look up Joan Miró. So I went up to Montmartre to see him. He lived in a sort of metal tunnel, a kind of Quonset hut. He was very affable and showed me one or two of his things, the rest having been sent to Brussels for a show. One of them was a big sheet of heavy gray cardboard with a feather, a cork, and a picture postcard glued to it. There were probably a few dotted lines, but I have forgotten.

I was nonplussed; it did not look like art to me. (A year or two later I traded some of my work with Miró for a big canvas.)

Miró arrived at my studio one day when I happened to be doing the circus. I guess he enjoyed it. A few years later, in 1932, having seen the circus again in his house at Montroig in Spain, he told me the next morning:

"I liked the bits of paper best."

These are little bits of white paper, with a hole and slight weight on each one, which flutter down several variously coiled thin steel wires, which I jiggle so that they flutter down like doves onto the shoulder of a bejeweled circus *belle-dame*.

At that time—1928—I met Ivy Troutman, wife of Waldo Pierce. She introduced me to some Americans having a group show at the place Vendôme. They invited me to exhibit a rearing horse made of wire, about two feet high. I got there rather late and was allotted a dingy corner. I went off to get a sheet of white paper to place behind my horse. When I came back, they said, "No paper." I said, "No horse." And I took it home.

Another time, Pascin got me to show with a group called Salon de l'Araignée, in some photographic studio near the Etoile. I had one wire acrobat standing on one arm on the chest of another one arching. I dallied about removing my object after the show, and there was an exhibit of movie equipment after that, and somebody needed a piece of wire to fasten something and cut out the forearm of my athlete.

About this time I was hoping to get a show for my own things somewhere in Paris, and Pascin introduced me to Emile Sittya. He took me to the Galerie Billet, 30 rue de la Boétie, directed by a Mr. Worms. For a certain consideration, he said he would put

Par je ne sais ~~par~~ mel miracle. Je
suis devenu membre d'un groupe
d'Ps de l'Art américain. Société
de peintres et sculpteurs très
arrivés, Hoho! Hoho! hazard de la
vie d'un peintre errant.
La même chance m'a fait rencontrer
le ~~très~~ Sterling Calder.
Absent de New-York, on notre _dernière_ exposition
d'en lieu ! je ne peux pas jurer de notre
effort, mais en tout cas, je te jure,
Mr Sterling Calder, qui est un
de nos meilleurs sculpteurs américains
~~et que~~ est aussi le plus ~~bel~~
homme de notre Society.

La Coupole

98-50
Tél. : Littré 98-49

RESTAURANT - BRASSERIE
BAR AMÉRICAIN

Paris, le

103, Boulevard du Montparnasse
PARIS

R. C. Seine 229,967 B

Revenant à Paris, j'ai rencontre son
fils

SANDY CALDER,

dont j'étais, le première vue, bien déçu.
Il est moins beau que son PAPA!
Franchement!

Mais mis en présence des _ses_ œuvres
~~du fils,~~ je ~~sais~~ _suis_ très bientôt il s'imposera
~~et j'espère que très bientôt~~
il ~~fera~~ ~~et dépasa~~ malgré sa sale
gueule. ~~Et exposera~~ avec un succès foudroyant
~~exposer à côté de~~ son PAPA
et d'autres grands artistes comme
moi Pascin, qui Vous dit.....

*Pascin's introduction to Calder's show at
the Galerie Billet. It was written while
Pascin and his friend drank on the terrace
of La Coupole*

By I don't know what miracle I became a
member of a group of exponents of American
art, a society of highly successful painters
and sculptors. Ho ho! Ho ho! hazards of the
life of an errant painter.
At that time I met old Stirling Calder. And
now absent from New York where our last
exhibit was held, we cannot enjoy the success
of our last effort! But at any rate I swear that
Mr. Stirling Calder, who is one of our best
American sculptors, is also the most handsome member of our Society.
When I returned to Paris, I met his son Sandy
Calder, who at first sight disappointed me. He
is frankly not as handsome as his father.
But now, having seen his work I know that
very soon he will be established in spite of his
ugly mug and that he will exhibit with terrific
success next to his father and other great
artists such as I, Pascin, who tell you ...

on a show. I decided to pay his fee. That evening, Pascin and his gang compiled my preface at a café table. Probably Robert Desnos and Foujita were there—or maybe I'm just bragging.

The show opened on January 25, 1929. There was a British policeman with a fat belly who laughed when you pushed him, wire acrobats, a rearing horse, and a number of things in wood that I'd done in Paris—a wood totem of acrobats standing on end, three high. Fortunately an English captain—a playboy but useful, I met him later—bought several of my things and got me out of the red.

On another evening, Pascin had a party in his studio on the boulevard de Clichy. He had lots of drawings made with "tacky paper," which he had covered with paint, then placed paint down on drawing paper, and drawn over finally with a stylus. These were piled on a table and the guests on arrival would look through them. There was a mass of them and as they were very slippery, once in a while they'd slide onto the floor.

I still have one of these that Pascin made especially for me, representing me as a young man reproducing Greek sculptural motifs in wire. In return, I made him a wire Josephine Baker.

Pascin used to enjoy his success and was very generous in cafés, where he would often foot the bills. When he arrived home in the evening, he would quickly say something about his ease and remove his tie and stiff collar, leaving a gleaming gold collar button.

At his home in Montmartre there was a sort of entrance hall with a little narrow staircase running up in a corner. Up the staircase there was a small window, close to the ceiling, which gave on his studio. At Pascin's parties, the little girls would go up and show their *derrières*. One evening a drunk was a bit too bold. He showed something else and everybody was horror-struck.

I had intended going skiing in Mégève, with some friends who had a chalet there. There were to be about eight of us. But instead, I worked on my show at Billet's. After the show was launched, I finally got to Mégève, but we stayed in a hotel in the village— I, and two very tall lean bastards. One of them knew a bit about skiing, and the other one was more gifted than I. They would disappear over a hill, while I struggled on the upgrade with my string-laced skis. I would arrive panting, to see them seated comfortably and talking. At my apparition, they would get up and put on their sweaters to sail downhill, without a word to me.

This was more or less repeated when we took a train, and then walked up a mountain slope. There were thirty or forty people, and when I got to the top, they were all having lunch in the sun and were finishing their coffee. As I arrived, they all got up and went downhill. The place was spectacular—sort of a saddleback

Pascin's caricature of Calder. Calder is on the horse at the right and Pascin and his wife on the one at the left. The drawing is in the style of Calder's wire sculpture. (Pascin's usual way of drawing is displayed on the five figures at the upper right.) Pascin advised Sandy that since his father studied the ancient Greeks in plaster, Sandy should do likewise in wire

95

A circus party on Rue Cels in 1929. It must have been a good party—Calder remembers few of the participants: Paul Fratellini, behind him, at his left; the Hungarian painter Medges, beside him, at his left. He does not quite remember, either, what is happening to the man in the picture at the far right

summit with a great chasm on the far side—and I also knew that I'd never get up there again, so I would have liked very much to spend the night there.

Instead, I had lunch all alone and came down all alone.

On the way back, I had my one chance to jump on skis, but before I knew it, the skis were planted in the snow with me in between.

So, I gladly returned to my studio on the rue Cels.

It was while living on the rue Cels that I went to a gym on the rue de Richelieu, in the heart of Paris, with Miró. Miró wanted to stay fit for posterity, so I accompanied him there. Our instructor was named Aimé Charbon.

Whereupon I said he must have been born in the winter.

I don't think Miró and I did much boxing, but we learned to inhale and exhale with gym movements. The air was drawn in through the nose and exhaled through the mouth with a great whistling noise. We used to have dinner together afterward.

One day, Miró said he would like to meet some American girls and learn how to dance. Recently I had been dragged to a Methodist affair where there were some little, rather cute finale hoppers, and I decided to take Miró there.

Miró arrived for dinner that evening very much spruced up with bowler hat and yellow bow tie, and looked very fine. When we got to the church affair, however, I began to dance and abandoned my friend to some young things who could speak neither French nor Spanish. So, I don't think Miró learned much about dancing.

96

February 5, 1965

5:00 p.m. to 6:30 p.m.

In the spring of 1929, a photographer named Sacha Stone came to the rue Cels to see my circus. He lived in Berlin and proposed that I go there.

So, sometime in March 1929, I took a train, third class, going from Paris to Poland through Berlin. On the toilet door there was a 00 instead of the customary 100 used by the French to signal such conveniences. I wondered if it was the Polish equivalent. I had with me fifteen to twenty wire sculptures of different sizes. They made a great open bundle five to six feet long and two in diameter—awkward but light.

I landed in Berlin. Sacha Stone had arranged a show for me at the Gallery Neumann und Nierendorf.

The day following my arrival, we took a cab to the Berlin station, with Sacha and my wire-sculpture bundle. He intended to take the official picture of my arrival. The bundle was so large that we had to get the cab driver to open up the top. And he said:

"What, for all that *Eisenschrott* [rusty iron]?"

Neumann, whom I knew quite well, had left the gallery and established himself in New York. So I had to deal with Karl Nierendorf, quite a nice fellow.

There was an employee in the gallery who was rather serious and he begged me to make a portrait of him. So I did, and placed it on a wire dachshund. He did not appreciate this, so I practically had to force it on him.

Unfortunately, Nierendorf opened the exhibition on April 1 and sent a lot of fake telegrams to announce it—but nobody believed anything.

After a while, the press took many photographs and I was bracketed on a news-service matrix with Charlie Chaplin and Yehudi Menuhin.

Chantal Quenneville was in Berlin. I guess it was she who had introduced me to Sacha Stone. She had been having a show of her portraits, which looked very mild for a square-jawed woman who smoked a pipe. She lived in a Berlin pension, so I went there too. Ed Biberman, a painter, was also there and we were finally joined by Paul Nitze, who turned up at my show, 32 Lützow Strasse, on a bicycle.

Riding in the streetcars, as always, I was trying to read all the advertising. For me, *Rauchen politzeilich verboten* meant "Smoking Politely Forbidden."

Chantal and I used to go dancing at the Café am Zoo; we were very lively. The room was round and had a balcony with little tables, and each table had a vase with artificial flowers. One day, we did a vigorous solo and everybody cheered and threw the flowers at us.

One of my best recollections of Berlin is that Nierendorf took us to see the *Dreigroschenoper,* the *Beggar's Opera,* by Bert Brecht and Kurt Weill. It was a great experience. I still remember Mackie Messer, in evening dress with white gloves, in a cage of chicken wire with his back to the audience. All of a sudden he pranced around, spread out his arms, and yelled . . .

In the middle of April, I confided my wares to Nierendorf and headed back to Paris.

One of the things I liked very much, and which I regret, was a wire woman walking with an umbrella and a man, with a soft hat and hands in his pockets, walking in the rain behind her. The title the Germans gave this was *"Mann steigt nach"* (which means, roughly, "What man is after"). That one, I wish I had now!

Finally, the only object sold was a small wire dachshund. I believe he was taken to Mannheim. I am always hoping to find him in the museum there, some day, but I have visited Mannheim since and there was no trace of him.

On the trip back to Paris, I hired a blanket and a pillow. The pillow, called "Siesta," turned out to be just right—the perfect softness. So when I had to change trains at the border, I stuffed it into my suitcase. But when the porter came in, he made me open my suitcase. He recovered the pillow and he said:

"Siesta geht nicht nach Paris." (Siesta is not going to Paris.)

On my return, the Keystone movie people wanted to make a short film of my studio on the rue Cels, so I got Kiki de Montparnasse to come and pose for me. She had a wonderful nose that seemed to jut out into space, and she eventually found a place at the Guggenheim Museum, thirty-five years later, alongside "Spring" and "Romulus and Remus."

I don't quite know what prompted me to go back to America at this point. Maybe the money was getting low. But I still had enough left to pay for another trip on the *De Grasse*, which had proved to be quite delightful the first time.

So in June 1929, I left Paris for New York on the *De Grasse*. Before leaving, I cut off my mustache. Several people had attacked it with scissors and I finally finished the job. I had kept it over eight years, since the days when I wanted to look more mature for the Truscon Sash Company in Ohio. With it, I had often been mistaken for Julien Levy, the painter, who nowadays often reproaches me for having seceded from his league. It had been all shapes and sizes and eventually was without wax, long and trailing.

February 6, 1965

10:50 a.m. to 12:50 p.m.

I am a pretty good sailor and I have certain theories on how to combat seasickness. The first rule is to walk around and get the sense of the motion of the boat. The second rule is never to lie down in a deck chair: that merely makes a spirit level out of your belly and one single bubble going round and round makes you dizzy. The third rule is to eat nothing but lemons if you should feel ill.

Edward Holton James with his uncle
Henry James at Rye, England, around 1910

Edward Holton James

Louisa James at left, aged two,
with sisters Olivia and Mary

"She was Louisa."
Here, sitting on the rail of the De Grasse

So once on board the *De Grasse*, I started walking the deck. I overtook an elderly man and a young lady. I could only see them from the back, so I reversed my steps the better to see them face on. Upon coming abreast of them the next time around, I said, "Good evening!" And the man said to his daughter, "There is one of them already!"

He was Edward Holton James, my future father-in-law.

She was Louisa.

Her father had just taken her to Europe to mix with the young intellectual elite. All she met were concierges, doormen, cab drivers —and finally me.

I still had a tuxedo in those days. In the evening I put it on and we danced rather violently—mostly to the tune of "Chloë." In the morning we played deck tennis and watched the flying fish from the bow. I guess I told her I was a wire sculptor. It did not mean anything to her. So the voyage went on. The night before landing in New York, I was short of funds and gave up drinking—I did not drink much anyhow, then. We sat a lot at a large round table. Louisa was opposite me and to goad me into action—I guess I was getting sleepy—she let fly a spoon and caught me on the brow. I got annoyed and turned in. Then she and George Parker, a painter, came and dug me out of my cabin.

Her father had traveled with her to protect her, but he had a bad case of asthma on the boat and could not do his duty.

Next morning, as we were approaching New York Harbor, I got up and got all spruced up to meet my family, but there was no one there. I guess I got a telegram inviting me to join my parents in Pittsfield, Massachusetts. Peggy and her boys were there in Pittsfield and I remember, one time, showing them my circus and at least one of the boys was sleepier than I usually was.

After a week or two, I heard from Louisa. She invited me to join her and her older sister Mary at Eastham on Cape Cod. They had a cottage right on the very edge of the dunes, so you could look out of the window and see the ocean right in front of you. It was marvelous swimming, and the beach was nice to run on.

We seemed to spend most of our time running errands, getting supplies of food. I remember Mary suffering from the heat one day; it was not bad according to my standards, but she hung wet towels and hoped the breeze would evaporate the water.

Elizabeth Hawes, who had introduced me to Miró, was designing clothes and had a showroom on Fifty-sixth Street. We'd agreed that I would run my circus in her shop and I went off to Cape Cod and wrote her nonchalantly. She was furious at my irresponsibility. We finally put the show on. It was a marvelous party with beer and hot dogs. Louisa was in Concord and I could not invite her.

In New York, I again occupied father's studio on Fourteenth Street, as he was in Pittsfield. I worked in wire as usual. That time I did what I thought to be a very nice horse. Harry Gould of the Oshkosh company happened to be in New York and stopped in to see me. He owned three pacers and drove them himself. I showed him my horse. He should have been an expert, but did not like my horse. I guess he did not feel it could pull him and his sulky.

Louisa came to see it, however, and thought it looked like a real horse. When she was a child, she was first a dog and then later graduated to being a horse, so she knew all about it.

Murdock Pemberton also came to see me in the studio and I gave him a small wire head of an animal, that he still has.

The man who made Wheatsworth crackers had been to see the opera of *Hansel and Gretel* and had become enamored of Joe Urban's scenery. So he got Urban to do him something similar in Hamburg, northern New Jersey.

Urban had an assistant, Sheppard Vogelgesang. Sheppard wanted me to make a spider that would run up and down the tower wall. The main part of the spider was a float from a toilet tank; the rest of it was wire and shining glass objects borrowed from bicycles and automobiles. I don't remember in whose car I traveled, but this job necessitated frequent trips to northern New

Jersey, where the applejack was excellent—and of course, we stocked up on Wheatsworth's crackers too.

In the spring of 1926 I had met Bob Josephy, who worked for Knopf in the book-production department. Well, Bob had had no illustration jobs for me at the time, but we had got to be very great friends. Now, in the fall of 1929, he had a very nice apartment on the top floor at Beekman Place and Fiftieth Street and he indiscreetly invited me to live with him for a bit—I stayed too long, I guess.

Josephy was very enthusiastic over my circus. This encouraged me and while at his house, I worked on it very hard. He helped me. We made the chariot race and the lion tamer, and it got to be quite a full-blown circus, growing from two suitcases into five.

All this while, I was quite unaware of the financial straits of the world, even of the stock-market crash.

While still in Paris the previous spring, I had met Miss Mildred Harbeck, who had asked me to design some textiles. To convince her of my worth, I had at that time showed her some of the circus. Arriving in New York, I had done the textiles, and we decided to give a circus party in the house where she and her sister lived on Lexington Avenue. I think we invited Frank Crowninshield, *Vanity Fair* art editor, Edward Steichen, the photographer, and Mr. Erhard Weyhe, at whose gallery I had shown in New York. There were also many other guests.

The next morning, I guess I delivered something to the Weyhe Gallery, and I saw him and asked:

"Well, Mr. Weyhe, how did you like my circus last night?"

And he, with a slight German accent, replied:

"Mr. Kalder, yesterday I lost eight thousand dollahr . . ."

This did not depress me and I went back to work with Josephy, improving my circus.

In December 1929, I had a show of all my wares at the 56th Street Gallery, which belonged to the Roman Bronze Works, one of the two New York sculpture foundries. That gallery was a real three-ring circus.

On the first floor, there was a show of Mestrovic.

On the second floor, the husband of a lady sculptor showed mechanical birds.

On the third floor rear was a Mexican with small wax caricatures. And I was on the front of the third floor with wood sculptures, paintings, toys, and jewelry.

Between the Mexican and me was still another room, a sort of black-velvet-lined locker with pictures hanging on the walls, and there was a man and a woman who would usher their prey into this den. And somehow, I felt they locked the door so their clients

103

1929—Circus Year in New York

would not run away.

My visitors tried out my toys made of wood, which had eccentric wheels, so that when the kangaroo and others galloped across the floor they made a certain thumpy noise. This often disturbed my cloak-and-dagger neighbors.

Probably one of my best pieces in the show was a wire man on a wire horse, and I think another person on top of the rider. Mrs. Aline Bernstein said that if she got a job she was hoping for, in theatrical production, she would buy this object and would I please call her up on a given day. I called her up and she did not have the job. I said, "I would like to invite you to my circus, but I don't know just where I am going to run it."

She said, "You can run it here, very soon—it is often a circus here, anyhow—and by the way, we are having a party this evening, why don't you join us?"

So, Louisa and I went. There were lots of people and lots of fancy food and liquor. The sky was the limit.

In those days, for the circus, I always had printed invitations, which I did myself with a linoleum cut. I wish I had some of these left. Mrs. Aline Bernstein set the date and asked me to invite some of my friends—she would invite some of hers. So I promptly sent her a batch of invitations, which were green and white, and she must have remembered that I had a few friends too.

The evening set, I arrived.

February 7, 1965

10:15 a.m. to 12:45 p.m.

I arrived with my five valises and a very small gramophone. One entered on Park Avenue, but the place was really—at the end of a long corridor—on Madison. I was greeted by Mrs. Bernstein. There seemed to be four or five people around. The room was somewhat oblong. I pushed sofas back against the wall, then I removed a bust from a table behind me at a far corner. I recognized the bust as Noguchi's. The bust lady wore a monocle—she was the daughter of the house.

My hostess said, "That's a young Japanese sculptor." I said, "Yes, he's coming tonight." (I'd asked him to come and run the victrola for me.)

Her guests seemed to be dressed negligently or in negligees. My guests arrived and occupied the shorter of the two bleachers. They included Louisa, Bob and Jane Josephy, Millie and Sandy Knox, Val Dudensing and his wife, and Lee Simonson and others.

Millie Knox had a white fur coat, and Mrs. Bernstein's sister, who was in the clothing business, kept eyeing this coat—with I don't know what.

By and by Noguchi arrived and I had set up the masts, the various cords, and the curtains. As I spent most of the time on my knees when performing the circus, I had bought a pair of basketball kneepads and was trying to break these in.

Well, I performed the circus.

I remember Lee Simonson, who was right in front of me, being very careful to pick up his peanut shells and put them in a container to spare the "lovely" blond wall-to-wall carpet.

Finally the chariot race, the last act, came off and my friends went home. It was always a long job packing things afterward—like in the real circus—and I always did it myself, having the knack and the memory.

Mrs. Bernstein said, "It's a lot of work."

That was her only comment.

As I was packing up, I revealed a Bergdorf Goodman suit box —purple figures walking across a white field. Mrs. Bernstein's sister (who worked for Bergdorf Goodman) asked me, "Where did you get that box?"

It was her only comment.

I told her that Josephy, the friend with whom I was staying, had received it from his bootlegger with a load of liquor.

I was never aware that the great Wolfe—that is, Thomas Wolfe, the writer—was present at my circus performance. He did not have the good sense to present himself and I only heard from him much later—some nasty remarks on my performance, included in a long-winded book.

My next housing victim was Paul Nitze, who lived in a little apartment on East Fortieth Street. The building belonged to the mother of a friend of his—she lived on the top floor. After I had been there a few months, he asked me to present the circus to a few friends. Among them was the mother of his friend, the lady who owned the building.

I was a little late in setting things up and to get the right tension in the tightrope, I had to put two brads in the floor.

There was a chilly moment, and then the circus went on.

Nitze at Harvard had joined the Porcellian Club—and I kept making them wire pigs, pigs out of hose with doorstop teats, pigs that could swallow a marble with a gurgling sound. I even carved

107

him a female figure, as the mate for a South Pacific wood carving that belonged to the club—I guess it was my way of thanking him for his hospitality.

I still had the key of Josephy's apartment and I called on him once and found no one at home. But on his desk was a folder—an invitation from the Weyhe Gallery to a banquet in honor of Rockwell Kent. This was embellished by a drawing of Kent in which a young lady was doing a *grand écart* at the top of the page and at the bottom was a man flourishing a goblet. There were also some straight pins handy . . . I put the pins in the lady's *expectation* and by the time I was through, the goblet was quite full . . .

The next time I saw Bob, he was furious and demanded the key and expressed his hope that he could get another invitation by Kent, unsullied by my hand or thought . . .

About this time, somebody from Baltimore butted into my business and arranged a show in Eddie Warburg's gallery at Harvard. Warburg and Kirstein had hired a floor in an office building across the street from the college. I repeated my bundle of Berlin days, but Eddie protested that I arrived with nothing but a roll of wire on my shoulders and pliers in my pocket. I admit there was some truth to this, for I always traveled with a roll of wire and a pair of pliers. I took the circus along too, and showed it to the Harvard boys.

I stayed on a cot in Eddie's quarters in the Yard—the original Harvard Square. Eddie had a roommate named Phil . . . Somebody . . . and I came out one morning with him on our way to the Waldorf restaurant across the street. He saw a friend at the end of the Yard and whispered:

"Hello."

And getting no response, added:

"Oh! pshaw! My voice has no personality."

He was confusing personality with decibels.

I must have made a little money, somehow, in all this—I sold a few wood sculptures: for $100, $200, and $500. . . . So, I was in a position to go to Paris again, by March.

Some friends had spoken of the Garcia and Díaz line of Spanish freighters and about the tenth of March, 1930, I sailed as passenger on the motor ship *Motomar*.

February 8, 1965

5:00 p.m. to 6:50 p.m.

We left from Brooklyn; mother brought me a crate of oranges. Louisa did not come, but her sister Mary did.

I was right under the bridge, next to the officer's mess. I was free to go up on bridge whenever I wanted to. As usual, the mate did not like the captain. He, the mate, used to sing ballads about Malaga to me. There were a lot of very fine young student officers on board, from all over Spain; they were taking their training. When they arrived on bridge, some would say:

"*Bon día.*"

I had bought a large dictionary to practice some Spanish, and found it contained no such expression. I would try to say the same thing and would be told:

"But no, it's *buenos días.*"

I was unaware of the existence of Catalonia. It was only some years later that I realized their differences of language.

I offered some of them mother's California navel oranges, but they weren't too enthusiastic, having their own blood oranges.

We had two meals a day—at 10:00 A.M. and 5:00 P.M.

I learned to enjoy the eggs fried with garlic and olive oil, but I had a little trouble with the codfish—nowadays, however, codfish is nostalgic of that trip. The custom was to pile five plates in front of you and remove them as the courses progressed. It was March and the sea was sometimes rather rough, and although there was a folding apron all around the table, it was not sporting to use it. Every once in a while, each would crouch over his pile of plates.

I think there was only one other passenger on board and he was working his way to Europe, peeling potatoes for the galley, I guess. I only met him once. We put in at Malaga, and I walked around the town and discovered a vegetable and fruit store with stacks of fruit all green and purple. Two years later, on the same run, but in early September instead of March, the same shop was yellow and orange.

They picked up a lot of fresh fish and we had delicious meals for the next two days on our way to Barcelona. In Barcelona, as I was the only one of the two passengers with much baggage, instead of the customs coming to the pier I went to the customs. I had a trunk, the five circus suitcases, the little gramophone, and a bag or so. A wagon came for me with four little wheels, an elderly horse, a little bit of a dog, and we went two blocks to the customs house. I thought they were going to play all the records before they let me out.

I went to the Hotel Regina, in a little room up somewhere high. It was then I decided that I liked white walls and red tile flooring. Ever since, all my walls have been white, wherever I was in control, and I have put in tiles when I had the opportunity. I tried to find Miró, but I guess he was away in the country. I went to a bullfight, and then on to Paris by train.

This time, I was supposed to get some fifty dollars a month from the Oshkosh toy company, so I thought I could chance renting a studio. I discovered a new studio building at 7 Villa Brune, in the *quatorzième arrondissement*, next to the *ceinture*. The concierge's face was like an enormous piece of chewing gum and she asked for a tip as big as her face. I promised it to her without realizing that I was being had.

On the ground floor, opposite the entrance, there was a sculptor from San Francisco who had brought along with him a lot of ponderous statues from America. He was garbed in a raincoat, whatever the weather. And his name was Voisin, but he pronounced it Voyzen.

The concierge said to me, *"Ce monsieur est vraiment quelqu'un."* (This man is really somebody.)

Whereupon I said, *"Moi aussi, je suis quelqu'un."* (I, too, am somebody.)

And she replied, *"Oh! Nous sommes tous quelqu'un."* (Oh! Every one of us is somebody.)

I looked up my old friends, particularly Marc Réal and his gang. I noticed that whereas when I first met them they used to drink *apéritif* and the second time I had dug them out they were drinking whiskey, this time they were drinking orange juice.

Rupert Fordham—one of my two old ski absentee-companions, by the way—owned the old studio I had rented on the rue Cels and still had an apartment above it. He also had a thirty-five-foot sailboat in the Midi. It was all teak and built by a German. He used to take friends as members of his crew and I had tried before to volunteer on several occasions, but he did not trust me as a sailor. However, at this time, he had taken his boat out between France and Corsica all alone and spent a night hove to. I guess some marine police boarded him and objected to this manner of navigating. For I got a telegram in Paris, inviting me to join him at L'Ile Rousse in Corsica, which I was delighted to do. We soon worked our way along the coast to the west, to Antoni and then to Calvi.

After we were tied up a sirocco commenced, and to strengthen the hold of his anchor, Fordham let out more chain and unwittingly fouled his rudder on the cable of a big dredge boat.

This did not prevent me from enjoying the two-day trip, and

from walking alone uphill where I discovered a farm in full harvest —what they call in France *la saison du battage*. There was a circular space paved with big stones, on top of which the wheat was being pitched, and a horse was running around in a circle dragging a big stone. The horse's driver was himself seated whip in hand on a donkey—quite an assembly. They offered me a drink of wine, and strangely enough—I was so modest in those days—I declined!

I also investigated the town of Calvi, quite fine, medieval. I don't think it was ever taken. I was particularly interested in the public toilet atop the thirty-foot-high fortification wall. Its housing and a twenty-foot beam, on which people sat, overhung the wall— plumb over a thicket of cacti. It was still in use.

I also wandered around Calvi picking up bits of what had been blue pottery, and with these and some wire I made a necklace which I sent to my mother for her birthday.

The third day, the sirocco seemed to have abated and we prepared to leave. Fordham went into town to buy supplies and I forget what he told me to do—probably to put some order in his rice, jam, and crackers—but it was not to wash the dishes, which is what I did. I'd bought a big chunk of white native goat cheese. As I slept forward, I hung the cheese there, on a string from a beam. When Fordham got back he was very much annoyed with me—whatever I'd done was not the right thing—so we shoved off in the late afternoon.

That night, the cheese stank so that I gave it a yank and tossed it out of the open hatch. I must have felt rather queasy—the sea might have remained rough after the sirocco—because I remember applying my theory of the lemon.

I held the wheel in the small hours of the morning. We were supposed to head for St-Tropez, but Fordham had given me the precise minute fraction of the compass to steer by, and I chose a bigger marking next to it—it was easier to keep track of and I believed it would get us there, within a mile or so, just the same.

The next day, the rudder ceased to respond to the controls. Fordham had a sweep—a big oar—and we rigged this over the side with the proper rope arrangement so we could still steer the boat.

In the old days when we lived in Berkeley and used to go riding with the Hayeses and Mrs. Patterson, my greatest enjoyment was when we had a flat tire. It gave me something to do instead of just being driven along, and I could learn something practical. Here again, I was using my ability to avert trouble. Finally we ended up at Villefranche, not St-Tropez. We parted company.

I put up at the hotel "Welcome," of which I had heard glowing accounts. After a short while, the proprietor, who had seen me come off a boat with a seabag on my shoulder, began to worry about his rent. But some fellows I knew who had a house on Cap Ferrat reassured him.

During my stay, I swam across the harbor—one-and-a-half miles—several times to get to the beach on Cap Ferrat. There were a couple of French gunboats in the harbor, and I had to keep my eyes closed tight while swimming by them, because of the chlorine.

Once, I was returned to my hotel by Val Dudensing—in his Lancia. He dealt in Picasso, Matisse, and others. I had known him for years, he had seen my circus, but he always seemed to patronize me rather than take me on into his stable.

February 9, 1965

10:30 a.m. to 12:00 noon

Just before I left Paris in 1929, I could more or less be said to belong to quite a gang: Pascin, Foujita, Man Ray, Kiki, Desnos, and many others. I felt very much at home with them and they usually held forth at the Coupole Bar. I would have much preferred to stay in the open air on the terrace, but I was fond of this gang, so I ended up in the smoke of the Coupole Bar.

When I returned in 1930, I walked past the Dôme and discovered seated some lesser lights from last year's gang. I was going to sit down with them, but they said, "Come on over to La Rotonde, across the street." I went and sat there and later was given to understand that those people no longer belonged to the old gang.

Louisa James had been traveling, with the intention of visiting Paris, during the summer of 1930. She first took a tour of Ireland by bicycle with an old friend of hers named Helen Coolidge.

On the *De Grasse*, when I first met Louisa, she had a lot of fairly short hair and the wind was always up, which is true of any boat, so her hair took the form of snakes and I dubbed her Medusa. The hair was still there, but the breeze was lacking, when I met her in Paris at the Hotel Foyot.

She arrived at about the time Fredric Kiesler—a Viennese architect who had done a few things in Paris and then gone on to New York—was having a fling with my circus. From previous years, Kiesler knew Fernand Léger, Karl Einstein, the critic, Le Corbusier, Mondrian, and van Doesburg. He gave me a list of whom to invite for the circus, so I invited them all for the same

Louisa James and Helen Coolidge toured Ireland by bicycle in the summer of 1930

night, at the Villa Brune. Another Einstein—from St. Louis, this one—was to be my *chef d'orchestre*.

I saw Kiesler before the performance, and there was great consternation in his camp because I had invited van Doesburg with the others. He apparently was a friend of Mondrian, but on cool terms with Karl Einstein and maybe Léger.

That was Paris, and I never understood the battles of these coteries—and somehow or other I remained aloof from all this.

But Kiesler insisted we must head off van Doesburg at all cost, so we finally sent him a telegram, explaining that there was some error and that he could come the following day.

Kiesler and his gang came to the circus, and this time I do not remember any reaction. However, Léger was interested in what I did and we became very good friends.

The following day, van Doesburg came with his wife Petro, of whom Louisa and I later became very fond. They also brought their two little dogs—they would rush and yap at every shot of a pistol or crash of cymbals. But I got more of a reaction from Doesburg than I had from the whole gang the night before.

The St. Louis Einstein had a smattering of knowledge on all these people which he had picked up from books. The next day, he called on Mondrian by himself. He came back to Villa Brune and recounted marvels, so I went with him to see Mondrian.

Mondrian lived at 26 rue de Départ. (That building has been demolished since, to make more room for the Gare Montparnasse.) It was a very exciting room. Light came in from the left and from the right, and on the solid wall between the windows there were experimental stunts with colored rectangles of cardboard tacked on. Even the victrola, which had been some muddy color, was painted red.

I suggested to Mondrian that perhaps it would be fun to make these rectangles oscillate. And he, with a very serious countenance, said:

"No, it is not necessary, my painting is already very fast."

This visit gave me a shock. A bigger shock, even, than eight years earlier, when off Guatemala I saw the beginning of a fiery red sunrise on one side and the moon looking like a silver coin on the other.

This one visit gave me a shock that started things.

Though I had heard the word "modern" before, I did not consciously know or feel the term "abstract." So now, at thirty-two, I wanted to paint and work in the abstract. And for two weeks or so, I painted very modest abstractions. At the end of this, I reverted to plastic work which was still abstract.

Shortly before this, I had lacked money for my rent. Some

"Léger was interested in what I did, and we became very good friends"

113

friends suggested that I run the circus for four dollars a seat. I bought planks, pinched some boxes, and made bleachers. I handled thirty people an evening on, I believe, four evenings. At the end of my professional run, the concierge came and said the proprietor who lived in the front could not get to sleep on account of the cymbals. But it was all over and I was able to pay him again.

The St. Louis Einstein had just somehow joined the group of artists called "Abstraction-Création," which included Arp, Mondrian, Robert Delaunay, Pevsner, and Jean Hélion, among about thirty in all. The invitation to join was extended to me after an investigation by several members. They came to the studio at Villa Brune and saw what I was doing. So, I became a member too.

During the "Abstraction-Création" days, I also came forth with this statement:

"Disparity in form, color, size, weight, motion, is what makes a composition. . . . It is the apparent accident to regularity which the artist actually controls by which he makes or mars a work."

February 14, 1965

11:00 a.m. to 12:30 p.m.

Sometime in the fall of 1930 Louisa decided to go home, and it took a lot more correspondence before we decided to get married. About the middle of December, I in turn went home, on the *Bremen*.

Being in tourist class, I naturally was on the stern, and the vibration of the partitioning panels was amazing. It was on this trip I met a girl from Texas, Alice (Lila Ray), who had fallen in love with a Hindu poet. And after she had gone to England and married him, she was disowned by her parents in Texas. I believe they were of German origin. (Later she went to live in Santiniketan, in west Bengal, and Louise and I visited her there some twenty-five years later, in 1955. Her marriage was successful and she had five children as well.) As Mr. James was in India at that time, I arranged to take her to tea at Mrs. James's in New York. My mother was there and this girl adopted my mother as hers, and they corresponded forever afterward—till my mother's death.

I had brought my circus as usual and I borrowed a little store from a friend on Fifty-seventh Street and Seventh Avenue. I wanted to sell tickets for my show, but after investigation showed there was only one toilet and as the door did not open outward, I

"I took her to tea at Mrs. James's . . ."
Louisa Cushing James and Mary Holton James, Louisa's mother and grandmother, taken in Paris in 1910

114

was not allowed a theatrical license. So we passed the hat—a rather doubtful procedure.

My friend and erstwhile client, Mr. Hearst, Jr., sent me a couple of cases of beer. I had done for him a mural of animals in a Gold Room and billed him for $1500. He had had a fireplace moved into that room and later told me he had settled that bill of $500 for $250, and asked that I be content with similar treatment.

Finally, Louisa and I got married on the seventeenth of January, 1931. I took the circus to the James house in Concord, Massachusetts, and ran it the night before the wedding.

The reverend who married us apologized for having missed the circus the night before. So I said:

"But you are here for the circus, today."

Bill Drew, my old Stevens fraternity brother, was my best man. I was rather fortunate, because he insisted that I wear black shoes, not the brown pair I was so fond of. Finally, I had to put on a blue suit to match "his" shoes.

The official wedding picture. In front: Louisa and Sandy (the hat was Drew's). In back: William B. F. Drew, Helen Coolidge, Charlie and Beatrice Prescott

115

I had known a little jeweler in Paris, Bucci, and he had helped me make a gold ring—forerunner of an array of family jewelry—with a spiral on top and a helix for the finger. I thought this would do for a wedding ring. But Louisa merely called this one her "engagement ring" and we had to go to Waltham, near by, and purchase a wedding ring for two dollars.

For supper that night, Louisa and I invited Helen Coolidge, Charley and Beatrice Prescott, and Bill Drew. After dinner we wandered around and found a little photographer's shop and Helen offered us a round of photos. When she paid, she gave the fellow a ten-dollar bill—which he took, slapped into the cash register, and banged it closed. Whereupon he said:

"It will be a dollar-fifty more."

Then we saw on the wall, in fine writing, that each group photo had to be bought at the rate of six prints for each individual on the picture.

We sought the cop on the corner, but he saw the writing on the wall.

Louisa and I shipped for France a few days later on the *American Farmer*. The bunks were uncomfortable but there was all the ice cream you could stand. I still had the place in Villa Brune. According to the precepts I had learned at the Hotel Regina in Barcelona in the previous spring, I prevented the proprietor from painting the walls, thus preserving the white plaster and securing for posterity a few interesting graffiti—they weren't very exciting, maybe, but there is always something on a studio wall . . .

My apartment was rather amusing, because the building consisted of eight studios, three vertically on either side and two over the central entrance. And I was located right over the entrance, so you had to shinny up a staircase and go through a passageway to get to the apartment.

Louisa and Sandy leaving for France on the American Farmer *a few days after their wedding*

Louisa between Alexander Stirling Calder and Mrs. Calder

Remembering the whistle-punk with his ropes to the donkey, I had rigged all the doors with string, and I could even open my front door from the bathtub without moving but a hand. We had pleasant neighbors—Campigli, the St. Louis Einsteins, Vytlacil, a Czech, Julian Trevelyan, and George Reavy. We found living there very pleasant.

Early in our married-life career we went to Romano, an Italian restaurant, off the Grand Boulevards near the Comédie Francaise. They knew how to make zabaglione. So when we got home, we tried this out, but you have leftover quantities of egg whites. We thought we would make prune whip or plum duff, and we kept quite a bowl of whites on the kitchen ledge. However, a day or two later, a hairlike mold arose over the whites—two or three inches high.

I think I'd bought the single cot bed from my ancient proprietor of the rue Daguerre, but the bed turned out to need some "Hello Dad Insect Powder," for one morning Louisa found a beastie on my chest. So, we retired to a hotel for twenty-four hours while the place was being fumigated. When we returned, the chlorine fumes were thick around us, but the exterminators advised us to set a few bowls of ammonia around and let it evaporate—that did the trick.

Einstein lived on the ground floor, across the court; he and his wife had a *bonne* who came and prepared coffee for them. We butted in by extending a wire from his window to our window on a slant across the court, which in guise of teleferic would permit us to pull a string and share their coffee.

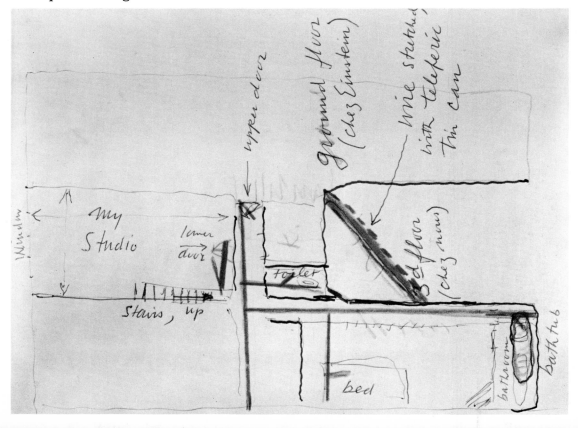

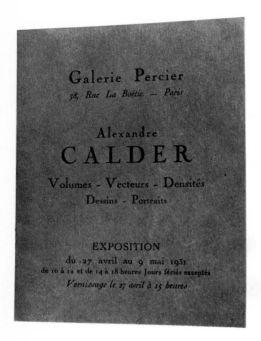

Due to the efforts of some friends in Abstraction-Création, I arranged for a show in the Galerie Percier and Léger wrote the preface. I still had some planks from Villa Brune; we put these on champagne boxes and painted everything white. The objects all ranged around the gallery, one or two were located in the middle, and on the walls overhead were wire portraits. In the window, we had two drawings of the circus.

I remember Mr. Level, the owner of the gallery, objecting to the size of the breasts of one trapezist and Mendès-France, the painter, who had introduced me to him, saying:

"Mais dans l'autre vous voyez le trou du cul du cheval . . ." (But in the other, you notice the asshole of the horse.)

These were things I had been making the previous fall and currently. I continued sawing off some circus bleachers, making square bases for my abstract objects.

There were two slightly articulated objects that swayed in the breeze. One was a more or less horizontal rod with a square sheet of tin on one end and an ebony counterweight on the other. The second object was an almost vertical rod, slightly inclined, about a yard long with at the top a little wire loop with a counterweight at its far end, and another little piece, with another counterweight —there were three elements. I rather liked it.

Six months or so later, a Polish poet—he said—came and collected objects from the members of Abstraction-Création for the museum of Lodz. I wanted to keep the last object described, feeling it was the most exciting, but it was the one he wanted, for probably the same reason, so I gave it to him. Later on, we heard he had been given some money to buy these things—poetical omission.

Louisa took all my new objects and my work without any demur. She seemed to accept them, and it did not occur to me or to her to discuss it.

February 15, 1965

10:45 a.m. to 11:45 a.m.

About the same time, the group Abstraction-Création had a show, Porte de Versailles, and I exhibited there too.

I also took the circus there and gave a performance for them, but it was raining outside and the drum got moist. The place was sort of a large tent, the sounds got lost, and it turned out to be

April 1931 show at Galerie Percier, Paris

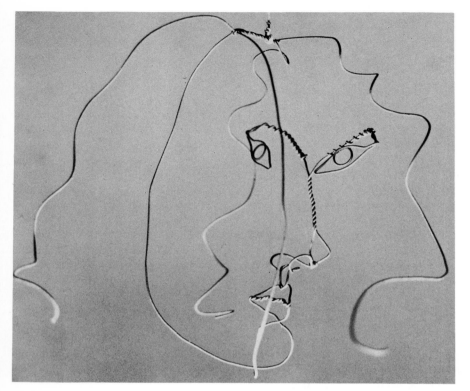

Portrait of Louisa

Portrait of Marian Greenwood

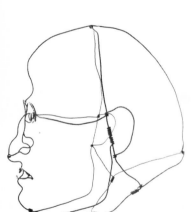

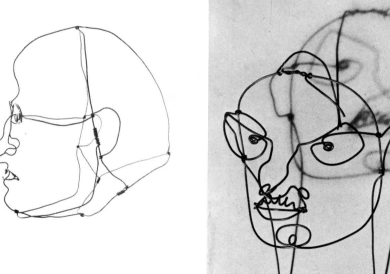

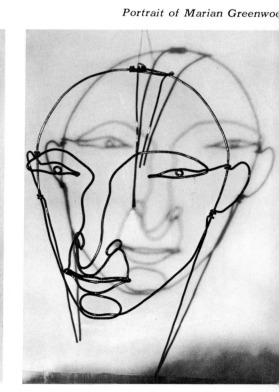

Portrait of Sheppard Vogelgesang

Portrait of Amédée Ozenfant

rather lugubrious—my circus needs good acoustics and not too vast a space.

Louisa had a very dear friend, Pauline Cauchie, who had been her governess and that of her two sisters when they were small children in Paris. She was married now and had a son, Marc-Antoine. Her husband was in the post office—the P.T.T.—and was also a musician. While looking for an apartment, she discovered a whole house, which was too much for themselves but just the right thing for Louisa and me.

This was a three-story house at 14 rue de la Colonie, in the *treizième arrondissement*, not very far from the place d'Italie. There was a studio on the top floor, because the husband of the owner had been a painter (he had been killed in 1914). There was also a garden. This was all very spacious and comfortable, and we whitewashed all the walls, painting the woodwork a shiny black.

We had barely moved in when we came home one night to find placarded on the wall, close to the entrance, a list of furniture to be sold at an auction. We first believed it would be worth while to attend and see if any suited us. So, the next morning we looked at the list more carefully and realized that the furniture corresponded piece for piece to ours in the house! We realized we were being seized. This, because the previous tenant had departed without paying his last quarter's rent and was charging it to us—on his own. Previously he had imposed upon us, before allowing us to move in, some pink and gold furniture, which we eliminated finally.

However, we were soon well installed with our own furniture, and Louisa had a piano. A lady even came in and applied for a job as a *bonne*. A Corsican woman with a square face. She used to make breakfast and lunch and disappear. She took care of her son and would never allow us to have any fish because the boy did not like it. She brought breakfast to our bedroom and would never fail to say:

"Maintenant qu'est-ce que j'ai oublié?" (What have I forgotten now?)

A year or two later, Louisa was in the hospital for a moment and Mr. James arrived to spend a week or two with us. Before we could head him off, he had told Madame Battini that he did not like anything reheated, so she could take home any leftovers with her.

That evening, Mr. James and I sat down before six lamb chops and a huge platter of green beans.

Louisa had always been fond of horses and dogs. One morning as we were having breakfast in a café, rue de Tolbiac, she saw a very fluffy puppy prance by. Its owner was a mason who had to travel from town to town. He readily parted with the dog, with

121

"My father dabbled with the possibility of asking me to supervise the installation . . . On the other hand we had heard a lot about Majorca . . ."

a proviso he'd visit it once in a while.

This dog got the name of "Feathers." He was white with a gray head and two or three black spots, and very fluffy when dry. But when he'd been out in the garden in the rain, he shrank in size and resembled any nasty little fox terrier.

February 16, 1965

5:00 p.m. to 6:30 p.m.

The summer of 1931 was coming and father was completing his statue of Leif Ericson for Reykjavík. He dabbled with the possibility of asking me to supervise the installation. On the other hand, we had heard a lot about Majorca and especially about the Hotel Mediterraneo in Palma, so we did not know whether to have a hot summer or a cool one.

Finally we decided on Majorca. By that time we also had a cat—Picken. He was black. We left Feathers and Picken with some friends and went off to Barcelona by train and continued by boat to Majorca. In the hallway of the boat, I swiped a wind scoop and fixed it on our porthole, so we had plenty of fresh air despite the heat.

We hastened to the Hotel Mediterraneo and enjoyed the spacious rooms, each with a terrace to the south. Pilar Miró came from Palma and she had directed us to look up her family. They were easy to locate because they had a pointed blue-tile roof on their tower. We spent pleasant moments with the Juncosas. They were all sizes and ages, and for the small ones there was a *chaise-percée*, where they sat.

We took a short bus trip to Paguera and stayed for a month in a small hotel there—with two English ladies, a Spanish professor, and his two children. There was a fine beach with the water just the right temperature. I remember one day seeing a little boy tending a herd of pigs on the beach. Most of the pigs loved to wallow in the water. When time came for them to go, the old boss would not come out and the little boy had to throw clods at him.

We projected a walking trip to Sóller on the north side, and in preparation I had a pair of boots made in Palma. So, one day we took the bus to the end of the line to Andraitx to start out on foot the next morning. Each of us had a knapsack; in mine, I had a flyswatter. We walked half a day, ten miles or so, and reached

Estellenchs. A festival was going on there and they had a band that could only play one tune—a *pasodoble*—which they did, marching to one end of the village and then to the other.

It had not rained in Estellenchs for two years and they only had enough water for the next three months. There were some clouds overhead, but nothing doing—they went away. The water systems were probably all alike in these little villages. In Paguera there was a cistern underneath the building into which a tin bucket was lowered when water was needed. The ground floor was always much larger than the second floor, and it had a flat roof which formed a terrace for the upper part. During the rainy season, if ever, they would wash down the roof and terrace and direct the water into the cistern. But if it does not rain at all, this does not work.

Behind and above Estellenchs, which was very sloping and covered with stone terraces built probably by the Arabs centuries ago, there were three or four springs, too salty to be drinkable, but which nonetheless served in a very orderly system to water all the gardens. Everybody had his allotted moment to draw his precise share of the water.

We stayed in a little hotel there and the girl in charge was always crying:

—*¡Mucho calor!*

And I got out my flyswatter and went to work.

Then we proceeded on our hike. We followed the coast afoot on a path high above the sea and came to Bañalbufar—this too was beautifully terraced. We stayed there a day or two before walking all the way to Sóller, twenty-two kilometers (close to fourteen miles), which we did pleasantly in a day.

The boots had long since been abandoned; they were strong but they wore my feet down, and we were both wearing espadrilles —*alpargatas.*

We passed Deyá, famous resort of Chopin and George Sand, but did not peer in—it was quite off our track. Several times Louisa and I had agreed to quit saying, "Look at that beautiful olive tree," but we kept breaking down, and we got into Sóller quite late. We were given a hotel room on the ground floor, and were awakened at about three in the morning by a cock crowing furiously right into our window. The next morning we took the electric train back to Palma.

Upon our return, whom did we discover but my old friend George Thomson, to whom I had sent a postcard some days before, saying there was a lot of sun. Being English, he had come to make the most of it.

The last day in Palma we bought a great handsome stack of

123

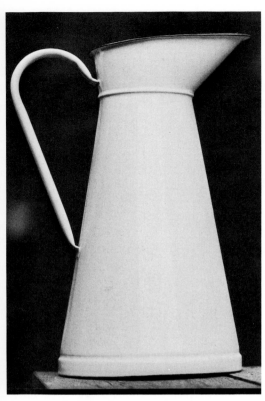

"A broc is a beautiful thing . . ."

dishes, simple, white, with either blue or red circles round the rim. To get to the boat we had a little cart with a little horse, carrying our luggage and the box of dishes. George Thomson returned to Paris with us. On the way by train from Barcelona, I started to read and put a visor on my head against the glare. A fellow passenger—a curé, I believe—said:

"You must not do that; strengthen your eyes with 'L'Elixir de l'Abbé Barbe.' "

I followed his advice for several months, squirting two types of this liquid in my eyes every morning. It must have been quite efficacious, because my eyes are not bad yet.

George stayed with us a few days, rue de la Colonie, in Paris, and I did a portrait of him in oils.

Soon after our return, in anticipation of her mother's arrival, Louisa decided to add a cook to Madame Battini. We had some swank friends who lived in *le seizième* and Louisa went with one of them to an agency there.

The first cook, who came from the agency, did not accept some beautiful aprons we had bought in Majorca, and called them *"criard"*—that is, loud. She explained to Louisa that she could make a rice pudding with one, two, or four eggs, according to the importance of the guests. At the end of three weeks we discovered she had only been marking time till her customary mistress returned to Paris, for then she left us.

The second cook seemed a bit nicer, but she explained to Louisa that her previous mistress always took off her shoes and put on bedroom slippers before entering the house to avoid scuffing the parquet.

I forgot to mention that in preparation for the advent of these cooks, Louisa had gone off to buy a *broc* and a washbasin. Now, a *broc* is a beautiful thing of conical shape, tall and slender—and instead she had bought a pitcher, fat and dumpy, while the basin had a flat bottom.

She said, "You won't see these things anyway, because they'll be in the cook's room."

But I was furious . . . and took the two objects down to the cellar and drove a spike through each.

I feel that if one accepts things which one does not approve of, it is the beginning of the end, and by and by you get more things of a similar nature. This is akin to the stunt of giving objects away which you don't like. Then the people think you do like that sort of thing, and pretty soon they'll give you back something of a similar nature. Bad taste always boomerangs.

About this time, Helen Coolidge announced her imminent arrival. Kiesler had introduced me to Varèse, the composer, and he in turn brought Jean Painlevé to see my circus.

Jean Painlevé—the son of Paul Painlevé, mathematician and French prime minister in 1917 and 1925—has made films of undersea life, *Spiralis* and *Bernard l'Hermite*, among others, and also *The Fresh-Water Assassins*. His work often took him to Brittany, where he had many friends in Port-Blanc, Côtes-du-Nord.

When not in Brittany, Jean Painlevé spent most of his time in Paris, in the second basement of the Institut des Arts et Métiers, where he had set up his laboratory for film making. He also shot close-ups through a microscope. So he often lived underground, close to his darkrooms, sometimes staying in his cellar for several days on end, sleeping on a cot when not busy working. He thus became, when away from Brittany, an underground ascetic, sort of a Bernard l'Hermite himself, satisfied with a cellar view, indifferent to daylight or fresh air.

Sandy and Louisa always loved the Tréguier area

Maybe that is why he loved Brittany so, and sold us on the idea of visiting his favorite area of the Côtes-du-Nord, Port-Blanc, in front of which Lindbergh and Alexis Carrel owned their island. Toward the end of the summer we arrived there and stayed in a little hotel, with Helen and Feathers. Picken stayed home with Battini in charge; I remember this particular point because he messed up some of our letters.

The Port-Blanc beaches are rocky, but the sand is pretty flat, so the water comes in and withdraws very fast. At low tide, there are great expanses to roam over. There is a fine town not far off, called Tréguier, which overhangs a river and is accessible by a steep hill. The stone steeple of its cathedral is pierced with geometrical shapes, through which one sees the sky. There used to be a narrow-gauge railroad which ran from Port-Blanc to Tréguier.

So we left Feathers at the hotel and set out on foot to Penvenan to take the morning train for Tréguier. I carried a roast chicken in a knapsack. By and by, there was a fork in the road; then we could hear the train coming. So I rushed ahead to hold the train a bit, but I chose the wrong road and broke into a run. It had been raining. The train passed me. I kept on running, slipped in a puddle, and, chicken and all, I skidded home right in front of Louisa and Helen, who had just arrived by the proper road. We made the train, which did not seem to be in a hurry anyway.

Part of the railroad bridges were knocked out during the war

125

and it is too bad they don't exist now as they stood then. No one felt the urge to rebuild things the same way. Many of those trains have been replaced by jammed buses. Nonetheless, a section of this railroad is still in operation and one can make a small excursion by train from Paimpol, have lunch, and return to base.

In Tréguier, we found a bistro in which we had a drink and ate our chicken. Then we found some wonderful clothing shops. In one of these, Louisa and I bought each a postman's cape and Helen got a raincoat and a pair of boots—heavy leather boots, so I called her Hindenburg. The boots she abandoned on the walk to Perros-Guirec the next day—they were indestructible but her feet weren't. So she traded them for espadrilles.

I have always remembered Tréguier with pleasure. And in later years, I have always been pleased when we went there again. These northern beaches are rocky and not very good for bathing unless you are the intrepid type, which keeps the throngs away.

As Christmas approached, Louisa thought of her friend's little boy, Marc-Antoine Cauchie, who was seven. She wanted to give him a real Christmas party. So we invited all our friends who had children—there must have been twenty-five or thirty kids. We had a fine-looking tree. I had made most of the stars with aluminum, sheet aluminum, complete with wire candleholder. We had gone down to the center of Paris to buy jokes and gifts. Louisa had some ten or eleven small leather Arab purses and quite a number of other things. We had placed them in a large suit box, left open and standing in one corner of the room. Among the jokes and tricks we had a burdock-made thing called *"accroche-légume"*—catchy vegetable. When tossed at a person a papier-mâché carrot or onion would stick to his clothing and raise hell with a silk dress. After a furious battle with the *accroche-légumes,* somebody found the gifts and annexed all the purses. All this time, Marc-Antoine was home with a cold.

After the party, everybody took what he could reach off the tree; the stars and candles disappeared. Next day, Pauline brought Marc to see the tree—it was green again.

All that winter, I had been working on things with a little motion, some with more motion. I had quite a number of things that went round and round, driven by a small electric motor—some with no motor—some with a crank.

I had met Mary Reynolds when I went to pick up some photographs, rue de Montessuy, and again in Villefranche when I came off Fordham's boat. We had gotten to be very good friends—as a matter of fact, she got one of the best stars off Marc-Antoine's Christmas tree. One evening, she brought Marcel Duchamp to the rue de la Colonie, to see us and my work.

There was one motor-driven thing, with three elements. The

thing had just been painted and was not quite dry yet. Marcel said:
"Do you mind?"

When he put his hands on it, the object seemed to please him, so he arranged for me to show in Marie Cuttoli's Galerie Vignon, close to the Madeleine.

I asked him what sort of a name I could give these things and he at once produced "Mobile." In addition to something that moves, in French it also means motive.

Duchamp also suggested that on my invitation card I make a drawing of the motor-driven object and print:

CALDER
SES MOBILES

The show opened around April and there were fifteen objects with motors and some fifteen others, all of which had moving elements. As I used to run a string as a belt around numerous corners —nostalgia for the whistle-punk days—these strings had to be tightened up every so often. And as I made most of the reduction gears myself, there was a good deal of greasing necessary. I spent most of the day of the opening leaning over my gearing, greasing and adjusting my babies. Louisa went home and got a clean shirt for me, but I had quite a beard by the end of the afternoon.

In the meantime, we lost Picken. Somehow or other, Helen did not like our cat Picken. One day, when we were out and she was there, she kindly opened the front door into the street for him. Why shouldn't he take a breath of fresh air? We never heard from Picken again.

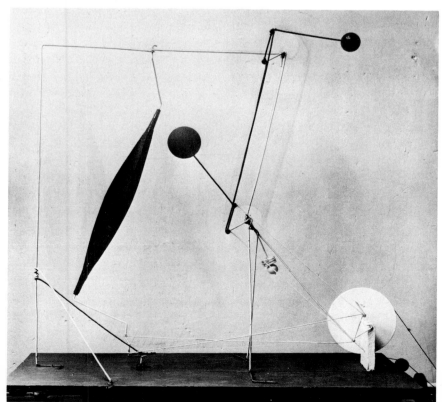

The motorized mobile that Duchamp liked

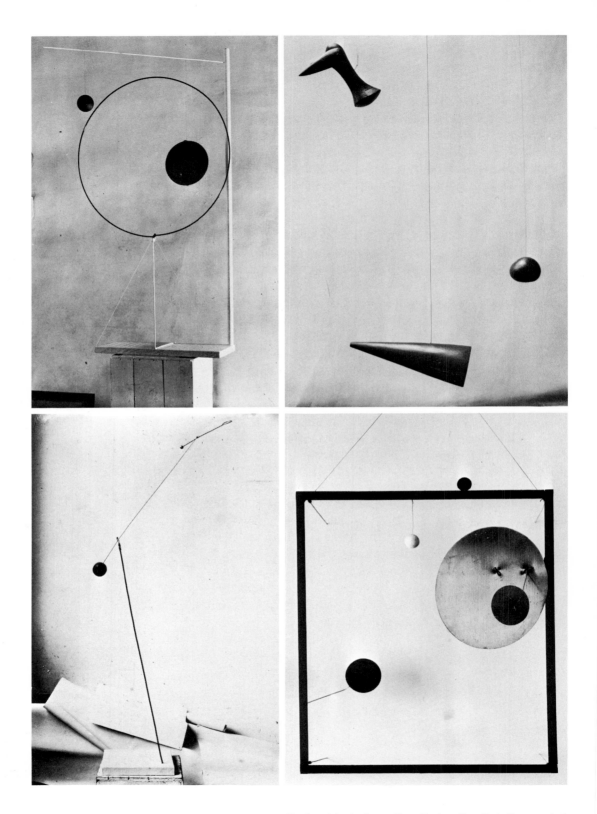

Early objects from the Abstraction-Création period

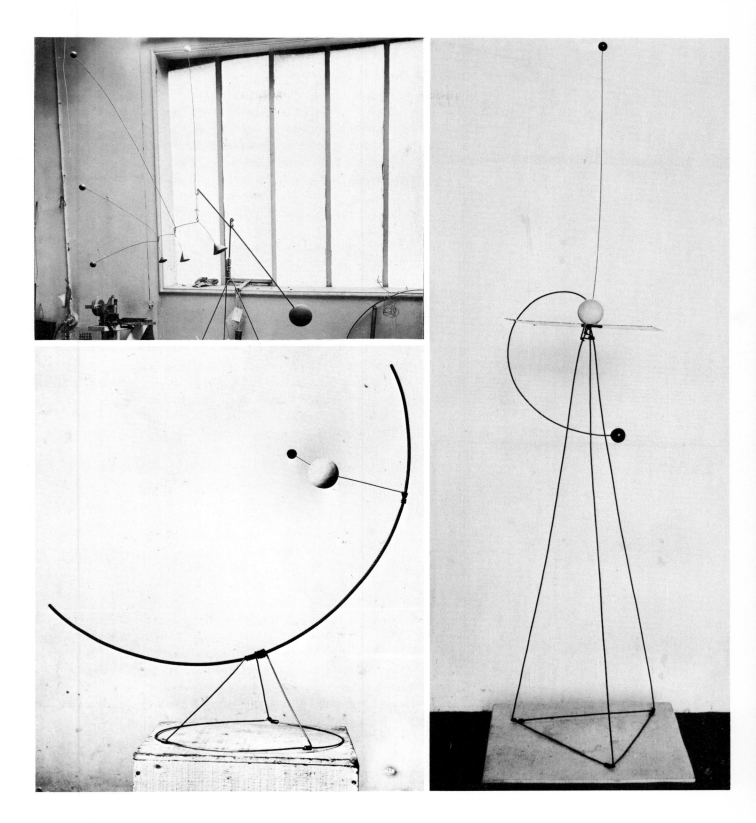

February 18, 1965

11:15 a.m. to 12:45 p.m.

I guess all the members of Abstraction-Création came to see my show. Moreover, their publication came out about this time. They kept it going for several years—one issue a year. At the end, they were hard up for funds and it was suggested they invite some successful artists to have their pictures printed alongside our own—they'd pay a bit more than we to carry the publication along. Somebody suggested inviting Picasso, and Delaunay became furious.

They did invite Brancusi. He sent a photograph, but no funds.

It was about this time that Jean Arp said to me, "Well, what were those things you did last year [for Percier's]—stabiles?"

Whereupon, I seized the term and applied it first of all to the things previously shown at Percier's and later to the large steel objects I am involved in now—such as "The Guillotine for Eight," shown at the Guggenheim in 1964.

The journalists did not seem to understand anything I was driving at. There were notes about *"l'art automobile,"* and a photograph of one object, likening it to a gear shift. They just did not, or would not, understand.

My fellow members seemed to understand. However, some of the lesser lights asked me, "What formula do you use?"

All this while, Louisa and I were enjoying the house at the rue de la Colonie very much. We saw Campigli, whom we had met at Villa Brune. Campigli was a very good cook. When buying a chicken, he would sniff it—you know where.

Sometimes, we almost had a full reunion of Abstraction-Création at the house. Mondrian used to listen to records and say very seriously, with a shake of the head:

"Ça, c'est bon.

"Ça, c'est pas bon."

One day, I had gone to see him and he surprised me greatly by saying, "At Le Boeuf sur le Toit, they painted the walls blue—like Miró."

I was amazed to hear that he frequented such cabarets or acknowledged Miró.

I was also making the most of the studio being so close to our living quarters, working for hours every day, but feeling free to knock off if something worth while came along. Once in a while I would pull the workbenches around, link them with planks, make the bleachers for the circus, and we would have it three nights running. Sometimes, we had nearly a hundred people. There were

"Bucéphale" in front of the Saché studio

"Teodelapio": two views

Saché, 1963. Several stabiles in front of the studio (following pages)

regular aficionados and occasionally some new people; others were bringing someone along. In the front row, there was always a place reserved for Louisa's great-aunt, Mrs. Alice Cuyler, who was quite elderly but enthusiastic.

She was also enthusiastic about the lights I had made—aluminum cones on wooden stalks—and as she played bridge very often, I made her a light with a long slender cone hanging from a long sloping slender post, with a chicken's foot underneath. She took this to her home, 8 rue Picot, and it seems it was successful.

Eric Grate, the Swedish sculptor, used to come to the rue de la Colonie and we used to have dinner and go dancing. There was also a delicious Hungarian named Tihanyi; he was quite deaf, had trouble with his speech, and had what might be called a lugubrious face, but he always kept trying to break the barrier—he could speak German and French, with a strange foreign pronunciation, and his English consisted of a few words. When one would go to light a cigarette with a match, he would say:

"*No est modern.*"

And bring out a *briquet,* which might or might not work. He invariably wore a flat gray hat and a long corduroy coat that almost reached to the ground. He was a painter, one of those who did not work too hard—maybe because he and his brother got a little money from a café they owned in Budapest. He lived on the rue Froidveau, and once as he was going home at night through the cemetery somebody hit him over the head. He became quite a hero, showing his abrased scalp.

He came to the house on the rue de la Colonie once and wanted to make some mayonnaise. He went around to the corner store and bought one egg. This did not work, so he went out again and bought another egg. Then a third egg . . . Then we gave up. However, he had one dish with onions, carrots, and peas which Louisa repeated successfully.

Tihanyi was quite adventuresome and one winter turned up in New York to arrange a show of his abstract paintings. Finally it took place in Romany Marie's Tavern. It was during one of those moments when I was in father's studio on Fourteenth Street. He came in once and said he'd like to telephone to Hugo Gellert, a fellow Hungarian by origin. So I called Hugo, whom I knew quite well, and Tihanyi talked to Hugo in Hungarian. Hugo talked to me in English and I spoke to Tihanyi in French—but he got what he wanted.

About May 1932, Louisa and I took a Belgian freighter for New York. Before leaving for Antwerp, we had a big party. Mary Reynolds brought Gabrielle Picabia, the first wife of the painter. The next day we had a *pneumatique* from Gabrielle Picabia, asking us if she could occupy one room and the bathroom while we were gone. We consulted with Mary, who seemed to think that would be fine.

So we went off to Antwerp with Feathers, the circus, and a bale of my stabiles and mobiles, about a three-foot cube. In Antwerp we had to put this bundle on a cab roof; then on the boat it got rained on again.

The other passengers were a missionary from Chicago, his missionary wife, a Negro from Liberia, and Mrs. André Roosevelt, the wife of the maker of movies on the Far East. We soon got to know Heidi (Mrs. Roosevelt) very well, and she was horrified to hear that we had allowed Gabrielle Picabia to use our house. She knew Gabrielle and also the rest of the gang, Duchamp and Picabia. However, we could not do anything about it then, because we were to remain on the ship for over nine days. Later, we decided to take a chance and leave Gabrielle there anyhow.

The woman missionary seemed to have been taken over by the natives. She tried to explain that she had seen a snake with two heads—one at each end. She also had another story about a colored boy who had been swallowed feet first by a python. He was rescued, but his lower part was all bleached out by the experience!

The mate had been in charge of a boat which had run down some fishing trawlers off Newfoundland, and this woman missionary would insist on trying to make him tell the story. One might ascribe it to a lack of tact, but again it sounded vicious, and I have had my doubts about missionaries ever since.

Arrived in New York, I arranged with Julien Levy to have a show in his Madison Avenue gallery. He already had on a photographic show, but as I did not need the walls, I was allowed to place my objects on pedestals in the open space between the walls and the front windows. Several of these were motor-driven.

Father came to the show and could not dissociate himself from a screw eye and a pulley which drove one object around; he said he could see nothing but a man on a motorcycle making laps. He was at least puzzled by what I made. Later, when I had exhibited some things at Stockbridge, near Pittsfield, where he lived, he put two of my objects on his lawn when they came back from the show—thus displaying a good deal of interest.

1932 — Harrises seeing us off
on Spanish freighter
I had poison ivy on my chin
and Sandy in his left cheek
, says Louisa.

February 22, 1965

11:00 a.m. to 12:30 p.m.

I think we spent five months in the United States that time.

The previous year, Bob Josephy had sold me an old Dodge, which I gave to mother and father, and now Louisa and I went barnstorming around in it to see friends and acquaintances.

Feathers made a great hit with everybody, and while we went swimming in a pond, near by to father's house, he finally learned from a Cairn terrier, who rushed across the dock and plunged into the water, to do likewise when we threw a stick for him.

We returned to Paris, via Barcelona, on the Garcia and Díaz Spanish line—another motor ship. We had a fine time—fourteen days to Barcelona in early September. Again the cooking was very good, and we became accustomed to eating *membrillo*—quince paste—with cheese at the end of each meal.

We passed the Straits of Gibraltar late at night, and the water was somewhat phosphorescent. Porpoises overtaking us, sometimes swimming three or four abreast, outlined by the phosphorescence, would scratch against the bow of the boat—a truly wonderful sight.

Again we stopped in Malaga, and this was the time I sought my fruit store and discovered it had changed color. In the streets, there seemed to be thousands of *limpiabotas*—bootblacks—and every one of them took out a pair of scissors and offered to trim Feathers' hair.

This time, we had taken precautions to find out where Miró really was and we planned to visit him for a week in Montroig.

On the way down by train from Barcelona to Montroig, which took four hours, was Tarragona—and here in Tarragona they took all our baggage out of our compartment, circus and all, and I had to go with the two tickets to stand in line and reregister everything from Tarragona to Montroig.

Miró was on the farm belonging to his mother, who also had an apartment in Barcelona. He had done a fine painting of the farm which Hemingway had acquired years before. This is one of the series of paintings of the farm which is very strong; some of the others are purple and green with views of plowed fields, grapes, trees.

I had long since abandoned my physical culture, but Joan was still at it and I joined him on the roof of the chapel, built on the farm, one morning. He made so many whistling noises that I gave up in a fit of laughter.

We had brought the circus along as usual, and I presented it before the Mirós and various farm hands and neighbors. That was the time he told me the next morning that what he liked best were those bits of paper that floated down. To my mind, it was obvious that these were pigeons.

While in Montroig, one day we took the train with Joan, two stations away, to Cambrils. Here we watched the fishermen bring in their catch. They had large flat baskets, one yard in diameter, resting on the ground, and stacked with fish arranged in spiral motifs. It was very pretty. Then, there being one person more than the number of baskets—with handles on either side—they all stooped at the same time and picked up the baskets in a queue and proceeded into the square. There, the first man turned in a circle until the others followed up around him in a spiral. Then, they all posed their load.

They proceeded to auction each basket as an entire unit. They would start with a high number like ninety and go down to eighty-nine, eighty-eight, eighty-seven . . . till someone nodded

Calder, Dolores, Pilar, and Miró on beach

assent and they decided it was sold. It was the reverse of what I had known and seemed somewhat more modest.

We managed to buy one of the empty baskets, because we liked it as an object, and when we got on the train, we had to ship it specially as an "empty container."

Miró hired a car and one Sunday all of us went to Tarragona. Again my Spanish was lacking. We stood around for thirty minutes to one hour without being able to figure out what was going on. The Mirós seemed to be waiting for some event to take place—and nothing happened. We just got back into the car and returned to Montroig.

A few days later we left. The car Miró had rented was supposed to come and get us, but it never showed up. We heard the train whistle in and whistle out of the distant station. A half hour later the car dashed up—the chauffeur had not been able to start it. We piled in with Miró, Feathers, and all our luggage, and dashed to the station a few miles off as if there was a chance of catching the departed train. After that, we sat in the station for three hours—with Miró not saying much of anything.

The trip down from Barcelona to Montroig had taken four hours. We returned from Montroig to Barcelona in two hours—something I have never been quite able to fathom.

We spent a Sunday in Barcelona with some friends, who took us to see Gaudí's cathedral and also to the park to see the Catalans dance the sardana.

Arrived in Paris at the Gare d'Orsay, we had so much luggage that we had to hire a special taxi. Feathers crawled under one

140

of the lateral benches of the vehicle and found a rubber ball.

When we got to the house on the rue de la Colonie, Gabrielle Picabia, who had remained during our American stay, was out. No one was there; the confusion justified somewhat Heidi's alarm. But I did find four hundred francs in a pocket of an old pair of pants when I put them on.

February 23, 1965

11:15 a.m. to 12:30 p.m.

Back in Villa Brune, I had tried my hand at stone sculpture. I had bought a couple of pieces of very soft limestone, *pierre de Paris*, through which one works like through cheese . . . or at least plaster. One of the things I had made was a horse; the legs were in bas-relief around the solid base.

On the rue de la Colonie, we had no sidewalk and a puddle always appeared right in front of the entrance steps when it rained. So sometime in the previous spring, I had buried my horse in the pavement to plug up the water hole—not being very enthusiastic about my sculpture. Mary Reynolds and Marcel Duchamp had paid a visit to Gabrielle Picabia and discovered the horse in the sidewalk. They dug it up and took it home, leaving me with the hole that continued to catch the water, worse than ever.

They thought they had discovered a Roman ruin.

In the winter of 1932, we had a visit from Mrs. James. She stayed with us at the rue de la Colonie.

The three of us went to have lunch at Jamet's, boulevard Arago—about a mile's walk along the rue de la Glacière. Feathers was with us. During the repast, I insisted on eating two *tartes à la crème* and Louisa was very annoyed with me. Occasionally, Feathers went to the bathroom and due to his long hair had some difficulty—maybe the bootblacks of Malaga were right after all. Louisa was behind us with Feathers and suddenly hastened to get in front so that I could see what was in store for me . . . I was the cleaner-upper.

In the spring of 1933, Jean Hélion, who was quite a friend of Pierre Loeb of the Galerie Pierre, arranged with him to have a group show of six artists: himself, Arp, Miró, Pevsner, Seligmann, myself.

There was a Bessarabian critic who wrote something on each

of us. His name was Anatole Jakovski. The text was not too interesting; he was trying to be poetic, and all I can remember is the following sentence:

"*Pas besoin de boussole dans le pays de Seligmann.*" (You don't need a compass in Seligmann's land.)

I can't even remember more than one of my objects: a cone, two feet long, of ebony and an ebony sphere six inches in diameter and a sort of a helmet shape made of two pieces of ebony. These were hung at the far end of two bars as eveners, and they rotated and floated up and down.

I went to the gallery once and was alarmed to discover that Pierre and some of his friends were amusing themselves by throwing all the elements of this particular object up in the air at the same time, thus succeeding in bending the bars and spoiling its motion.

For some reason, I did not repeat the show of the previous year at Marie Cuttoli's, but had one at Pierre Colle's, on the rue Cambaceres. I ran into Dali during one of the visits to the gallery before my show. As he lived not far away from the rue de la Colonie, I decided to call on him. He was busy sorting dirty postcards, but took time out to give me a little green book, *Babauo*, which was a scenario for a movie. He had written it and had it printed.

A few days later, I returned it with a remark that there were in it "too many restless inner tubes, pumping up and down." He immediately took offense, and this coolness has existed between us ever since.

About this time, Louisa had a late miscarriage in a Paris clinic. I had taken her there and returned home for the night. The next morning, Madame Battini asked where Louisa was. I said, "*Elle a eu une fausse-couche.*" (She has had a miscarriage.)

And she said, "*Ma mère elle en a eu des fausses-couches.*" (My mother, she has had many miscarriages.)

And I asked, "How many children are you?"

And she replied, "*Dix, ca fait quinze avec les fausses-couches!*" (Ten, that makes fifteen with the miscarriages!)

February 24, 1965

11:00 a.m. to 12:45 p.m.

There were so many articles in the European press about war preparations that we thought we had better head for home. Louisa hoped to have a baby in tranquillity and Europe did not seem tranquil at the time. So in June 1933, Jean Hélion and we took an American boat, whose name I forget, for New York, having given up our lease on the rue de la Colonie.

Upon landing we went to Concord, Massachusetts, to visit Louisa's parents. There, we bought a secondhand 1930 LaSalle touring car. It had a cloth top, removable, and could seat nine,

Calder in the LaSalle with daughter Mary, as seen by Saul Steinberg many years after the car's purchase in June 1933

with broad seats front and rear and jump seats as well. It was in good shape; I kept it a long time and enjoyed it. You got plenty of air in this vehicle. And often I took my wares to open a show in New York in it. (All in all, I kept this LaSalle for over seventeen years!)

Shortly after its purchase we drove to visit my parents in Richmond, Massachusetts, close to Pittsfield. There too, we did not spend very much time and started off in search of a dwelling.

My formula was that we wanted a modest house with a barn out of which to make a studio. I had gone up and down the Housatonic River with my parents in 1928, when they were looking for a house. It was a pleasant valley and we tried that again. There was nothing doing.

Then we went over to Tarrytown and looked around there with Louisa's brother-in-law, Chanler Chapman. After that we headed for New City, Rockland County, west of the Hudson, in New York State. For there we had friends such as Henry Poore, Billy and Wally Fleisher, and others. Well, we saw nothing around there

143

Roxbury, 1933

either. Then we headed for Long Island where our dear friends Jane and Reggie Harris lived. Jane and we drove all the way to Yaphank, quite a ways out—a camp during the First World War. We spotted a rather important house which had a big barn and a ballroom over the carriage shed. It also seemed to have a still in one of the barns. We were really enthusiastic over this, but it belonged to one of the big estates and it was painted green to efface it. Moreover, this house would not have been suitable because it was in a dull neighborhood, with flat countryside.

Next we went to Westport, Connecticut, and stayed there with Bob Josephy. One Sunday we traveled as far as Sandy Hook and saw nothing, although we called on an agent. The next morning, on a Monday, we borrowed ten dollars for gas from Josephy and set off for Danbury, Connecticut, and there we visited an agency. The manager was not there, but we were received by his assistant, a little man who took us around.

We saw one or two places and finally, driving over the brow of a hill . . . we now each claim to have been, Louisa and I, the first to exclaim, "That's it!"

But I am convinced it was I who said it first.

We walked out in the pasture and saw a great rocky mound on top of a gentle hill. That sealed it. Of course, the barn had been burned two years before. I later found several finial ends of the old lightning rod—a sort of sunburst of copper, full of hay. I liked these objects and saved them, tacking them up on my shelves.

Many years later a man came to sell me, not lightning rods, but lightning protection. I showed him this finial device which had failed to protect the barn full of hay and he said, "Oh! Yes, that is one of ours."

And I said, "You might as well be running along."

The little agent was glad to sell us the house and eighteen acres for $3500, of which 10 per cent was required immediately—and of which I had none. I telephoned my faithful friend Bill Drew, who immediately sent the required check to the New York office of this real estate agent. So, we heard by phone that it had been done.

For the rest of it, I had a vague life-insurance policy that I had subscribed to in an inadvertent moment some years before, and on which I could borrow $1100—with a mortgage for the rest. This took care of things for the moment.

We were also obliged to take out a fire-insurance policy, which later stood us in very good stead, for in 1943—ten years later—a good part of the house burned down, through a short circuit, and the policy, which had been doubled, worked out.

This was Painter Hill Road, Roxbury, Connecticut, which we have now occupied for thirty-three years, with occasional trips to Europe. Since then, many other buildings of mine have gone up on these eighteen acres—I even purchased two adjoining acres for more than the original price of the whole house—and some people describe it as a small village. There was the room that replaced the one burned, a guest house, and two studios.

We returned triumphantly to my family in Richmond, Massachusetts—we owned our very first house, my first house and I was thirty-five—and we brought the family down on a picnic to investigate the new acquisition. Everybody liked the land; it was a nice day in August.

Pepe de Creeft lived with some friends in New Milford, near by, and we decided to stay there a month or two while refurbishing the house.

We picked up a strange crew of carpenters, painters, and even a plumber who used to study *Popular Mechanics* and undertook to put all the plumbing and heating in the house for $1100. He also wanted us to let him shield the house with asphalt shingles over the wood walls, and claimed that at fifty feet no one could then tell that it was not made out of brick—but we resisted this temptation. Later another plumber, who worked on the house after the fire, remarked that our first expert had not even reamed the pipes after cutting them. Nevertheless it all worked till we could afford to improve it.

We had a coal-burning furnace, which would blow off steam at fifteen pounds. Many times I ran down cellar, cursing *Popular Mechanics*, naked, to shovel ashes on the bed of coals and keep

Roxbury, 1938

Roxbury, 1935

Roxbury, 1966

the steam down. Years later, we replaced all this by installing an oil burner in the coal burner and finally by putting in a whole new furnace, which has a safety device to cut it out if it gets too hot and also if water is lacking, and an automatic water injector. This makes life much simpler.

Adjacent to the farm, there was an old icehouse, dug into the ground on two sides. Heavy posts on the outside held the boards together. I got some second-hand windows, stuck them in, and made it into the first studio I had ever owned. But at the end of this improvised studio there was a fireplace that smoked, and I always had to open the door. I finally built the hearth up with stone and got it to work. I found that when this result was achieved, the area of the chimney opening was about twelve times that of the flue—which verified Benjamin Franklin's principle. The chimney no longer smoked. Later, when we transformed this room into a living room—a whole new studio having been built —while installing a level brick floor I discovered the room was not level, being several inches higher around the hearth. But we maintained this by building a semicircular ledge in front of the hearth.

That winter, Gertrude Stein's opera *Four Saints in Three Acts* was produced in Hartford, Connecticut, at the Wadsworth Atheneum. We decided to go and called up Virgil Thomson, the composer. We arrived in our open car at eight in the evening, bedecked in all the clothes we could muster, including a yellow fisherman's shirt from Barcelona, and were greeted by Eddie Warburg, in evening dress, who said, "You look as though you'd driven up from somewhere."

Which was in fact the case.

After the performance, we were invited to have dinner at Chick Austin's. His house had been constructed from a photograph he had taken of a house seen during his wedding trip in Italy. As a result it was like a stage set, and the rooms behind the façade did not necessarily correspond with what was going on in the façade.

There was a barroom in a cellar, with a very narrow set of stairs leading to it. Julien Levy got rather tight and blocked the passage. Whereupon, Louisa suggested that Jim Soby and I put him to bed, which we did. He came down shortly after, very indignant that we should have called attention to his inebriety, and remained in that state of indignation for about twenty years, first blaming me and later Louisa. However, we have become good friends again—and I hope this account does not make him angry once more!

By taking out a partition between a small room and the biggest one to the south—it had been a kitchen and had a sink which we removed—we turned these two rooms, exposed east and south, with a door going directly outside, into a nice sunny living room. We made the kitchen in the north corner of the house; we like the sun but we wanted the living room to benefit from it most. At the time we bought the house, there was also a small dining room, but after the fire we melded it with the kitchen.

Our furniture and effects had come from Paris in six or seven large cases made out of some North European white wood. Out of one of these, I made a corner cupboard for the new kitchen, in which to hang pots and pans. Later on, after the fire, I made another cupboard—it looks Old Dutch or Early American—and for that one I used a large case which came with some of my jewelry back from the Museum of Modern Art.

All these bits of furniture, I painted with barn red—which is probably the secret of my success. All the walls were whitewashed as per the permanent teaching of the Hotel Regina in Barcelona.

There was a lot of wood left from the house construction and with this, I built a large outdoor table. I also housed in the legs of the sink and put a hook of my own manufacture on the door, in the middle. This has been photographed several times—and my daughter Mary has often described it as "the way to the cellar," because our cats used to come out of the cellar through it and stick a paw under the ledge of the sink door.

At the time we bought the house there were really only two trees: an old split apple tree that we patched up—under this one, we sat to eat in summer and in the spring—and a maple planted by the front driveway. Henry Karrmann, the farmer next door, from whose mother we had bought the place, went in the early spring with his horses and a stoneboat up into his woods and hacked out several large trees, with roots and clod frozen in a lump. This has resulted in our having a fine ash east of the house and a maple in front of the garage. Several other such attempts elsewhere ended in failure. But once, we brought two dogwoods from Henry Poore's in New City. One of these is still growing and blossoming every spring near my present studio, and the other we planted near the woodshed. It was burned in the fire. And after the carpenters had tripped over the stump for three weeks, they finally sawed it off at ground level—it never reappeared.

A maple three or four inches thick next to the fire was sawed off temporarily, seven feet from the ground. When it began to grow again, it started off a foot from the ground. I was advised to saw it off again slantwise, which I did, and now, twenty years later, it is a fine tree.

Then we invested in thirty or forty young fruit trees that we planted north and east of the house. The peaches to the east did beautifully for a few years, then died. We never had any success with peach trees, later. We also put in two cut-leaf maples; they are very large now.

Practically all the eighteen acres we had were pasture with no trees because Karrmann's grandfather, Charles S. Hurd, had been a hellion about keeping the place clean—he had had the boys up at 5:00 A.M., cleaning up the brush under lantern light.

We made it a habit to lend the eighteen acres to the farmer next door for pasture, to keep the place clean, but a new young whippersnapper farmer came and he was doubtful of our intentions in lending him the grounds. The fields went to seed and wild apples grew up.

But the year after the cows ceased to graze, the blackberries were wonderful. In 1937, we also had a row of red pines planted, but they were irregularly set and too close together, so they did not grow well. Several times, I cut down the deciduous trees to give the others a chance. Now, however, poison ivy seems to have taken over and it is a fearsome spot.

In the spring of 1934, Mayor La Guardia decided to have an exposition of art in some New York public building and I sent two things, one of which was objects suspended in a vertical circle of wire—this was bought by Alfred Barr for the Museum of Modern Art. (He later exchanged it for a motorized "universe.") This, after my selling two small objects to the Pittsfield Museum and another object to a lady in Rochester, was my first break since our return from France and the rue de la Colonie.

In Paris, I had met Pierre Matisse and he had come to the rue de la Colonie once. So I asked him for a show in his New York gallery, and had one in the spring of 1934.

For about eight or nine years thereafter, I had shows with him almost every year. When we had the group show at Pierre Loeb's in Paris, I had met James Johnson Sweeney, of whom Léger had spoken several times. He wrote a preface for my first Matisse show and I gave him an object—but he insisted on giving me a modest payment.

Most of the objects in my first Matisse show I had made during the winter of 1933, in Roxbury, but the object Sweeney chose I had made in Paris. The Calderberry-bush: a two-meter rod with one heavy sphere suspended from the apex of a wire. This gives

148

quite a cantilever effect. Five thin aluminum discs project at right angles from five wires, held in position by a wooden sphere counterweight. The discs are red and the supporting members, including the heavy sphere, are black, while the wooden sphere is white.

Another object started on a vertical sheet of tin used as a panel, painted white, in front of which three rather flattened jelly beans rotated, red, black, and white. This particular object always embarrassed me because people never failed to peer over the top to see how my string belting was faring and what corners it went around.

There were a few faithful friends at the opening and I used to stay in the show and try to explain my wares. The president of Stevens came, but I missed him. I wrote him a letter in which I tried to explain what my ideas were and used such expressions as "composing," "torques," "vectors of motion," and so forth.

He must have been nonplussed, for I never had any acknowledgment of my letter—which I have always taken as a proof that the college was not really interested in my work. Later, they seem to have changed their minds. And I have developed an attitude of indifference to the reception of my work, which allows me to go about my business.

CALDER
PAINTER HILL ROAD
R. F. D. ROXBURY,
CONN, U R A

2 Oct 58

Dear Miss Bush

One of the problems confronting me is to get enough free time to *work*, and not to go around talking about it. So I beg to be excused.

Another of the problems confronting the contemporary artist is Mr. James Johnson Sweeney — who / implies he wants him to make an object for a certain place, but does not come around to see what ideas have been developed, if any. So would you be so kind as to bring this to Mr. Sweeney's attention?

"Also, how long is a "student generation"?

Cordially yours
Alexander Calder

Since 1933, Calder has practically given up trying to explain his work, and he normally avoids discussing it. This October 1958 answer to an invitation to lecture at Wheaton College is typical of his attitude. However, he never sent it and it was later found in his "Oubliettes"

149

Somebody came walking up the Painter Hill Road—about 1934. We invited this someone for a drink and he talked about Peter Blume, the painter, whom I had known previously. We discovered he lived in Sherman, Connecticut. So we set out to find him, and after asking our way a few times we located him.

Mrs. Blume's sister, Ann, had just married her dear old friend Heber Blankenhorn. During the evening, I discovered they had no wedding ring, so I found a piece of copper wire and made one for them.

Through the Blumes we got to know Malcolm Cowley, Matthew Josephson, and Bob Coates, who all lived within a stone's throw of each other. Thus, we expanded our acquaintanceship around the Roxbury countryside.

Bob Josephy also had bought an apple farm in Bethel, Connecticut, twenty miles away.

So things went on and I continued to work assiduously.

During the fall and winter of 1934–1935, Louisa retired to her mother's home in Concord, Massachusetts. She had decided she was going to take it very easy so as not to have the misfortune she'd experienced in Paris. She was set on having a child. So, I shuttled between Roxbury and Concord.

I once took Louisa a mobile I had made with mirrors, tilted at forty-five degrees to catch the late afternoon sun and project it on the ceiling. These spots of light would go around suddenly in very small circles, according to their tilt and that of the sun, and Louisa could not stand it and I had to take it down. So I sent this object to Tom Taylor, who was with Bausch & Lomb at Rochester, New York, to see if his optical firm would like to produce it. He said no, they would not, but that many of the employees who had seen it had copied it at home for themselves.

One weekend, the Sweeneys came up to visit me on their way to Boston. I had been instructed by Louisa to pick our Roxbury tomatoes and put them in the house before leaving for Concord. So Jim had to help me with this chore. The resultant crop rotted on the dining-room floor.

The two Sweeneys and I had a pleasant trip to Concord and we all spent the night at the Jameses'. Louisa felt the necessity of celebrating the change of scenery—the new faces—and sent me for some whiskey, the first in months.

Mrs. James occupied an old-fashioned wooden house, with old-fashioned rugs and furniture, in the center of a four-acre plot. Mr.

James, who wanted to be a bit aloof, had built himself a house in the corner of the lot, straddling a little brook. Being asthmatic, he had made very large windows that opened fully. On the ground floor was his study and one large living room. Upstairs was his bedroom, right above, and two other guest bedrooms, one of which we occupied. There were bands of red and green and gold around the top of all the rooms, the doors were natural varnished wood, the ceiling was low, and it was very pleasant.

Mr. James used to play the violin atrociously but assiduously, preceding and following a gramophone on which he had devised a foot brake. That was in his study. In the cellar were workbenches and also a pool he had made, diverting the brook into the basement.

Edward Holton James was at war with undertakers. So, he'd had a pine box made which was big enough to take care of him or of his wife, who was a good deal taller than he. It was in his bedroom, probably full of junk.

The heating system was called "pipeless furnace," so there was a large grid in each floor, making privacy difficult. Once, I had been up to my bedroom at the end of the house. I hesitated at the top of the stairs before going down, and I peered down at the box in his bedroom and he said:

"What are you doing in my room?"

And I said:

"I want to look at that pine box, because I might have to screw the lid one day."

He laughed.

"Mr. James used to play the violin atrociously but assiduously . . ." Here drawn by his own granddaughter Sandra Calder

March 4, 1965

6:00 p.m. to 7:15 p.m.

On my frequent visits to Concord—for I kept on working at Roxbury—I made many gifts of flowers to Louisa, things that I don't like very much nowadays, perhaps, things that seemed cute and were growing in little boxes.

Mrs. James became perturbed because it was with Louisa's money that I was buying all this horticulture. Once, she took me aside and made me promise to be a good businessman.

I said I'd do my best.

Louisa, at some stage during her pregnancy, decided to learn to play chess. I think we were struggling with some knight's move when she said, "Let's go to the hospital."

*Sandra at five painting
in Sandy's Roxbury studio*

So we got into the LaSalle and drove over. I think the top was down. It was a fine April night of the year 1935 and we got to the hospital around nine.

After she was admitted, I took a nap in the car and must have slept quite a while. It was about one in the morning when I woke up. I went in to see how things were going. A nurse told me that everything was fine and that I should go back home to sleep.

I hesitated a moment. Then Dr. Johnston happened along. He said, "I'm glad to see you, because I'd like to get another doctor. She is bleeding."

So he got a doctor named Gustafson, from Boston. The baby had been born but the mother's womb had collapsed. Dr. Gustafson put his hand in and pushed it back into place.

Mr. James arrived early in the morning to see how Louisa was and when he heard that Louisa had bled—it was stopped by then —he collapsed on the lawn in front of the hospital. He was a brave man, but did not like the thought of blood. (He had a row of false teeth, thanks to a cop who beat him up one day when he would not move on in the Boston Common. He was protesting the Sacco-Vanzetti sentence.)

Louisa had a fairly long convalescence, over two weeks. She had two very nice nurses—a day and a night one.

I think the hospital wanted to know the name of the infant before allowing her to depart. Somebody gave us a rather amusing book, written by a cultured theatrical producer, on how to choose the name. I wanted to call her Rana, which in Scandinavian means "goddess" and in Spanish, "frog"; maybe something of this first choice took, for she does nothing but draw frogs lately—1965.

Illustration from Sylvester the Lead Frog
(Éditions Maeght, Paris)

Mrs. James was most perturbed that she could not tell her neighbors the name of her dear little granddaughter . . . because she didn't have any. Finally we called her Sandra. I suppose it was after me—Alexander, Alexandra, etc.—though we had started out to call her after no one.

We hired a nurse for a while to go back to Roxbury with us. So we went: the four of us and Feathers.

As Louisa had been knocked out as a source of milk, the baby was put directly on Carnation milk. "It's good for you"—as long as someone else can punch the hole in the can.

We bought a little gray canvas baby carriage and used to put it out under the biggest maple, right in front of the house. Until a few years ago, there was a triangular stone we used to block the wheels with—but that's getting sentimental.

With all this, I forgot the show I had a few weeks before Sandra was born.

Sweeney knew Mrs. Schutz who ran the Renaissance Art Society at the University of Chicago, and he arranged for me to have a show there in March 1935. And from there it went to the Arts Club in the Wrigley building. So I spent a couple of weeks in Chicago, first at the university, then at a downtown hotel.

The only thing I sold was to Miss Katherine Dudley. Five ebony sticks suspended on threads from a semicircular arc of wire embedded in a slab of lignum vitae. She still has it at 12 rue de Seine, Paris. It was fun to see it when I came to Paris eleven years later —in 1946. I used to come to Katherine's at odd hours and muscle in on a meal. She was very fond of cats, and the cats were fond of the mobile.

I had taken my circus along to Chicago, and gave several performances, and I think one evening I hired out to a Mrs. Brewster. She had an elegant black-and-white marble floor into which I could not nail. So we got a storm door and nailed a stick onto it at each corner to moor my guy lines. To add strength to the sticks, we piled a few logs of firewood on each. Mrs. Brewster, who had rented me out for fifty dollars instead of the hundred I asked, thought that this firewood was rather shabby, so she had some cyclamens brought in to stand in front of it.

I got rid of these.

I made some very good friends in Chicago, such as Rue and Al Shaw and Rue's sister Dodo. Not to forget Bobsy Goodspeed, who was president of the Arts Club at that time. Tchelitchev was there too.

On the return trip I stopped off at Rochester to see Mrs. Charlotte Allen, who had been introduced to me by Fletcher Steele, the landscape architect—he had been interested in my show at the Galerie Vignon in 1932.

Mrs. Allen wanted a mobile for her garden which Fletcher Steele had designed—this was the first object I made for out of doors. As I remember, it consisted of some quite heavy iron discs that I found in a blacksmith's shop in Rochester and had then welded to rods progressively getting heavier and heavier.

Fletcher had laid out the garden so that it made a zigzag labyrinth round three sides of a pool and then back again, and ended up behind a hedge. By the pool was a large oak tree, and we were very much amused when Charlotte told us one day—Louisa and me—that she once had a bill from Fletcher:

$50 . . . . Concentration on tree.

March 5, 1965

11:00 a.m. to 12:45 p.m.

In 1936 I had another *vernissage* at Matisse's and there were very few of us. I remember Campigli—it was as though we were standing over a dying fire trying to keep warm.

Who should walk in but Edward G. Robinson.

Pierre's gas chamber—or high-pressure sales room—was attained by walking through the whole gallery, and Robinson went directly to that room. He remained there for at least two hours— that is, it seemed to be two hours—and when he came out he walked straight to the exit door.

Fifteen minutes later Pierre came out in turn, carrying Matisses and Picassos. Robinson was dressing up his hotel suite in expectancy of an important meeting—he only borrowed these paintings.

Next day, I asked Pierre what Robinson had said.

What he had said about my show was, "What the hell is that stuff?"

At one of my earlier Matisse shows, Jere Abbott bought an object for Smith College and Agnes Rindge—who had a show of mine at Vassar and was teaching art there—bought an object for her college.

There was a student of Agnes's, Ellen Coen, who did as a thesis an article on me—it was the first time I'd been written up so seriously. Much later, in 1954, when we visited Beirut, she was Mrs. Jawdat of Bagdad, Iraq, and she got me a job in Beirut with a young Lebanese architect. She wanted very much to have us visit Bagdad, but our host in Beirut, Henri Seyrig, did not seem to think much of Bagdad, so we did not go. I wish we had gone,

154

now, because they lived out in the desert.

A few years later, Jawdat was ousted by a revolution, being related somehow or other to the ruling classes. They now live in Rome.

In the summer of 1936, we heard from Paul and Francine Nelson, whom we had met just before leaving France, that he was coming over to be the architect for a large CBS building. They later asked me to do an object. A trophy for "HAMS."

In 1937, before sailing for France, Calder undertook to do an object for CBS. The model seen here is in wood painted white with steel wire. The completed object was in stainless steel and steel wire. Sweeney did not like it

*Roxbury, 1936. Sandy dancing with Sandra
while Louisa plays the accordion.
Calder here is thirty-eight*

So we wired them to use our apartment on Eighty-sixth Street. This was an apartment we had had for a year or two on the corner of Second Avenue. It was a railroad apartment, with four dark rooms and two light rooms—one north and one south, the only sunny one. There was a small grate in every room. While living in Roxbury we spent each winter there, for several years. I always established a workshop in some little store, sometimes up First Avenue, sometimes on York Avenue, or perhaps on a cross street. I cleared out every year when we left for the country and would settle the following year as best I could . . . I even had two such studios, during the same period, at some point.

These rented shops really worked very well. I would whitewash the lower half of the windows, not to be bothered by onlookers, and if the locale was on the west side of the street, as was often the case, the morning light was fine. I did a lot of work in such places.

In those days we used a lot of California wine and I was letting a gallon age under the sink. So Nelson on his arrival used it, and I protested that he had taken my old wine.

They were so pleased with our apartment that they later took the one across the hall.

Nelson also brought over with him Oscar and Ritou Nitzschke, and they all lived for a winter across the hall. During this period Louisa and I became acquainted with many architects.

I had bought a toy accordion for Louisa, with about eight notes, and she managed to play this. So, I bought one with ivory and "diamonds" in a hock shop. And she played this even better. Then Paul's birthday arrived and Francine Nelson went all out and got Paul a very fancy accordion. Louisa could play this one even better. So, I got her a better one still.

This was a winter of accordion music. The building project not having progressed, Nelson decided to return to Paris and they made us promise to come and visit them in Varengeville, on the Normandy coast, that following summer.

In May 1937, we sailed on a French boat, with lots of luggage. We had Sandra, aged two by then, and Dorothy Sibley to take care of her. We brought along a folding bed and a *chaise percée*, the five suitcases of the circus, seabags, valises, and so forth.

We used the LaSalle to transport ourselves from the Eighty-sixth Street apartment and made two trips—despite the fact it could seat nine. Tini Matisse took it off our hands on the second trip. As we were moving out of the apartment, there was a great pile of debris left in the middle of the floor.

Shortly before sailing, I insisted on trying to show Sweeney how to dance and managed to fall backward. His forehead hit my

156

Adam's apple and my voice disappeared. It was rather lugubrious. I recovered my voice later on, but have never quite managed to make the old noise of the seal in my circus.

The Nelsons in Varengeville expected a gay Calder. I arrived with a rather drawn visage and they wondered what was the matter. We were the last off the boat, due to the volume of our luggage.

The *douanier* said:

"Where do your things end? There?"

And I said:

"No, over there."

"There?" he said then, pointing further.

And I said:

"No, over there."

The first thing he opened was one of the valises of the circus, and he said:

"*Ca, c'est du cirque.*"

He passed everything.

I remember another time, we landed somewhere with an accordion in tow, and we were treated to:

"*Les musiciens.*"

The Nelsons had brought their car and—being forewarned—the butcher's truck. So, we packed Dorothy Sibley and the bags with the butcher boy, and the rest of us went in Paul's car. The French countryside was lovely with flowers and lush green fields.

After a few days in Varengeville we moved on to Paris—in search of an apartment. We were directed to Alden Brooks, for whom Paul had built a house on the boulevard Arago. Brooks had just sold his house to some French people, but he had the use of it for another three months or so. It was practically empty of furniture and was a big house. He invited us to move in for three months, in sort of a camping state. He and his wife stayed on, in part of the house, for several weeks.

We had a funny time in the kitchen with people asking:

"Is that our bread?"

"Is this their butter?"

But the wine was common to all.

There was a great passageway through the house for a car, and in the back corner of the garden was a triangular garage, with a turntable. I never saw a car on this turntable, and I used the garage for a studio. Once, we even had a lot of people. Many of us stood on the turntable and rode around in gay rotation.

In the hallway of the house, we improvised a banquet hall, using the kitchen table to which we appended wings made of planks. We sat on the box which had brought my tools from New York, and on a few chairs that did exist previously. Here, we entertained all sorts of people: Alvar Aalto, the Finnish architect, and his wife Aino; Alberto, the Spanish sculptor, who had done a large thing at the Spanish pavilion of the Paris World's Fair of 1937 and who sang to us beautifully in Spanish; and many other people.

It had been four years since we had left Paris, and we saw many old friends and I gave my circus. Possibly due to the Paris 1937 World's Fair, one day I went with my friend Miró to see the proposed Spanish pavilion where he was to do a large painting. I met José Luis Sert, the architect of the pavilion.

When I saw what was going on in general in this pavilion, which included "Guernica" by Picasso, I promptly volunteered my services to do something or other for it.

Sert was against this, for obviously I was no Spaniard, but later on, when he had received a fountain displaying mercury from Almadén, which looked like a plain drinking fountain, he called me in to get him out of the dilemma.

I was told that mercury was chemically very active and that the only things it would not corrode were glass and pitch. Whereupon I decided to make my object of iron covered with pitch. I had been to Lalique's to see what was available in the way of glass, and decided that "glass is not for me"—that is, the glass of Lalique. (I have made things, such as mobiles and several fish, with pendent pieces of broken glass selected by me—some eroded by sea and sand, which I picked up on beaches.)

March 8, 1965

11:00 a.m. to 12:30 p.m.

After a while the Brookses prepared to depart for the United States. We had a tremendous farewell party at Jamet's down the street—a nice restaurant. They gave us a room upstairs. We were close to fifteen: the Brookses and their daughter, Paul and Francine Nelson, Katherine Dudley and Annie Harvey, the Mirós, John Ferren, an English painter, Matthew Smith, and we.

The Americans got together and ended up throwing things around and being quite disreputable.

After the turmoil, we were left alone in the house on the boulevard Arago.

Finally the Spanish pavilion was ready and it was opened with special ceremonies. The part I liked best was a little old man who beat a tattoo with a mortar and pestle.

158

Paris World's Fair, 1937. The Mercury Fountain

Léger was there and said to me:

"Dans le temps tu étais le Roi du Fil de Fer, mais maintenant tu es le Père Mercure." (In the old days you were Wire King, now you are Father Mercury.)

To make the mercury circulate it was necessary to put a little water in with it so that it would wet the pipes and the pump; it would not work otherwise. The pump and a reservoir four feet across were located in a closet under a stairway. The reservoir was eighteen inches deep and full of mercury to maintain a steady pressure. The mercury was led to my fountain, underground, through a half-inch tube and then up thirty inches where it spewed onto an irregularly shaped dish of iron, lined with pitch. This dish was very nearly horizontal; otherwise the mercury would have rushed off. It trickled in turn onto another plate, differently shaped, and then from that onto a chute which delivered it rather rapidly against a sort of bat, attached to the lower end of a rod, which held at the upper end another rod—with a red disc at the bottom and in hammered brass wire the word A L M A D E N on top.

The impact of mercury against the bat made the combination of the two rods, the red disc, and the word "Almadén" weave in the air in a sort of figure eight.

The basin was seven feet and three inches across, but nonetheless we soon discovered that there were little particles of mercury being splattered on the cement floor all around. As the

159

Small mobile

"Snow Flurry," 1948

Mobile

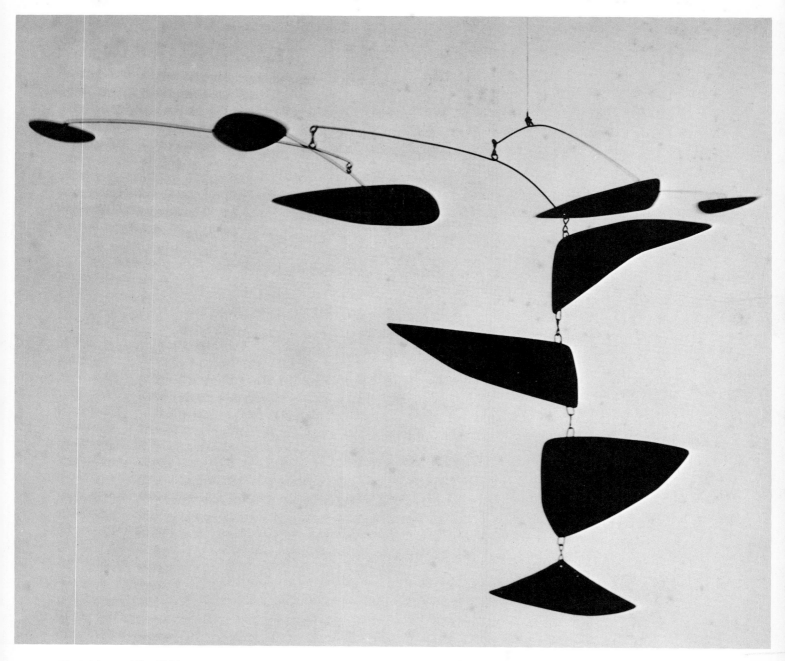

Model for mobile, 1946

mercury was very expensive, we tried to conserve it by making slowing-up dams in the chute. This was easy because all we had to do was to warm the pitch and stick in a piece of iron. I also made a labyrinthine spiral for the end of the bat to avoid lateral splatter.

But the most astute conservation stunt was not mine. Somebody took a folded-up fly screen and placed it just where the mercury dripped from one plate to another and this incarcerated the dripping mercury. Finally all worked beautifully, and there was no need to add any mercury to the fountain during the whole show.

It became the favorite pastime of onlookers to throw coins at the surface of the mercury and see them float. This did not gum up the functioning, as the mercury was drawn off from the bottom of the basin.

Some American journalist came through and dubbed me: "Calderón de la Fuente." But Lacasa, an architect and public relations man for the pavilion, claimed it was I who had thought it up.

In preparation for the summer we had rented a house in Varengeville, not far from the Nelsons—a sort of chalet, tall and shallow, facing the sun.

Jean Hélion, who had been to London a few years before, had put me in contact with John and Myfanwy Piper and Ben Nicholson and Barbara Hepworth, and we lost no time in inviting the Pipers and the Nicholsons, separately, of course.

We also had invited George Thomson and he was there when the Pipers arrived on the boat at Dieppe. George would not go to the boat with us. Such is British restraint. The Pipers, reluctantly, were the last ones off the boat. Such is British restraint.

The beach where we swam was down a very steep and winding hill, which cuts through white chalk. Here, the White Cliffs of Dover are the White Cliffs of Varengeville. And when you look up at them from the beach, you see layers of black flint placed regularly at different levels. This has affected the architecture of the locality, for many houses are built out of brick with horizontal stripes of flint in the walls.

We enjoyed ourselves on the beach, and even Sandra went wading.

Right behind the Nelsons' house was a rather big fake timber building belonging to a Mrs. Scott. There was a Canadian and his wife living there at the time and they were very cordial, so that when Jim Butler and his wife came on a walking tour, with their two Siamese cats in a basket he had made especially to go on his back like a knapsack, they were invited by the Canadians to camp in the garden behind the house.

They had a pup tent on one side; directly opposed was a small sheet of canvas to continue the roof line, and the cats were underneath that.

Well, one day on the way down to swim, we stopped to see the Butlers. Nobody was home but the cats.

We all looked in.

Miró said, *"Ou est-ce qu'on fait la cuisine?"* (Where does one do the cooking?)

He must have expected a little kitchen to scale.

March 9, 1965

11:00 a.m. to 12:30 p.m.

We were quite a band in Varengeville and mustered two accordions in the group, because besides Louisa there was Georges Braque who played the accordion well. He had a little concertina, and he was very gay and so was Marcelle, his wife. Besides the Nelsons, there also were Georges and Marguerite Duthuit, Herbert Reed, Pierre Loeb, Miró, and a young guy named Galannis.

I had a workshop composed of a two-car garage painted white, with an open mouth—there were no doors. It overlooked a vegetable garden to which a ramp of paving stones led.

I was surprised one morning to have a visit from Braque. The trouble was that he had just been awarded the Carnegie prize for painting and he was greatly disturbed. The arduous American awarder had gotten up at 6:00 A.M. and left Paris to do the awarding before Braque had had his breakfast.

We had quite a long and pleasant talk, he and I, and he came out with a statement that when there are people around and you are working, and you prefer to stop working for a moment and think of something by yourself, then the people who surround you wonder what in the world you are doing and why the hell you don't get busy.

As he left, I gave him a little spiderlike object that I had made.

The Nelsons had a *bouvier des Flandres,* Racco, given them by Braque, who had the parents. The Canadians next door had this dog's brother, Rollo. Well, once the Canadians left their *bouvier* in the Nelsons' yard and the gate was about six feet high. For some reason, the Nelsons and the Canadians took the precaution of tying the two dogs together—something like a bolo. And the dogs apparently took the fence together. They were found outside and unharmed!

At the top of the descent to the beach lived the curé, and he had a bitch of some sort. For long periods of the year she was kept within the limits of his yard. But when she came in heat, he thought it proper to let her out. So all the dogs of the neighborhood were after her, and Racco and his brother Rollo came to bites. Feathers was not injured in this melee; we could imagine him seated on a mound, observing and hoping for the best.

Feathers had almost been married once. One morning on the rue de la Glacière, we were having coffee and a taxi driver, out of work, talked to us about him. He said he had a female dog "just like him." She happened to be in heat at that moment. We thought that it would be nice to have Feathers' offspring. So, I took him in a taxi, somewhere on the rue du Temple. The chauffeur's wife was there too. We all sat on the big bed which occupied two thirds of the room.

The bitch, who turned out to be a sort of fluffy fox terrier, was quite willing and would back Feathers into a corner. He did not seem to know what was happening to him and I'm sure he did not think "he'd live to spend all the money."

By and by Feathers was all in and lay panting on the floor, without having achieved anything in particular. We gave him lumps of sugar to resuscitate him. Nothing seemed to happen. So we left. Halfway down the stairs he looked back. I thought he had changed his mind and took him up again. But there really was nothing to be done.

We intended spending the winter in London. So sometime about September we sold the Ford, which we had purchased from the Brookses, to Claude Laurens and took the boat from Dieppe.

Myfanwy Piper had found us a one-room flat in Belsize Park. Somehow or other I arrived first, and set to work whitewashing the walls. When our things arrived, a big red Moroccan rug I had bought at the Paris exposition made it rather pleasant.

Sandra, who was two and a half, went to playschool. The first day she came back, she said:

"Boy."

He turned out to be a German.

Sandra, at that time, had some trouble with her scalp. Heretofore she had had lovely golden curls, but behind the house we had had in Varengeville there had been a thatched peasant house, where an old woman took care of a lot of little children. Sandra used to go there and play.

One day, she came back with a very elegant hairdo.

The old lady had done a beautiful job and it had taken just the time of the voyage to London, and the time to get settled, for the lice to develop in this work of art. So Louisa, horrified, rushed

Sandra off to the Harper Method. But they were horrified too, and would not let Sandra in the building. Whereupon, some young woman took pity on Louisa and offered to come privately to the house. I think the cure was serious bathing and kerosene, that you have to rinse out in turn, rapidly. But Sandra's hair was temporarily cut short in the process.

The Pipers had a lovely old farmhouse, and still have it, at Fawley-Bottom, and I remember once we went out with Léger, who was in London working on a film of H. G. Wells. He came out to Fawley-Bottom Sunday morning and as we walked to the pub to wait for noon and the first drink, Louisa and I had on orange-and-yellow fishermen's undershirts we'd gotten in Barcelona, the Pipers had blue and red, so Léger suggested a ballet of the colors as we walked along.

I had the circus in London, of course, and gave several presentations, one of which was supposed to be rather elegant—so Louisa put on a white gown of raw silk that Francine had sold her before we had left Paris.

To see oneself in the mirror in our apartment, one had to stand on tiptoe and peer over the dustbin. So Louisa forewent the pleasure of seeing her reflection and just put on the gown, and off we went to my circus.

Louisa ran a gramophone quite blithely for the first half, but during the intermission she went to the ladies' room and got a glimpse of herself in a real mirror, and came back horrified by her billowing lines. I think the gown was finally given to Sandra, sometime much later.

As a workshop, I got one of a row of little studios in Camden Town, which was not very far away. I got some second-hand lumber and made a workbench. Some other people in the studio courtyard had milk delivered them every day and the milkman as he put the milk bottle on the sill would call out loudly:

"Poops!"

March 10, 1965

11:00 a.m. to 12:30 p.m.

In London we saw quite a bit of George Thomson, Duthuit, and also a German, Flaxlander, whom I'd known in Berlin during my show at Nierendorf's. Now he was a layout artist for a London paper. As early as 1933 he had been an anti-Nazi and had been jailed. After six months, his family had managed to pull the strings and get him out and he had gone to England. Later, when the London blitz was on, the British moved all people originally from Germany out to Canada—and him among them.

One of my reasons for wanting to go to London was to have a show there at Freddy Mayor's, in Cork Street. The gallery was small but the show was quite nice. About February 1938.

Some of the objects were very slender and filmy—little lines of fine wire—and I used to turn out the light and project them on the wall with a flashlight as they turned around. I also made a mobile for outdoors. Because of the low ceiling, I had to sling it on a low cord. John Piper has this one now and it looks powerful old-fashioned.

*"I also made a mobile for outdoors . . .
now it looks powerful old-fashioned"*

I also made a large stabile, and when I left London I confided it to the keeping of a young architect named Brown, who lived with his family on Berkeley Square. Brown agreed to house it if I would pay for the transportation. So, some stalwart men carried the pieces up two flights of narrow stairs of what was more or less a brownstone house. We set it up in his room, which had a drafting table, a bureau, chairs, and so forth. I had gone there to direct things in his absence. When it was all set up, you could barely creep between furniture and stabile. At that moment Brown, who was detained elsewhere, called up and I heard one of the ladies of the house say:

"Yes, it is here, but what is it?"

In a month or so, in the early spring of 1938, we sailed to New York, Feathers having already gone home to Concord to the Jameses' with Dorothy Sibley, to avoid six months of quarantine in England. Upon our return we moved to another apartment, in the same building on Eighty-sixth Street.

Two ladies came to see some of my jewelry one day. We had quite a big bit of mirror standing on a bureau, and one of the ladies was standing in front of it, trying one, then another necklace.

I decided just then that I was going to charge more, and nearly doubled the price. So when the lady asked, "How much?" I said:

"Seventy dollars."

In the mirror I could see Louisa's face get red.

The woman did not buy the necklace.

In our previous apartment, the first summer, Louisa had pulled all the blinds down, which caused the white walls to turn yellow. We had asked the superintendent to repaint the walls for us, but as our lease ran two years, he did nothing about it. So we went to a little paint shop around the corner, got some whitewash, and were advised to put plenty of salt in it to make it stick.

This time, when we had been installed in our new apartment in the building, the superintendent asked me:

"What did you paint those walls in your old apartment with?"

The subsequent tenant had put lovely flowered paper on the walls and the flowers had disappeared.

We had just been home in Roxbury in February or March of 1938, when a man came to see us who had just acquired a mechanical shovel and wanted to know if we'd like our pond dug out. The pond as it originally existed was about a foot deep, full of reeds, grasses, and muskrat nests. The man agreed to dig it six feet deep for $250, as he had a lot to pay on his shovel.

As a matter of fact, the shovel had originally been acquired by an unsuccessful farmer up the hill to dig drains in his pastures and the present owner had merely been retained to operate it. He had

167

worked so long without pay that finally the farmer owed him a sizable part of the value of the shovel. Whereupon the farmer sold the shovel to his employee, the mechanic—who in turn owed money to the farmer.

And therefore, the interesting proposition.

To empty the water from the existing pond, the enterprising shovel operator started digging well below the dam and came right through it. So, when the dam had to be replaced, he merely did it with an earth fill. The dam might have been large enough, but it certainly was not packed sufficiently.

The existing springs only existed in the spring, so the rising of the water of the new pond was rather gradual. Finally, it was practically full. And one morning, as I came up to visit it, I heard what I thought was a new source of water—certainly water was flowing. But when I got near, I saw the water was flowing out, not in—the dam was washing out.

We got some other fellows to rebuild the dam, with a stone face, of course, and this cost five hundred dollars.

At Roxbury, in the meantime, we resumed our old acquaintances around the countryside. Particularly with the boys from Sherman, Cowley and Blume and Coates and Josephson.

Malcolm and I decided we were practically the same age, two days apart. I think August 24 is Malcolm's birthday; mine always used to be August 22. So, we planned to celebrate together at our house. We went to an Italian bakery in Danbury where they made good bread, and had them make a special cake. It was built like a zoned building, stepped up twice. It was white, with lavender mocha. In mocha it said:

FORTY, FIT, FAT, AND FARTY

We got a couple of dozen pizzas as well, and the day of the party I made Jimmy de Tomasi, the new husband of Jane Harris —he claimed to be four years younger than we were—hold the cake in the air for the twenty miles from Danbury to our house. As a result, he was practically paralyzed for half an hour. We also got a lot of cubes of meat and prepared to roast them on spits.

March 11, 1965

11:00 a.m. to 12:30 p.m.

We knew Malcolm, but not most of the people he invited. His first guest arrived at two in the afternoon—a tall, lean, handsome, slightly mannish-looking girl in shorts. She had not been there half an hour when she shinnied up quite a tall maple, with no branches to help her.

After that—I lost track of the later arrivals. One of our guests was Pat Mestre, with his wife; he was at that moment the Dean of Bard College, and when Jim Soby got there he tried to confuse us, saying Pat was the Bard of Dean.

I still had my old shop in the icehouse—the new one was to be built that fall—and the electric wiring was rudimentary. The bar was in my shop and at a certain moment I was trying to plug in a light, so I did not witness the arrival of Adèle, our maid. She had placed the cake, all candles lit, on a big wicker tray.

Louisa, in preparation for the festivity, had mowed the lawn that afternoon, and as Adèle stepped off the stone step of the wood-shed door the cake skidded off the tray and landed upside down in the new-mown grass. To the lavender and white, a third color was added—but it was still delicious.

There were individual incidents, such as attempted drowning and even rape, they claim. We did find a pair of glasses up at the pond the next day.

We ended up about forty people and we'd completely forgotten to cook the meat. Louisa, discovering the pizzas just as people were leaving, distributed them as door prizes.

This party has always been referred back to as THE birthday party. But there were many gay gatherings.

In the fall of 1938, I had a show at Springfield, Massachusetts. Mrs. Cordelia Pond of the Smith Museum was very much interested in my work and organized quite a fine retrospective. It was at that time I met W. G. Rogers, the journalist. I plied to and fro to Springfield and back to Roxbury, in the LaSalle, delivering my show.

The day of the *vernissage*, we were surprised to have arrive on the train Alvar Aalto, the Finnish architect, Fernand Léger, and Sigfried Giedion, historian of architecture and sometimes of art. Aalto even made a speech for the opening of the show. Perhaps he was just exercising his new English.

It was quite a large gathering of my objects, of all categories—about sixty in all: wood and wire sculptures, abstract constructions, and mobiles—no outdoor objects or stabiles that I remember.

However, I don't think I sold anything at the Springfield show—it still was a good show. Or perhaps I did sell "The Flattest Cat" to Charlotte Allen of Rochester.

During the period of preparation for the show, while I was plying back and forth, I was also building a new studio on the foundations of the old barn east of the Roxbury house. My classmate from Stevens, Jim Horn, drew the plans for me, as he had experi-

"There were many gatherings"
Sculpture classique: *Calder, Rino Levi, the Brazilian architect, and Carlton Sprague Smith, the musician*

169

ence in construction work. I chose prefabricated factory sash for a great expanse to the southeast, thirty feet long and twelve feet high, and in the southwest corner, fifteen feet long and twelve feet high. To the west, which had been the high side of the barn, I put in sash about four feet high. We decided to conserve the silo as part of the building; it had windows too——in a semicircle.

This factory sash, as it was then made——I don't think they make it quite like that any more——was opened by pulling a chain which undid a bolt and tilted the window, top inward and the bottom up and out, making a wonderful funnel for air on the hottest summer day, and I worked amid these funnels. (In the summer of 1964—twenty-six years after the studio was built——I even got a kink in my back from this ventilation, having worked up a sweat in a cotton shirt, instead of the usual wool one I wear. I had to go to a doctor and learn the use of an electric pad to bake it out.)

Before saying goodbye to the carpenters, I asked them to put seven rows of screw eyes in the rafters, of which there were about twenty-two. So, my sky is studded with about 150 screw eyes. And when I want to put a pulley aloft with a rope through it——to suspend a mobile or some object——I have a long stick with a notch and stiff wire hook at the end, which holds another hook attached to the pulley, and I fish for the selected screw eye with this device.

One time I started painting, and I used to run the canvases aloft.

I don't remember exactly what happened, for quite a while, till Mary was born. About a month before this festive event, Louisa and my mother decided to hire a maid to take care of Sandra and do some cooking while Louisa was in the hospital. They answered some ads, and got an old Scotch lady.

Louisa decided to have this baby in New York, so we were in the apartment again. The kitchen was at the front end, next to the hall door. When I arrived in the evening, before I could pass the door, this lady who spoke like the gobbling of a turkey would recount all the catastrophes which had occurred during the day—such as spilled ink and other things. We went out occasionally, Louisa and I, in the evening and Sandra got into the habit of rushing after us and saying:

"When are you coming back?"

Through which we deduced that the old woman was frightening her with stories of our not coming back and so forth.

We decided we had to get rid of her. Louisa made one attempt, but the lady said Sandra was a nice little girl and that she liked her very much. So, I had to undertake the job.

I went out and cashed a check for her wages, while Louisa and Sandra went for the day around the corner to Elizabeth Grinnell's.

Roxbury, 1938. Building the new studio and · · ·

170

Then I proceeded to tell the lady that she must leave. I gave her her wages, and all she did was to hang onto the water faucet and drink glass after glass. After some time, I succeeded in persuading her. When she had packed her little valise and few effects, she asked if she could come back to collect them. I said no, that she must leave her affairs downstairs with the superintendent. Then I went to the Grinnells' too.

When Louisa heard that the maid was coming back to get her valise, she insisted we get into the car, Sandra, she, and I, and drive around all day till danger was past.

On our return, the valise was gone.

. . . as it is today

Two hours piecemeal

Louisa still wanted a maid. The next was a pretty blond girl, a German—Senta. We discovered later that the way she got Sandra out of bed so quietly was to stuff her with candy, but she seemed quite satisfactory.

After a month or so, she told Louisa she had to leave, because Der Führer was calling everybody back into Germany. But luckily for her, she had an older brother who was also in New York and he was dead against her going back. We think he finally succeeded in dissuading her, as a month or so later someone called us about her references.

As a doctor for Mary's projected birth, Louisa chose Dr. Richard N. Pierson and in due course he sent Louisa to Doctors' Hospital. Mary's birth was Caesarian, in view of the trouble Louisa had had with Sandra. I think that is why Mary's head is so round. Dr. Pierson was very much pleased with Louisa's speedy recovery and sent her home two days early, but unbeknown to Pierson and almost unknown to Louisa, Mrs. James, in Concord, Massachusetts, had gotten a healer somewhere in the vicinity to "work on Louisa" in absentia. So we don't know which to thank. Louisa never dared tell Pierson of this treachery. Mary was easier to name than Sandra, because of Louisa's dear sister Mary James—now Brown.

Mary was born on May 25, 1939. Thus Sandra, who had wanted a baby for the last four years—that is, from the very day of her birth—now had one.

Several weeks later, we were delighted to hear one day that José Luis Sert, the chief architect of the Spanish pavilion at the Paris 1937 exposition—at which the "Guernica" of Picasso had been shown—and his wife Moncha were in Cuba and expected to arrive in New York shortly.

The only way that Sert, who was a Spanish refugee, could obtain a visa was to get Walter Gropius of Harvard to invite him to give a few lectures. It was then that our New York railroad apartment and its six rooms came into action. And when we went back to Roxbury, with Sandra and Mary this time, we took the Serts with us. We gave them our room and retired to the attic.

We did a lot of Spanish cooking out of doors—at least, Moncha did. We built a fireplace up by the pond and I made a red-and-blue awning out of bunting and slung it horizontally between four masts. I had a grid of strings under it and occasionally it would billow into the sky. This was a very welcome spot of shade, as at that time the pond was in the midst of a prairie due to the digging operation.

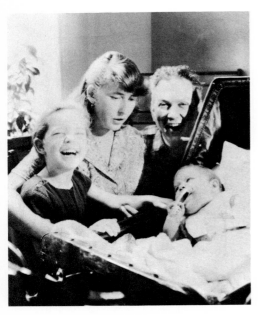

Four Calders now!

Sert and I used to take two swims daily, and I wanted to devise a system of changing one's clothes in public. So I made a hoop, about one yard in diameter, out of a heavy wire and to this I sewed a two-foot skirt of some more red bunting; this was supported by a rope going over my shoulders.

I was just practicing with it by the pond when four road workers from uphill came down in an open car. They were at some distance, so they immediately turned around for another look. By that time I'd changed—the show was over.

As I had studied Spanish while in college and then made several abortive attempts to expand it, I was glad of the opportunity to embellish my Spanish a bit with the Serts. It got rather mixed up with the Catalan language, of which I acquired a few expressions— Sert was a Catalan.

My best phrase was *tots foututs*—meaning "the jig is up."

We saw a lot of Herbert Matter, the Swiss photographer—had, in fact, since 1938—and Stamo Papadaki, the Greek architect. Herbert made many photographs of the children and of us too.

The *Architectural Forum* decided to round out their pages with a little magazine called *Plus*. This was very elegantly edited by Papadaki and Matter. Naturally, they had a lot of photographs of my objects, diagrams of a water ballet, objects, drawings, etc.

But people who advertised door hinges and knobs in the *Architectural Forum* itself could not see any gain in having this sheet inserted. They brought pressure to bear and *Plus* was quashed after about the third issue.

About this time, a plexiglass manufacturer wanted to get some publicity, cheaply. So he put up a modest prize and published a lot of rules about what you could do with plexiglass and how to work it. I entered this competition, but I did not like their suggestions on how to work it. I just used a hacksaw and a file. Anyway, they finally took my object and reproduced it—they thought— nice and smooth. Also, it turned out they did not have any black plexiglass, and where I was to have varicolored lights playing at the end of a two-inch stalk, they abandoned that as being too complicated, and made a horrible base for the thing, too.

In spite of this, I was awarded the prize, because I knew the jury—or rather, the jury knew me.

Henry Russell Hitchcock was an old friend of Louisa's. In 1939 he got me a job doing a well sweep in iron for Soby. This well sweep was a big thing, twenty-two feet high.

Hitchcock, at times, wore a fluffy black tie, so I decided to make him a wire tie pin comprising the two syllables of his name. He came to see me one day and accepted this with great pleasure. Then we went out to Soby's, where they said I was quite clever.

Later Ernestine Fantl, who was in charge of architecture at the

Museum of Modern Art, swiped the pin from Russell and wore it. One day Eddie Warburg said, "Ernestine, you should not wear that pin." Finally she lost it. But not before she got married and went to live in England.

When John McAndrew took over Ernestine's job at the Museum of Modern Art, he bought two brooches from me for his secretaries. One of the brooches was a piece of crumpled-up wire I found in the street. I flattened it out and put a pin in it.

This perturbed Alfred Barr, who said on two occasions, "What does it mean?" On the third occasion he said to its owner: "Did you look at it in the mirror?"

1939 was the year of the New York World's Fair and I had been commissioned by Harrison to do a water ballet for the New York Edison Company. They were all ready to light the ballet before I had made it. And I even had to give an interview to two boobs—where the light would come from, etc.—before I'd made it. They also had me give a sort of lecture to a batch of young students, boys and girls, who were to be guides in their Fair building. I made a couple of wisecracks and began to consider myself a lecturer.

The engineer in charge of the nozzles for the ballet wasn't interested in the project, so nothing at all came out of it, then. At any rate, they installed a row of jets of their own around the building —they were forty feet high—and these were put into action.

They had a bridge over the pool—where my ballet was supposed to be—and this bridge led into their building. To avoid any recriminations from ladies whose silk gowns might receive a drop of water, they built a cellophane tunnel over the bridge. I doubt whether this cellophane tunnel would have suited my ballet, anyhow!

Several years later, I proposed this same ballet to Eero Saarinen for the General Motors Technical Center, near Detroit. This turned out to be the most expensive fountain in captivity, but it really works, I believe, and I have received two or three compliments on it. They still have my rig, but they only show it for important people—so I doubt whether I shall ever see it!

As I said above, I started to consider myself a lecturer. At this time, our friend Oscar Nitzschke was teaching architecture at Yale. So he asked me to come up and address his students. I made a few notes in preparation, but left these behind, thinking I would consider things on the train. I left from New York, but I met Oscar on the train and we talked all the way. He took me to lunch, which Ritou, his wife, had prepared at their New Haven house, and it was topped off with a bottle of red wine. Then, I was led to the slaughter.

176

Some of the students had made what they called a "mobile," using among other things a corset and an open umbrella; this was hanging right in front of me while I stood up. I was quite nonplussed and my urge to speak disappeared. Also, there was an infiltration of students from the naturalistic painting and sculpture classes; they had come to heckle me. So, heckled I was. Some of the real architectural students have since become very good friends and always refer with pleasure to the hour or two I spent there. But I don't refer to it in a like manner.

I finally did speak and say a few things—I limped through it—and I decided never to try that thing again.

However, in India, many years later, we found ourselves on the dais before a mass of shepherds dressed wonderfully in red, and that time I was able to give them a dissertation on the raising of cattle in the east and west of the United States. This was translated into Hindi and seemed to meet with a certain amount of interest and approval.

March 15, 1965

11:00 a.m. to 12:30 p.m.

In the spring of 1939, when we returned to Roxbury with the Serts, I had the excitement of moving into my new workshop, which seemed vast and unencumbered. (It did not stay unencumbered for long.) Moncha Sert even made a paella in the hearth—the only time we ever had a fire in it.

With my 150 screw eyes overhead and two more or less blank walls to hang things on, there was plenty of room, the studio being twenty-five by forty-five feet, and it was beautifully lit from the south, thanks to the twelve-foot-high factory sash.

I discovered with pleasure that in the winter when the sun comes from the south and the angle of sunlight is low, it penetrates the room and warms you up. In the summer, when the sun is overhead, the roof throws a shadow straight down, more or less, and this, when the windows are rotated into funnels—according to my scheme of things—cools you in turn.

I had two workbenches built of laminated two-by-fours—the two-by-fours are nailed against each other to make a four-inch slab. The bench which had the biggest vise on it eventually received a very large broken house radiator of cast iron as its underpinning, to make it steadier when I yanked at something. And yank

I did. With a big monkey wrench and this vise, I was able to twist eyes into a half-inch steel rod.

And now, it was 1940. I had continued to have shows at Pierre Matisse's since 1934, with one or two years out. I'd done such things as "The Whale" (Museum of Modern Art, New York), "The Black Beast," of which I made a copy for Eliot Noyes in New Canaan (*Life* made a lot of photographs of it in the snow), and

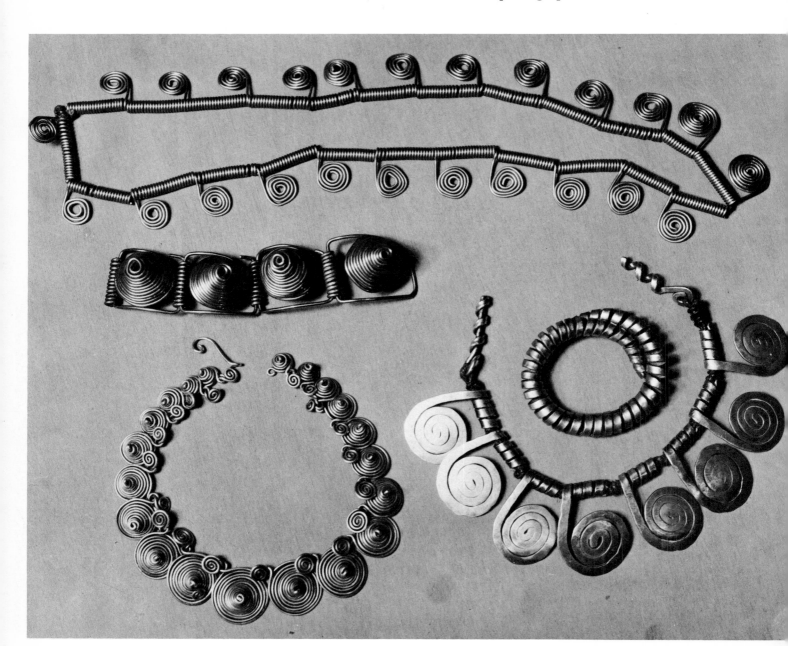

Calder's early jewelry—1940

"The Spherical Triangle," now in Rio. These were fairly large outdoor objects: "The Black Beast" is eleven feet long and almost nine feet high. They were the forerunners of the big stabiles to come.

In the fall of 1940, I had a show of jewelry at Marian Willard's gallery on Fifty-seventh Street. The show was relatively successful and I sold a few things.

The next year, I tried to repeat my success at Marian's with another jewelry show—we set it up on a Sunday. Louisa was supposed to come down from Roxbury the next day for the opening. But she called up to say she had had a little accident with the car. So I went back to bring her to New York the next morning. When I arrived, she said the Japs had bombed Pearl Harbor. It was December 7, 1941.

In spite of all, quite a few people came to see the show.

There was a young architect named George Dudley, one of Nitzschke's products, who had just gotten married. Monday morning, before I arrived, he'd made the show a success by buying several things for his wife.

One of my New York winter workshops, which I'd had for several years, was at Ninety-seventh and First Avenue, and one day for lunch I had walked a block or so further north and found an Italian restaurant with a bar and a dance hall next door. There, they held dances on Saturdays and Sundays with an accordion and a piano.

First of all I went alone to try this out and enjoyed myself. Then, I took a few friends all on the regular Saturday or Sunday night, but eventually I got them to have the music come at my expense. on a week night after a *vernissage,* and we had all our friends there for dinner and dancing too. This place was called Guerci.

This went on for four or five years—we had several parties a year. Finally the place was sold, and the new proprietor was Hungarian, I guess, and he installed a television over the bar and allowed the dance-hall license to lapse—so there was nothing doing any more!

In 1943, aluminum was being all used up in airplanes and becoming scarce. I cut up my aluminum boat, which I had made for the Roxbury pond, and I used it for several objects. I also devised a new form of art consisting of small bits of hardwood carved into shapes and sometimes painted, between which a definite relation was established and maintained by fixing them on the ends of steel wires. After some consultation with Sweeney and Duchamp, who were living in New York, I decided these objects were to be called "constellations."

"Constellation"

179

Calder and Yves Tanguy in Roxbury

Pierre Matisse must have thought Yves Tanguy and I were not doing so well, because he showed us together. I was mostly in the first room and Tanguy in the second room. In the constellations nothing moved, and it was a very weird sensation I experienced, looking at a show of mine where nothing moved.

The first constellation I had made was a small thing to stand on a table, with at one end a small carved thing looking like a bone and painted red. At the Matisse Gallery, this was standing on the floor and Jacqueline Breton, who was separated from André and affected an enormous Great Dane, came to the show with her mutt, and when he saw this bone-shaped object he menaced it and made as though to take a snap at it.

We had gotten to know the Tanguys quite well. As a result of the war Yves Tanguy and Kay Sage, ex-Princess San Faustino, came to live in New York, and as we found them pleasant we had them out to Roxbury. They liked the country around our place very much, and they bought a house in Woodbury. For several years we saw a lot of them. I remember one day when we lived in New York and I had to go to Roxbury. I drove up and first called on the Massons, André and Rose, in New Preston, north of us, and I told them he should put more red in his painting. Then I went to our house in Roxbury and got whatever it was—and finally I went to the Tanguys' and told Yves he should put more red in his painting . . .

We saw quite a lot of the Tanguys for a while and we even had a blackout drill together that turned into a blackout party— the four of us retired to the cellar, Louisa played the accordion, and we all drank red wine.

I think Yves started recalling the old days in Paris. He got tight and started to insult his wife. The old days were quite old—before he'd even been a painter. He was in charge of a trolley car once— I think he was the motorman—and he ran into a wagon with his trolley. He got down and walked off—that was that.

There were also the Paris days when he used to play chess with his friends, each chessman being represented by those small sample bottles of liquor. Naturally, as you took the adversary's pawn, you drank what was inside that pawn, no matter what.

Sometimes the Tanguys would come to dinner and would sit in our parlor, while Louisa was in the kitchen preparing the food, and I would go into the kitchen, too. This was Yves's first stage of being dead sober.

The second stage was when he'd get slightly tight. Then, he was charming. I remember once at Seventy-second Street and Second Avenue, in New York, in a Czech bistro, Yves was very pleasant with a poor unhappy lady; he got up and danced with her.

180

Then, there was the third stage, when he was really tight. If there was any dispute or argument, he'd go looking for his knife—which fortunately he did not carry.

Once, I took a friend to supper at the Tanguys', and Yves disagreed with this friend and menaced him with a table knife for half an hour, till I persuaded him to give it to me.

Another time we were at the Tanguys' with Ed and Sugar Gillette. We were sitting outside and I must have been in quite an advanced stage, for Sugar flicked a spoonful of water in my face and I replied with a whole glass of wine in hers. Yves was up, looking for his knife again . . . We loved him dearly, three-stage Tanguy!

During the war years we also saw quite a lot of the Massons. In some hotel lobby once in New York, I ran into Georges Duthuit and he was waiting for André and Rose Masson. That was the first time I really remember meeting André—although he seems to recall meeting me in the days of the Spanish pavilion. They had just come from France by way of Martinique, along with André Breton, his wife Jacqueline, and his daughter Aube. The Massons had two sons who were born in Spain during the civil war: Diego and Luis. I immediately invited them to come and visit us in Roxbury, so they came. And as they were looking for a place to live, Louisa scouted the countryside with Rose to help her find something. They found a house in Washington, Connecticut. It was rented to them by one of the men about town, and later when he discovered that Rose was Jewish he was all in a dither, because Washington, Connecticut, kept its fly closed.

They nevertheless stayed there some six months, and then they found a sort of summer house with little heating, belonging to a Mrs. Brown. They were there about three years, although Mrs. Brown also proved to be anti-Semitic—when Yom Kippur came, she would tease Rose with silly postcards.

Finally the Browns forced the Massons to leave, by some legal procedure, and they moved to yet a third house for the last few months of their stay in America.

The Massons, of course, were very well received by all our friends in Sherman, some of whom they had known in the old days in France before Malcolm had written *Exile's Return*.

One evening we picked them up and took them over to a party at Bob Coates's. I drank some wine and slept all evening. When we got ready to go, I was to drive. Rose sat next to me and André and Louisa were in back. It was a little foggy, and at one point I had to get out to see which way the road branched out. When I got back, Rose thought I was driving too fast and she finally insisted André and she would rather walk home. Louisa had some harsh words for me, and before we started the car up again the Massons had disappeared in the dark, walking in the direction of New Milford.

After some discussion between Louisa and myself, we proceeded to try to find them and I, gathering we'd overshot them already, hastened along to find a place to turn around. Louisa grabbed my hair and started to shriek.

It was at this precise moment we passed the Massons, without seeing them. We turned around later, but still could not find them. So, we went home.

Next day we called on them, and they told us they were wondering whether I was murdering Louisa when they heard her shrieks in the fog.

The Massons explained they had been picked up by a car, by some rather tough-looking men, and that they were very glad to spend the night in New Milford, where they had been admitted to a hotel—after declaring they were man and wife.

This reminds me that in nearby New Milford they made cigars. These were sold in a big barn and horse harnesses were sold outside. On the porch, there was a beautiful white wooden horse. He came in every night.

They had a type of cigar called "The Spanish Crook." You got a hundred in a box and on the lid it said:

Wine Dipped
It's Full of Pleasure

I wouldn't vouch for the wine, but apparently when they were picked out to dry, the pinch between thumb and forefinger made the kink—so you could not look straight down your cigar at your enemy.

During the war the kink was eliminated, as a matter of economy, and "The Spanish Crook" became "Maid of Norway" and later on "Top Hatter." Most recently they're called "Black Ripe." I have smoked them through all these names.

I had a box of the original Crooks in the car when we went with mother and the Serts to visit Jane and Jimmy de Tomasi for a Thanksgiving dinner. We had a flat tire, and when we got out the spare it only had two pounds pressure. Some cops came along and offered to take the tire about a mile to get it inflated. When they got back we showered them with Crooks.

Jane always gives one too much to eat and it's a battle to resist. When Thanksgiving dinner was over, mother said:

"Jane, that was almost good."

Jane said, "What do you mean, almost good?"

And mother said, "All, most good."

182

11:00 a.m. to 12:15 p.m.

I remember one morning in 1942 when Louisa went off with some other ladies to be a nurse's aide at Waterbury Hospital and I waved goodbye—because I was out in front of the house digging in the garden as a war measure.

At about this time I was called to Washington, Connecticut, to be interviewed by a very nice man who asked me whether my family was dependent or had independent means. As Louisa had certain means of her own, I was put in 1-A. I was forty-three.

In preparation for a possible mobilization, I went to some pains to study camouflage and took a course, but most of the people in the class were interior decorators or antique dealers—they wanted to eke out a living while their businesses were at a standstill. I even went down to Fort Mead, Maryland, to see Saint-Gaudens, the son of the sculptor. He was the head of camouflage.

I did not see him, but I saw someone else. When I had got on the bus at the railroad junction, near Fort Mead, the driver said he would let me off at the right spot. Then he forgot. As a result I made a whole tour of the camp in the bus before arriving at the proper place. I had ample opportunity to see the double barbed-wire cage for prisoners of war and army wives and army brats.

And when the officer said, "Do you want to do civil or military camouflage?" I said, "Civil."

During the war, I continued to try to be a *"camoufleur"*—civilian grade. And I was also asked by Marian Willard, who had a friend working with army hospitals—in occupational therapy—to go to Staten Island to a big military hospital, which I was glad to do. I spent the whole day there, making tin ashtrays, little toys to encourage and inspire the wounded to make things of a similar nature.

One day I was asked to go to Bernardsville, New Jersey, where a Mrs. Cutting had a rest home for merchant-marine sailors, not for the wounded but for the shocked and weary. So I went out there, armed with tin cans, tinsnips, hammer, drawing ink, pen, paper, and so on. I spent the whole day doing little stunts; finally I ended up at a loss what to do and just made caricatures of anyone who'd pose for me.

The matron of the establishment kept saying, "These men don't do anything but listen to the radio."

Finally, I collected my wares and tools, and went home on the train, getting in about 8:00 P.M. I discovered it had been D-Day.

183

In the meantime, during the spring of 1943, there was a meeting at the Museum of Modern Art and though I was not mentioned, Jim Sweeney and Monroe Wheeler got together afterward and decided they had both meant to bring up my name as a person they would like to have exhibited.

So then I was to have a show in the fall of 1943 at the Museum of Modern Art, in New York. Sweeney was to direct it and we got Herbert Matter to assist us.

With each exhibition at the Museum of Modern Art, the museum produces a catalogue, and a good many of these are excellent books. Sweeney, as my promoter, wrote one on me. Of course, it did not make the deadline, but it has been the standard and practically the only book on me up to the present writing. Subsequently Jim has undertaken to write about various other people, but he is a stickler for the very finest language and correct facts. He has always had a great difficulty giving birth to a new baby. I think I have a younger brother—the architect named Gaudí . . .

At any rate, I am very grateful to Sweeney for this noble effort on my behalf. He is one of the very rare critics whom I can believe —probably the only one—and his book encouraged me, and many others, to believe I had something!

I spent many days, like an ant, collecting my objects here and there and taking them to the museum. I know all the back roads of Connecticut, now.

All three of us—Sweeney, Matter, and myself—were active and full of energy. But I, in preparation for the actual *vernissage,* decided I wanted to get a shoeshine. I could never quite figure out where to do it, not having any polish myself. One day the shoeshine boy, on his rounds of the museum, came to the gallery where we were working and I subscribed to his attentions. Whereupon Sweeney and Matter accused me of being lazy: it was the first time any of us had sat down.

I was pleased with what success the show had. It was even extended into 1944, and the museum had a short film made of it.

It was sometime in 1943 that Feathers died. We had been off somewhere by car when we came home to Roxbury, up the steep hill, and discovered him playing with the neighbors. As he always wanted to ride, he raced after us and almost caught up, only to disappear as I turned into our driveway. I stopped the car and looked out: he had dropped in his tracks! We called up Rose Peterson, whose father was an Irish vet, and she said to give him some whiskey. And . . . poor Feathers, we gave him whiskey against his will. He had always been a teetotaler.

So then we buried him by the pond—a white stone at his head.

In the spring of 1944, Paul Nelson, who was vice president of

France Forever in Washington, D. C., asked me to show the circus for the benefit of this organization, and to have an exhibition of my work in their offices.

In January of 1944, while my show was going on in New York, I was introduced to Ivy Litvinoff, who seemed to want to buy an object of mine and I showed her one——in excess of the show.

She said, "That's too big. It would be nice to give that to the Museum of Western Art [in Moscow]."

But she did not buy anything.

However, I did not mind her idea. I even thought it was quite nice——to give an object to the Museum of Western Art. So Monroe Wheeler wrote and asked them if they would accept this gift, and they replied in the affirmative.

The mobile, composed of about fifteen black discs——"The Black Lily"——was to be shipped to the Russian embassy in Washington and then unpacked and flown to Moscow.

While in Washington, I told Nelson about this, so he called up the Russian embassy to find out whether they'd lend the object for his show. They had it at the embassy and were agreeable, so Paul and I went around to get it. We were admitted by a very tall Russian in a tunic. He spoke no English. Somehow or other he must have been informed, because he brought out the mobile in its packing, as received from the Museum of Modern Art in New York. Then he got an immense butcher knife and started to attack the bindings. That did not suffice, so he got a hammer.

I said to Paul, "If we stay much longer, he'll bring out the sickle!"

Apparently "The Black Lily" was delivered to Moscow, but I have never heard hide nor hair of it since.

March 18, 1965

11:00 a.m. to 12:30 p.m.

During the fall of 1943, I had a jewelry show in Chicago. Rue Shaw was now president of the Arts Club and she invited me to show my jewelry there. I had been invited a year or two before, when I made "Red Petals" for the Arts Club, but I had not gone.

"Red Petals," by the way, was made during the war for a little octagonal room lined with rosewood. As I become professionally enraged when I see dinky surroundings, I did my best to make this object big and bold——to dwarf these surroundings. As it was during the war, I went to a junkyard and bought a big chunk of an old boiler. It had a pebble grain due to the action of the water in the boiler, which gave it a very fancy surface. I cut out a big somewhat-leaf-shape, which standing on end came to seven feet high, with an arm standing out at the top. This was held vertical by two leaf-shape legs behind it. From the arm overhead, I hung some red aluminum leaves—they might well have been remnants of the boat of the Roxbury pond.

So, this time, I arrived in Chicago with my jewelry and tacked it on the walls of the self-same room—the rosewood octagonal room.

I spent a week or so in Chicago, then came back to New York where we were living on Seventy-second Street, and Louisa said quietly that we'd had a fire at the house in Roxbury several days before. But she had waited till I came back to tell me—which I thought showed a good deal of courage.

Louisa had been at the Serts in New York, and had had a whiskey or two, when our wonderful colored maid Maud called her up: she had been told by neighbors of ours in Roxbury that our house had caught fire.

Roxbury after the fire

Apparently, the Roxbury fire engine was often balky, but on this night it had worked very well. First to respond to the fire alarm was Joe O'Brien, a farmer, our next-door neighbor, followed by other neighbors. He knew where things lay. The fire was in the rear. Joe forced open the front door, near the road, and was met by smoke. So, he went back up the road to the barway that leads to our pond. He got the engine to draw the water there and not much time was lost.

My old workshop—where the fire started—having been an ice-house, was dug into the ground, so they had to attack it below steep steps on the east side to get to a vantage point. Apparently, five men coming down these steps went flat on their faces when the hose ceded—as in the movies. They all came up again and got the house under control. At this point, they thought they had the fire licked and went home—except for two boys who found a jug of hot white wine under a burnt floor. They embarked this against the rules and have been running around town ever since. Sometime past midnight, another neighbor saw a flame coming out of a ridge of the main house. He called the alarm again. Fewer men responded this time, and they had to smash part of the roof ridge to get water down and douse the fire for good.

The one thing I was really worried about, should there be a fire, was a gift of Miró, a 1933 painting he had given me in Paris, a canvas five feet by four. I had placed this in the front hall, which was very small, with a special unhooking device of wire loops on nailheads—in case of an emergency.

186

Louisa and Malcolm Cowley went there next day and spent half an hour getting it loose. The painting was badly smoked—it took all the blue out of it and most of the red—but it is still a beautiful picture.

When Miró came to Roxbury in 1947, he was very much interested in this picture, because he could see himself as an old master.

What was destroyed was the icehouse, my original workshop, where the electricity had probably shorted, and the woodshed and a corner of the bathroom. The toilet, which was of china, had exploded. It must have been a dreary business for Louisa and Malcolm to drag all they could save to my new shop—this seemed to fill it completely when I got there. Gone were the unencumbered spaces.

The insurance people were very considerate and introduced us to a man who had a few war contracts and could scrounge a little material to patch us up with. They squared off the main house and rebuilt the woodshed. One day, I was quite horrified to hear the contractor boss say to his carpenter:

"Say, Al, fake that corner in."

Which was exactly what I wanted, but it was couched unfortunately.

As we were celebrating Christmas in Sherman in 1944, mother called up: father had gone to the hospital; it was very serious. So, I took the train for New Milford next day. I shuttled to and fro between Roxbury and the hospital. He died a week later in New York.

Louisa and I went to the funeral, leaving the children with Rose Masson in New Preston. Albert Sterner said a few words of farewell.

We came home by bus in the afternoon, expecting to be met with the LaSalle, which had been left in the garage to have its gas tank cleaned. We were met by one of the gas boys at Carl and Walt, our favorite garage. He snickered:

"Your car burnt up."

We discovered that some bystander had been smoking while they took the gas out of the tank. The top was burned and the tires blistered. I replaced the top with one of my own making. I ran a piece of canvas from the rear over a wicket made of a steel rod, and attached it to the top of the windshield. I drove this car around for four or five years longer before retiring it.

At one time, when I delivered one of my works to someone near Philadelphia, I was amused to hear the son of the house say to his father:

"But how can he drive such a thing?"

March 30, 1965

11:00 a.m. to 12 noon

Some architect appealed to me to make one or two very small mobiles to go with the model of a proposed building. I made these, took them to New York, and stopped at the Sweeneys', where I met the Serts. Everybody shouted:

"He's not such a good architect!"

And Laura Sweeney grabbed one little object and Moncha Sert grabbed another one. The architect never saw any of them.

These two little objects are the forebears of a line of very small mobiles I occasionally make. I got rather excited making them as small as my so-called clumsy fingers could do them.

". . . a line of very small mobiles . . ."

Then in the fall of 1945, Marcel Duchamp said, "Yes, let's mail these little objects to Carré, in Paris, and have a show."

So a whole race of objects that were collapsible and could be taken to pieces was born.

I discovered at that time that a package eighteen inches long and twenty-four inches in circumference was permissible. Well, I could squeeze an object into a package two inches thick, ten inches wide, and eighteen inches long. Using the diagonal, I could even squeeze in a nineteen-inch element. Some of my plates bolted together and the rods unhooked and collapsed, and I kept mailing these to Carré, who had replied in the affirmative to a cable of Marcel Duchamp. So by June 1946, I had quite a stock of objects in Carré's larder and I took a plane over. There were even some quite large objects, such as the "Lily of Force." We set about photographing these things with Carré's photographer. The photographic material was very poor that year.

It was in the middle of the summer and I still don't understand why the show was put off—probably because the middle of the summer is a dead season in Paris. So I decided to go home again, via England where I got a plane.

I came back to Paris in October 1946. Jean-Paul Sartre had been in Mexico the previous year and on his way back, during a stay in New York, he had visited a few French artists. André Masson brought him to see us in Roxbury and I saw him again in New York, where he came to my little shop. I gave him a mobile bird made out of Connecticut license plates—there is nothing tougher than these; they look like aluminum, but they hang on forever.

During my first visit to Carré, we decided to ask Sartre for a preface, and he agreed. When I came back to Paris the second time, the catalogue was about ready.

One day, Carré said, "You go to Mourlot, the lithographer, and see what I have been doing for you." I went, and discovered a beautiful catalogue, in which the indifferent photography was replaced by a sort of line drawing—the contour of my objects—with color fillings.

Unfortunately, I found the thing a bit monotonous, as all the backgrounds were gray, and I suggested a few blue and yellow backgrounds as well.

However, the lithographic printing process is quite inexorable; you can't go back on what you did yesterday.

The following day, I got a *petit bleu*—telegram—from Louis-Gabriel Clayeux, the right hand of Carré at the gallery then, saying, "*Catastrophe!*"

Carré was furious with me and threw out the yellow backgrounds.

Finally Sartre's preface arrived and it all made a fine little book, with some of Herbert Matter's photographs, as well, of objects in motion.

In the show, there were several objects composed of a heavy metal plate, hanging horizontally close to the floor from a davit that came up from the floor through a hole in the plate; above this were some foliage and berries.

Carré wanted to put these on some pedestals and I said, "No, my wife insists these must be right on the floor."

And Carré said, "*Ce n'est pas noble.*" (It is not dignified.)

There were two mobiles of the epoch of the constellations—the war period—made of bits of hardwood, carved, painted, and hanging on strings at the end of dowel sticks. Carré had previously deleted these from what he wanted to show, so I gave them to Mary Reynolds, who was back in Paris. And she always refers to them, ever since, as the "*Pas Nobles Mobiles*" (the undignified mobiles).

These now belong to the Guggenheim Museum.

The show at Carré's opened on October 25, 1946; there were a lot of visitors and even Henri Matisse. The gallery was in the *huitième arrondissement*—there are a lot of electric-power users in this section, and from five to six in the afternoon they would turn off the electricity to save coal, as a postwar economy measure.

189

GALERIE LOUIS CARRÉ · PARIS

S'IL est vrai que la sculpture doit graver le mouvement dans l'immobile, ce serait une erreur d'apparenter l'art de Calder à celui du sculpteur. Il ne suggère pas le mouvement, il le capte; il ne songe pas à l'ensevelir pour toujours dans le bronze ou dans l'or, ces matériaux glorieux et stupides, voués par nature à l'immobilité. Avec des matières inconsistantes et viles, avec de petits os ou du fer blanc ou du zinc, il monte d'étranges agencements de tiges et de palmes, de palets, de plumes, de

RED PYRAMID
MOBILE, 1945
LARG.: 1 M. 30

STEEL FISH
MOBILE, 1934
HAUTEUR : 3 M. 05
COLLECTION PHILIP L. GOODWIN, NEW YORK

MORNING STAR
STABILE, 1943
HAUTEUR : 2 M. 01

BABY FLAT TOP
MOBILE, 1946
HAUT. : 1 M. 50

Horizontal mobile

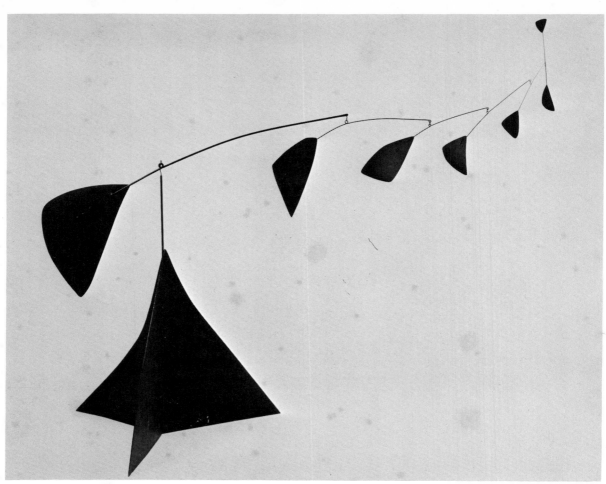

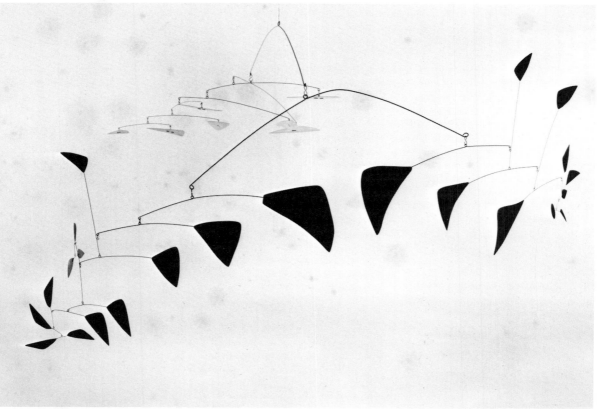

"Sumac," 1961

"Semaphore," 1959

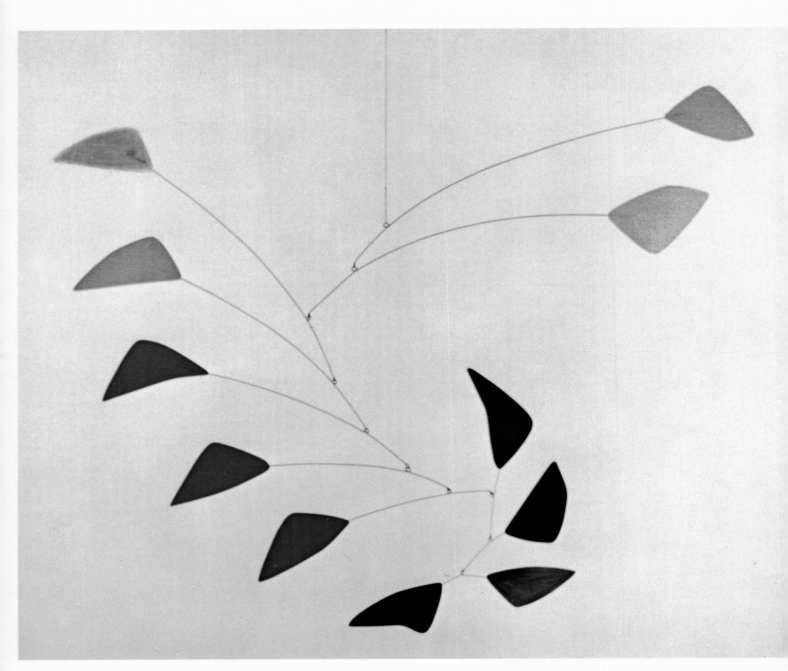

Mobile, 1956

"Little Leaves"

So, we put a candle on the floor under an object with a multitude of small leaves and made it rotate. It was very fine with the shadow going around the candle on the ceiling. This object is now in the Basel Museum.

This time, for the return trip, the State Department was so kind as to get me a passage on the *John Ericsson,* which had been the *Kungsholm,* an old Swedish cruise ship. It was wonderfully steady and had a continuous deck, around which one could walk without going through a door.

There were one hundred English war brides aboard, with their babies. They used to bring the children up occasionally to air them on the deck. One day, a baby stuck out his arms to me and the mother said:

"No, child, that's not your grandfather."

This makes me think of the time when we lived on Eighty-sixth Street. I went to Fred Leighton's, the Mexican shop on Eighth Street, and bought quite a number of dishes and bowls. As it all came to a good deal more than I had in my pocket, I said to the lady, "Will you take a check?"

And she said, "What's your name?"

So I said, "Alexander Calder."

Whereupon another lady said, "Oh! I used to know your son!"

I only had two young daughters, aged eleven and seven, but I went over and patted her on the shoulder and commiserated with her on our advancing years!

March 31, 1965

11:00 a.m. to 12:15 p.m.

I had left Pierre Matisse at the time of my show at the Museum of Modern Art, after some misunderstanding, and for a year or so had been without a dealer.

Curt Valentin inquired about me several times, through André Masson, and I finally joined his stable. He had very few Americans. He had Lipschitz, but he used to purchase things in Europe— Moore, Piper, Beckmann, Picasso, Miró, Juan Gris, and so forth —and he sold these things in the United States.

The first thing we decided to do was to put out a book that I would illustrate.

Previously, I had done one for Monroe Wheeler in Paris, in 1931: *Les Fables d'Aesope,* translated by Sir Roger Lestrange and published by Harrison of Paris.

This time, we got James Sweeney to collect the material, the basis of which was old English rhymes. I worked hard at the drawings and repeated many of them several times. Finally we chose the title from one of the rhymes for which I had done the most complicated and successful drawing:

Three Young Rats.

We also included one American rhyme which goes like this and has a bumptious tune:

You never know as the hearse rolls by
When it may be your turn to die;
They wrap you up in a big white sheet,
And drop you down about sixty-five feet.
They throw in dirt, and they throw in rocks,
And they don't give a damn if they break the box,

Everything's fine for about a week,
And then your coffin begins to leak,
The worms crawl in, the worms crawl out,
They play pinochle on your snout,
They invite their friends, and their friends' friends too.
You look like hell when they're through with you.

A controversial drawing

I did this over very many times, making a cadaver and coffin six feet below earth with many worms.

First of all, Curt Valentin felt badly about the terrific number of worms, so I did it over several times. Then Sweeney objected to where they were placed. Finally I sent them a drawing, this time from the country, from Roxbury, with only one worm—rearing his head from you know where.

Whereupon Sweeney wrote: "This will about do."

This, however, was not the one published. I think Sweeney must have sequestered it.

Curt exhibited the original drawings when he presented the book to the public in the fall of 1944. As most of the figures are naked, there was one in particular climbing up a chimney that Peggy Guggenheim, in her own manner, discovered as being very obscene.

The previous spring, Wally Harrison had suggested I make some large outdoor objects which could be done in cement. He apparently forgot about his suggestion immediately, but I did not and I started to work in plaster. I finally made things which were mobile objects and had them cast in bronze—acrobats, animals, snakes, dancers, a starfish, and tightrope performers. These I showed that

195

fall at Curt's, I guess it was at the same time *Three Young Rats* came out.

This was rather an expensive venture and did not sell very well, so I abandoned it for my previous technique. It was also disagreeable to have to check the manipulations of some other person working on the objects at the foundry. However, I play with the idea, from time to time, of going back to this medium.

At about the same time, I made some projects for other objects, but never achieved them, having gone in another direction. And here is such a drawing I discovered recently that I had made at the time.

Curt was a very gay, affable fellow and he was very good friends with a lot of museum people, naturally. One time he got together a birthday party, and I think Alfred Barr of the Museum of Modern Art was to supply the cake and I was requested to design a candle for it.

I took two plumber's candles for the legs and one for the torso; the shoulders and arms were made by a fourth candle, and the head was the butt end of a burnt plumber's candle. The penis I made with the stump of an ordinary red candle.

All the wicks were carved clean so they could be lit, and when we proceeded to do this the revelation was disastrous. Apparently, red wax burns quickest.

Curt Valentin was really quite gay. He was a German and as a dealer he went to Europe by plane two or three times a year to buy pictures. He also liked to drink and he used to say that he could not afford to take a boat:

196

"Look at all that liquor I'd have to buy!"

In the spring of 1948, I met Burgess Meredith, the actor, at a cocktail. I had heard that he was interested in my work, so I presented myself, not having been introduced. He talked about things. He was launching himself in some movie production and had bought some equipment. Later, he came up to see me in Roxbury. I showed him the studio. We put him to bed on a sofa, in a room with a lot of plants. He woke up with hay fever, which was not very propitious for our relationship. At any rate, I kept telling him that he was such a good actor that I was not sure whether I liked him or not.

He wanted to make a film on the mobile and me. I suggested that he call on Herbert Matter, because Herbert always made fine still pictures of my work, and I was sure he'd like to use a movie camera.

So, we got organized and made a few trial runs and things seemed to be going along pretty well, except for one moment when everybody came to dinner in Roxbury.

Meredith had told me that he and Paulette Goddard, his wife of the moment, had paid five thousand dollars to learn French. And during the meal, he said something in French. Upon which, I said:

"Ça, c'est dit avec l'accent de deux mille cinq cents dollars." (You said this with a $2500 accent.)

I was thinking that he had paid the five thousand dollars for the two of them.

Whereupon he got up from the table and left. He only came back the next day.

That summer, Louisa and I were arranging to go to Brazil and Meredith went to Paris to do some stupid thing about "the man in the Eiffel Tower." This left Herbert all to himself. As he lived near Montauk, at the east end of Long Island, he came to borrow things and took them to Long Island. Some of the things he stood in the water and some he hung over the water. He even put quite a bit of money into buying film for the purpose.

Meredith had thought of having a little boy in the picture. As Matter's little boy Pundy was just the right age, I suggested him.

Next fall, Louisa and I were both back from Brazil and Meredith was back from Paris, and we saw what had been done. It looked pretty good. But it dragged on, because Herbert was a perfectionist, like Sweeney. And at times I'd say, "Can't you take some of those trees out?" and Meredith would say, "Yes, and take out some of the sea."

The final wait was about a year till John Cage came back from Europe to do the music. Herbert would not have anybody else, especially not the two Russians that Meredith tried to impose.

I'd always understood that a simple dated letter is a good contract, so we drew up a letter. Meredith was to get his expenses first, and then 50 per cent, and Herbert and I each of us 25 per cent. About the time we were due to receive something, I got my lawyer to work on it, but on account of delaying tactics, the seven-year statute of limitation, or what do you call it, ran out—and Meredith, now, gets the whole thing.

It so happens that our niece, Eva Hayes, was visiting us the first days Meredith ever came to Roxbury. She lived in Berkeley, near my sister Peggy and her husband Kenneth. When Meredith came to San Francisco in some play, Eva told my sister to look him up. He took Peggy and Ken to the show and to dinner, then to some night club. And then he disappeared, leaving Mr. Hayes holding the check.

April 1, 1965

4:30 p.m. to 5:30 p.m.

In New York in 1944, we had met a Brazilian—Henrique Mindlin. He had been intrigued by a small mobile he had seen somewhere, and wanted one for himself. It was sort of a little chair, made out of a bent piece of metal, with three legs and a feather sitting in a notch in the top.

I made him a similar one which could be taken to pieces—legs taken off, metal feather removed—so he could fly it to Rio without any trouble. I often regret not having made him a cloth vest with pockets, each the color of the part contained.

Mindlin was very enthusiastic about my work and said that I must come to Brazil. So four years later, in 1948, having made various shipments of my work to Henrique in Rio, Louisa and I set out for Brazil—but our route was very devious.

We first drove across the continent and left Sandra and Mary with my sister Peggy in Berkeley. Then we flew from San Francisco to Los Angeles, Mexico City, Panama, Trinidad, and Rio.

At first, we had both decided we should travel on different planes, but Louisa said in San Francisco, "Let's fly this first trip together," so I said, "Let's take the whole works together"—which we did.

In Mexico, we had to stop over for twenty-four hours, from seven in the morning to seven the next day. I had written my friend Fernando Gamboa, director of the Museo de Bellas Artes,

198

and he and his wife came to meet us at the airport. He took us to a hotel and we both slept a few hours. We were tired on account of the altitude. Then they took us to lunch, and we walked around town in the afternoon. In the evening, we had dinner with Luis Buñuel and Jeanne and the Buñuel boys.

Next morning we were off again. The first stop, after Mexico, was Panama. We were rather weary on arrival there, because we got in very late. We stayed in a very old wooden hotel, with high ceilings and openings above eye level from the rooms into the hall, for ventilation.

I insisted on taking Louisa in a taxi to Panama City, to see the crazy traffic and open buildings I had seen sixteen years before, when a fireman on the S.S. *Alexander*. It was not as exciting as I had hoped, so as we were quite weary we went back to the hotel. Then on the following morning we took the trip to Trinidad. The trip was quite amusing because the DC-3 made many stops in the coastal towns on the way. There were often ladies in evening garb, who traveled with us for a hop or two—they were going to some party.

When we got to Trinidad we were still weary, despite a pleasant trip. As it was muggy, we chose an air-conditioned room at the hotel there. We were serenaded by a Negro orchestra; in fact, they were playing for themselves.

Next day we took a plane for Rio. We found John Dos Passos on board. He was going to round up all of Brazil, in a few days.

When we crossed the Amazon River, the moon shone in spots from overhead on the river and cut out great black islands of different shapes; this was not always very distinct, but when you could grasp it, it was stunning.

We came down shortly after in Belem and were all ushered into a sort of small Quonset hut, with benches on either side. Shortly afterward, four or five gentlemen in white tunics came over carrying a big white jar with thermometers in alcohol. They stuck one in the mouth of each traveler. They came back a few minutes later to read them and stuck them back into the same jar. I suppose the alcohol gets changed through evaporation, or maybe, if they read a high temperature, they would not put the thermometer back into the same jar?

Louisa had at first been against going to Brazil, because of her dislike for a lot of society ladies in black silk dresses, having their tea parties. So, as Henrique had expected me to come alone, he had arranged one such party on the first day. It was not so bad as all that, and we took Dos Passos along and shared the honors with him.

This reminds me that when we landed in Rio it was very foggy

Calder traveling by plane, seen by Bob Osborn

and I was much amazed by the dexterity of the pilot bringing us down. He landed on a large island in Guanabara Bay, on the military air strip, and we had to be ferried across to the mainland in a small launch with large windows on either side. We sat next to Dos and he looked up and said:

"Oh! There's the Sugar Loaf . . ."

And then (he was almost blind from a recent accident in which his wife had been killed) he exclaimed:

"Oh, no! It's my straw hat."

It was, in fact, its reflection in the window.

April 2, 1965

5:00 p.m. to 6:00 p.m.

With Henrique and our good friend Dotty Kidder (her husband was second secretary of the United States embassy) we went to work collecting objects of mine from private owners, in addition to those I had specially shipped for the show.

In a few days we were ready to set up the show on the second floor of the Ministerio do Educaçao, which I consider one of the most beautiful buildings going, influenced by Le Corbusier, with supporting columns under it. It was built and designed by Niemeyer, Costa, Moreira, and others.

The hanging was not done without difficulty, because of a certain Dr. Paulo. (I noticed that everybody in Brazil called everybody he liked by his first name. You could say Vargas was Getulio and I was Sandy—not that I met Vargas, because he was dead then.) This Dr. Paulo insisted on using pea-green screens with sticks nailed across the top from which to hang my objects.

He said, "Your things are very light," putting his hand—while talking—under a big chunk of wood and not noticing that the counterweight went down when his hand went up. But we had to knuckle under because he was in command and would not budge.

Louisa sat around watching and some of the various loans got rather "interconfused." All of a sudden, Henrique said:

"No, that's not right."

And he walked over to one object, took an element out of it, and came back and inserted it quite properly in another object on a table in front of Louisa, who was sitting there.

Incidentally, for furniture we borrowed the stock of the local Alvar Aalto store—mostly stools, with three legs and a plywood top.

200

Everything seemed to be taking shape nicely when, around five in the afternoon, in came Niemeyer, Roberto Burle-Marx, Mario Pedrosa, and others. They immediately began to rehash the whole setup, taking one object from here and putting it there, bringing back the other where they'd started from.

Dotty, being in the embassy, had said that I should send my card to the United States ambassador. As I had no card, but a paintbrush full of black paint, I took a fairly large piece of cardboard and painted my name on it and sent that.

Before leaving Roxbury, I'd taken the trouble of having my monkey suit let out and even had bought three shirts with frills at a New York haberdasher's. When I got into one of the shirts, for the opening of my show, the frills finished short of my belly button—so there was a half-moon on my front. I said, *"Tant pis."* (The shirts were all alike.)

But nobody, including Mr. Ambassador, seemed to notice my half-moon.

I guess this is about enough about this opening.

Except that they had a book for everybody to write in and there were some long dissertations in Portuguese on my art, including one given by Pedrosa. We had met in New York, in 1944. He had looked me up and we had become very good friends.

While he spoke, I sat in the front row to hear better, but as it was in Portuguese, I dozed off. Finally the press took a picture and woke me up for this purpose. But as Mario was on the far side of the stage, all eyes were turned toward him, except mine that looked straight into the camera.

Lota de Macedo Soares thought I ought to do some work while in Rio, so she took me to the district where one found hardware stores and I bought a hammer, an anvil, tinsnips, sheet aluminum, steel wire. I already had my favorite Bernard pliers (they have a parallel bite), which I take wherever I go.

At first, I worked on the second floor of a mechanic's shop. He was very nice, but there was a terrific current of air—even too much for me. I worked up a sweat and my fingers got so cramped that I could hardly open my hand.

I hastily took a piece of aluminum sheet and fashioned a *figa* —the Brazilian good-luck piece, which is also an emblem of fecundity and is composed of a hand in which the thumb passes under the forefinger. This seemed to do the trick, so I continued working, and finally I put a wire pin on the *figa* and gave it to Lota, who often wears it as a barrette.

Then Lota found another place for me. A dear friend of hers, Eugenio Lage, was in New York, and he had bought a house with a garden and a garage in the middle of Rio. But he did not have, then, enough money to undertake the renovation. So she wrote him, asking if I could work there. We moved in before his answer arrived. I elected the garage as my studio and built a workbench, set up my anvil and my tools. Things were arranged in such a way that I could drag the workbench into the garden and cut and hammer in the sun.

Louisa and Dotty used to come for a picnic lunch sometimes, and the flower beds and hanging ferns were lovely. They were attended to by a barefoot gardener whom Lota referred to as "Gostoso"—the tasty one. She once remarked that Gostoso must wonder about me: "A guy who looked like a general and made such strange toys!"

One day soon after our arrival, we'd gone dancing with Dotty, Randy, the Mindlins, and their friends in Rio. A girl named Branca, who was almost as big as I, danced with me and found me rather stubborn, so she wheeled me around, practically off my feet.

After a few weeks, we flew the show over the mountains to São Paulo—that is, I packed them and Henrique flew them to the Museo de Arte there, publisher Chateaubriand's museum. Louisa, Dotty, and I followed Henrique the next day.

In São Paulo, the wife of the museum director did the installation all herself—she did a good job. Previously she had come to Rio and studied the installation.

A few years before, the architect Rino Levi had come to our house in Roxbury and now he gave us a party. Of course, there was a wonderful samba orchestra.

After the opening of the show we returned to Rio, where we were feted quite a bit, here and there.

We met Kelso Peck, who had King Carol's suite on the top of the Copacabana Hotel. We all danced the samba violently, but Kelso did not know how to dance. So instead he would do cartwheels and every time he went round all his pens and pencils fell out on the floor. We kept picking them up for him.

Once, a lady living in what she thought a "modern house"—she was a sculptress—invited us. There were a dozen guests around a big round table. In the center, in a bowl, there were so many bird-of-paradise flowers that they became vulgar. After lunch, she insisted on taking me alone to her studio.

There were several things of hers and she showed me the first one she'd ever done. Then she rummaged in a drawer and took out a large jacknife and she said:

"I did it all with this."

So I said:

"Next time, why don't you use a shovel?"

202

April 3, 1965

11:00 a.m. to 12 noon

We occupied an apartment on the Copacabana which belonged to a French diplomat and his Argentine wife. They had gone on vacation, leaving us a charming Argentine maid.

Every other day—or so it seemed—we had to call Dotty to bring us some toilet paper. Delia the maid remarked, "But my boss only uses a new roll once a week."

One evening we went to a *macumba*, somewhere in the Rio countryside. There were women in white dancing around in a big circle. We got into it too. I danced with a colored lady. Some Russian photographer took a picture of us and published it in *Fon Fon*, a Rio scandal sheet.

For years we never did see this photograph, because, as Dotty told us, the Kidders got called on the carpet about this by the embassy and she had "flushed her copy down the toilet." The affair did not bother me, except for their sake.

Before we were to leave Rio, we decided to have a party. Heitor Dos Praceres (Hector of the Pleasures), a Negro painter and friend of ours, had an excellent samba band, so we decided that they should come sixteen strong. The smallest member of the band was a young boy. He had a mustard can, which he banged with a big spike, keeping perfect rhythm. It was quite uncanny, the damnedest thing . . . he just beat that thing right!

The party took place in the little house where I worked. Two days before, Lota wrote to Eugenio in New York, saying that if he did not see any objection we would have a party there. The little house was bare and built around a tiny court and we decorated it with signs saying:

DON'T DO IT HERE

And things like that.

Dotty got the embassy caterer, an English gentleman who only knew whiskey, to supply the drinks. But we also wanted *cachaca*, a local cane derivative—it is very strong and is usually served in *batida,* or punch. After four or five hours, most of us were the worse for wear.

At one moment, Louisa said, "Where are all the people?"

And somebody replied, "Haven't you looked outside?"

A few days later we flew home by way of Puerto Rico, Miami, and San Francisco. We'd been gone two months and were very glad to see our daughters. We had some fun with the Hayeses in

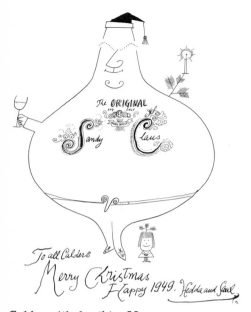

Calder with daughter Mary,
seen by Steinberg

Berkeley, before leaving. (They made a terrible punch, with muscatel as a base.) We stopped in Los Angeles to visit Alden and Hilma Brooks; they had moved to Topanga Canyon.

Crossing the desert, it is very difficult to find a decent place to eat. We stopped in New Orleans, and the first morning in Louisiana we were astonished how good the coffee was. I had some business with a young architect there. He showed us around and took us to Antoine's, the famous restaurant.

One is supposed to have only two Sazaraks.

But we had three.

So finally, the maître d'hôtel came and asked us whether we'd like to see the cellar.

We found the old French quarter very pretty in spots. But most of the town—in spite of Senator Fulbright—is quite dull.

We stopped in New York, on our way to Roxbury, to see mother. She now occupied our apartment on Seventy-second Street—but it was large enough for the whole family to stay there, at times.

April 4, 1965

11:00 a.m. to 12:15 p.m.

Arrived home in Roxbury, Louisa taught me the rudiments of the samba. It is really quite simple—a shuffle that I had never grasped before. We then tried to indoctrinate the countryside. But aside from the John Whites and the Teeb Clapps, we were not very successful. However, occasionally a "samba-ista" arrived on our doorsteps and was well received.

One time, Sweeney brought a busload of art critics and museum directors. They were a bit late, of course, having been waylaid by Soby and Philip Johnson. We gave them something to eat and there turned out to be a Brazilian in their midst who asked to hear a samba. And so, the party was on.

The bus driver called his wife three times and said he'd be late, later, and still later.

By the spring of 1950, Louisa and I felt the whole family should take a trip to France. Sandra was fifteen then, and Mary eleven. We hired from a friend her apartment on the rue de Penthièvre in the *huitième arrondissement*, strangely enough, in the middle of a chic quarter of Paris. But the apartment was not so chic.

After seven or eight days at sea, we arrived in Paris on the boat

Spring 1950. A familiar moment at the
Deux Magots

204

train at about ten or eleven in the evening. We went to a very funny hotel, rue des Saints-Pères, a sort of family hotel: Le Bon Lafontaine. We put the girls to bed and went to the Brasserie Lipp on the boulevard St-Germain for a drink, and the first guy I ran into was our dear friend Rubem Braga, whom we had met two years before during our stay in Brazil.

Christian Zervos, who edits *Cahiers d'Art*, had very kindly put me in touch with Aimé Maeght, who had a very good gallery in the *huitième arrondissement*. And I brought over to Maeght lots of the Roxbury mobiles, and had a show there in June 1950, following a show by Miró.

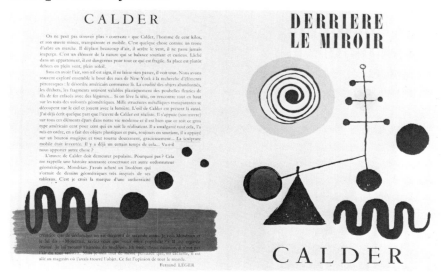

June 1950. Calder's show at Maeght. Fernand Léger presents it and sort of forecasts the gigantic stabiles to come. "Mobile sculpture was invented quite a while ago . . . Will he bring us something more?"

The Maeght Gallery is a handsome combination of two large rooms with a lot of windows on the avenue de Messine, and a cross-draft, if desired, through the room called "yellow."

I had many of the medium-sized hanging objects and these hung in profusion. They were very light and airy. I think Sweeney saw this show and was impressed by the manner of hanging. It was the beginning of a long association with Maeght.

At Maeght's, I found my old friend Gaby Clayeux, who had been with Carré in 1946.

Toward the end of Miró's show, Maeght took us all out to supper at a fish restaurant in Montmartre. Miró was having sea urchins and oysters, so I said to him:

"Joan, what difference do you find between the oysters and the urchins?"

Whereupon he went into a huddle, all by himself, and finally came out with this statement:

"The urchins have a very delicate flavor, but it is the oysters that give you the strength."

205

Gigitte Maeght and I did a polka when the orchestra happened to play one. We became very popular and received much applause —nobody else was dancing.

Some time later, we went to see Ritou Nitzschke, now Bac, at La Roche Jaune in Brittany. We went by train and were met at St-Brieuc by Jacques Valentin, with a two-ton truck that had an open body.

Ritou's house is an old shelter for guardians of the oyster beds; it is located on the edge of the Tréguier River, a mile from the sea. But the oyster beds having been moved further down toward the sea, she was able to acquire it. It looks like a small fort, has a room and a half and an attic, but I don't know how many people we crowded into it on army cots—anyway, it was very gay.

A mile or so downstream, at the mouth of the river, was a house we could see on a mound, completely isolated. The mound was an island at high tide. Here, a lady lived who kept her husband chained to an iron bedstead—or so the story goes—because he had a ladylove in the neighborhood. It was a most spectacular spot.

We went on various trips in Jacques Valentin's truck, standing up in the back and peering over the boards, and once we were stopped by a police officer who was afraid we were competing with the bus system.

Maire Gullicksen, who had an Alvar Aalto house in Norrmark, Finland, had long wanted us to visit her. Especially at the season when one eats crayfish in Finland—this turned out to be August.

When I went to the Finnish embassy to get visas, I saw a map on the wall and realized how near Russia we were going to be— and I was rather impressed.

We took the train to Antwerp and from there we took the Finnish ship *Arcturus*, which seemed to be the only one left after the Finnish war. I think it had been sunk and refloated. On the way to Antwerp, we sat in a compartment with a lady and a gentleman and struck up a conversation. The lady smiled at Mary and said, "What do you think I do?"

And Mary said, "Cleaning lady."

She was a television and radio star.

The *Arcturus*, to my mind, was a fine little boat, the weather was wonderfully sunny and the water slightly choppy, but our daughters seemed to collapse on deck and many young students did likewise. We got Sandra out of her berth later, on the Kiel Canal, but she went right back to it.

Somebody gave me a little dictionary of the Finnish language and I memorized from one to ten—about all I could do.

Arriving in Helsinki, we went to a hotel to await for Maire, who was coming in from the country. The girls were very hungry and

I tried to order a few ham sandwiches in my new-found language. The girls thought my effort very funny. Louisa did too.

Soon Maire arived with a big car and took us all to the east, to Sunila, to see her paper mills. This plant, too, was designed by Aalto. There were great wheels in pairs, rolling on paper pulp in vats, about a dozen pairs of wheels—to me, they looked like circus elephants doing a stunt.

Then, back to Helsinki and off to the west, to Norrmark. It was an all-day trip. We stopped to see a fine old church, of very modest materials, with large wooden sculptures. And then, we arrived at the home of some friends of Maire's, whose tongues were hanging out—we were over one hour and a half late for lunch. The Finns had resisted till we arrived. But the climate, uncertain at times, and the great spaces make the arrival of people somewhat problematic.

Finally we got to Norrmark and the house turned out to be very handsome. They had a sauna and swimming pool, both of which we hastened to sample, and the crayfish, of course, were served for dinner, with potatoes and dill. Since that trip, Louisa uses dill in profusion in her own cooking.

From there, one day, we took a five-hour trip to see the Bjoerkenheims, who have one of the few remaining big farms in the north of Finland.

They could not find any United States flag, but they had four Finnish flags up for our arrival—they were very cordial. We went to the top floor of the house, where the children, of which there were many, had decorated the walls with winter scenes. Here, we revived with aquavit and various other potions and were given snacks and smorgasbord. When Louisa and I thought we had finished dinner, we all went downstairs to the real dinner.

During our stay there, our hostess suggested I look at the two privies—one for men and one for women. The one I saw had eight seats in a row and was very neat.

The countryside is a good deal like Maine, with small pines a foot or so in diameter everywhere. Almost anywhere, one can leave the main road and discover a pond or small lake over the intervening ridge. We had several barbecues of crayfish by the edge of such ponds. There are forty thousand lakes and it is somewhat repetitious.

April 6, 1965

11:00 a.m. to 12:15 p.m.

At the end of a week we left.

After two or three hours by car, we got to Turku and took a boat to Sweden. We spent a couple of weeks dodging traffic, which comes at you from the wrong side.

We saw some old friends from the Paris days—Astrid Grate, now remarried, and her former husband, Eric, also remarried and with a lot of kids. We went to visit Eric's family out in the country.

While waiting for him to come home, we stayed in a little country inn and I climbed up a hill to say hello to Astrid's present brother-in-law. His was a very old house, and there were bunks built in the walls. There were house thermometers on each side of the living room.

A few years before, a man named Skillberg had come to Roxbury with his wife and bought a little mobile for two hundred dollars, and on account of exchange regulations he had not been able to extract the funds to pay for it. We met him, this time, quite a ways out from Stockholm, and he paid our railroad ticket back to Antwerp, where we were now supposed to take a ship for New York.

The value of the object did not quite get the four of us all the way to Antwerp, so I had to chip in. When nearing Antwerp, we discovered the train went all the way to Paris. As we had a three-day wait before the boat sailed, we decided to go all the way to Paris and return in time for the sailing.

Well, the ship was called the *Europa*. The previous *Europa* had been sunk during the war. This was a big old British steamer, probably too slow for the fancy trade; it had been called the *Remutaka*, and was now operated by an Italian line. We had booked this passage through an agency in New York.

There seemed to be some disorder on board. They took our passports away. As I had been told that one should guard one's passport with one's life instead of guarding one's life with one's passport, I was greatly perturbed. So I went back and protested at the desk, and the steward said, "All right, take it."

I fumbled in a big wooden box and got our passports back.

It was a ten- or eleven-day trip, and we read with a certain amount of concern that there were typhoons in the West Indies and that it seemed possible they could veer north and meet us on our way to New York.

However, we used to gather about ten strong, before meals, for whiskey sours.

We arrived home in September 1950, and we bought a third car—it happened to be a Dodge convertible. As our Roxbury garage only holds two cars, there was always one left in the driveway. And of course, I used that one.

The old LaSalle, its battery gone dead—we'd now had it seventeen years. John and Leonie White had often used it with us to go on picnics. So I called up Charlie Burdick, the hot-shot mechanic, and gave him the car—asked him to take it away.

I had been invited to have a show at M.I.T. and I went up to arrange for it. I stayed in Cambridge with Olivia, my sister-in-law. One evening, I went to have supper at Concord. On the way back, I fell asleep at the wheel and missed one turn on the road. I ran into a traffic island and ended up in an Arlington hospital. Later, Olivia put up bond for me, and I finally came out of it all without any permanent scratch.

When Louisa heard in Roxbury that I was hurt, she started dreaming, she says, of a list of people whom she should inform of my demise.

Mother's only comment was, "You spoiled your fun."

Fortunately, Sweeney was on the job and put up the M.I.T. show for me. I was up and could see the show, before it was over. Ezra Stoller, the photographer, had arrived one day at noon, when the doors were locked, but through the glass walls he took two excellent pictures of the show.

I must have met Henri Pichette at lunch with Giacometti in Paris. Now he wanted me to decorate his new play: *Nucléa.* So in the early spring of 1952, I flew over to Paris. The troupe included Jean Vilar, Gérard Philippe, Jeanne Moreau, Françoise Spira, and quite a number of others.

I was interviewed by a journalist once and told him I was learning the play "through osmosis," because I never did see a complete copy of the text.

Gérard wanted an extra stage, two meters above the other, on pipe columns, but I cut it into ribbons and had a semicircular band in the rear of the stage with a ramp sloping down to the footlights and ending with a few steps . . .

At one moment two large panels, "the clouds," descended from above, rotating on themselves, displaying white and black sides. I will always remember the lines:

"*Nuit et jour.*" (Night and day.)

And:

"*Jour et nuit.*" (Day and night.)

There was also a big stabile, painted red.

The first act was about war, the second about love. Pichette's war seemed much more dramatic than Pichette's love. At any rate,

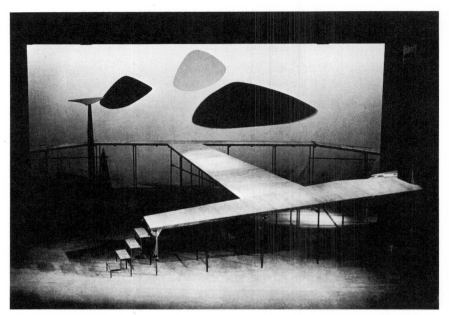

"I cut Gérard's stage into ribbons . . ."

the play did not meet with much success, despite certain merits.

The following year, it was revived for a few occasions and Pichette tried to catch the public by having the love first and the war after—the public refused to be held captive by this dodge.

Vilar was very nice, but more serious than Pichette and Gérard Philippe, who were very gay. Vilar, having the responsibility of the Théâtre National Populaire on his shoulders, was a target for attack from jealous people.

I remember many gay reunions with Pichette and Philippe. Pichette lived in a maid's room, 29 rue Octave Feuillet in the *seizième*. His maid's room belonged to a wealthy patron of the arts who lived downstairs. It was a long pull up six flights, especially when loaded with bottles, but it was very gay in the little room when you got to the top.

And of course, Pichette could talk much faster than I could understand. But when I did get the gist of it, it was very good news.

He loved to imitate the noises the animals make. He would declaim:

"The dog barks,
"The horse whinnies,
"The cow moos,
"The owl hoots,
"And Pichette . . . *déconne* [blabbers]!"

Louisa came over for the opening and afterward we went to visit the Massons in Aix-en-Provence. Rose had won at the French lottery and bought a car. Amazingly enough, she had even learned how to drive it. She took us around the countryside, and we were

210

so enchanted with what we saw that we decided to come back to France and to Aix the following year. So, we rented a little house for the next year, from June 1953. A very pleasant little house, without much electricity or water: Le Mas des Roches.

That spring, I had already left Roxbury a month or two earlier, when the Museum of Modern Art decided to expose me in the Venice Biennale. They got Sweeney to install my things and he made a list of what he wanted. So Curt Valentin, then my dealer, sent out a young man to pick the pieces in Roxbury and he and Louisa did very well—although there was "The Red Lily," into which they found it impossible to insert the lily. But the things got to Venice, where Sweeney, too, found it impossible to hook the red lily in place.

I arrived a few weeks later to take a look and I found this piece lacking, but the show looked pretty good, so I said, "I'll leave it as it is."

I was already back home in Connecticut and we had gone to see Sandra at Putney School in Vermont, when a wire arrived at the school for "Sandy Calder," from Curt. But Sandra was called "Sandy" too—she got there first.

Well, I had won the thing, in spite of the red posy.

In September 1952, some time, I was invited by the German State Department to tour West Germany. I reported for the flight at Idlewild and was surprised by the number of clerics going too; there was one fellow with a big gold cross on his belly—I think he was a Methodist. There were also two or three librarians of Congress, a fellow named Bill Friedman, ex-architect and curator of museums; also a little lady who was running around to find black offspring among the white people of Germany—or something like that—and I.

We first flew to Bonn and were briefed, and then in small groups we went off under the guidance of a godfather. I was bracketed more or less with Friedman, so much so that I got to know he had a portable electric razor, but that for foreign use he had a transformer, which weighed five times as much, in his other pocket.

I was sent off to Munich almost immediately. For two days, I met various people, among them Bruno Werner, a journalist who had happened to write up my 1929 show in Berlin. Curt Valentin had given me a list of all his friends and Werner was one of them.

When I finally got to Berlin and saw the Gedächtniskirche, I happened to write Bruno Werner that day, explaining that I thought the Germans should keep it in its present state. It was ugly, but the bombing had made it beautiful. Werner published my letter in a Munich paper.

The next stop was Mannheim, where I went on an all-day trip

from Munich. I claimed the train was late, but my German host in that town countered, "German trains are never late; you took the wrong one."

Mannheim is a remarkable town, with each block numbered or lettered—it is contained in a bend of the river and does not have any chance to expand.

We went to Darmstadt, Berlin, Hanover, Bremen, Cologne, and back to Bonn. In Hanover, I met my very good friends Al Henzen and his wife.

In Hamburg, I met Rudolf Hoffmann *"der Nase"*—of the handsome nose. He took me dancing with other people on the Reeperbahn. We ended up dancing together, which had quite some success.

In Bremen, there was a tall medieval figure of Roland, Charlemagne's buddy—this figure must be eighteen feet high and is built of stones, piled on top of each other. The knees came where I could see them best. They were composed of iron spikes strapped to the stones. This and the Gedächtniskirche are what I liked best in the way of sculpture. Which shows that airplane bombs have a medieval quality too.

I did not meet Carl Hartung, but I consider him the best German sculptor. His drawings are good too.

I met several others, whose work I did not like at the time but who seem to have developed considerably since.

So, I returned to Connecticut, with my impressions in a rather confused state—you could feel they wanted you to approve of them and you did not quite know whether you should or not.

April 9, 1965

11:00 a.m. to 12:15 p.m.

A year or two before, sometime around 1950, I had a show in the Gallery of Contemporary Arts in Washington, D. C. There I met Jean Davidson, son of Jo, the other sculptor. We got along very well, and I invited him to come to Roxbury for Christmas.

Apparently, some fifteen years before and in Paris, Jean had seen two things of mine in the apartment of Mary Callory and he had been struck by them—to the point of having some violent discussion with his father as to their merit. When he arrived in Roxbury, I presented him to my mother and upon his saying he admired my work, she answered:

"Oh! But you should have known Stirling—he was a sculptor!"

During the Christmas holidays, I presented my circus. Jean became very enthusiastic about it. So the year following, when I told him I'd do the circus again, he invited what seemed half of Washington, D. C., to see it.

One time when we were visiting Dotty Kidder in Washington, D. C., Jean came to lunch. As he ate two helpings of dessert I passed the following drawing on to him. Afterward he wafted me to his farm in Clarksville, Maryland. He had a marvelous chassis, with a 300-horsepower Chrysler engine, and if he ever noticed flames spurting out of the hood he had to go faster to gobble them up. Now he was going 118 m.p.h. on Route 40 and he pointed at the speedometer—the dial was right in front of me—and said:

"We're hitting 120."

This was no time to argue.

A year or two later, in France, I got into his Allard for a ride to Tours from Saché and I was given the alarming command:

"Please hold that door shut. It unlatches with the wind pressure!"

In the spring of 1953, which was to be our year in Aix, we fiddled around without booking our passage for quite a while. So we ended up in first class, against our will, on the *Flandre*.

Independently, Jean, who had had enough of Washington, D. C., after eight years of covering the White House for *France Presse*, decided to go back to France to settle down, he thought, in Brittany. He took the Allard with him. The first thing he did upon his arrival in France was to visit his brother Jacques in Jo's old house, in Saché, Indre-et-Loire, south of Tours.

Half a mile away from Jo's old Manoir de Bécheron, Jean had discovered a mill on the Indre River. And he lost a few thousand francs daily to its proprietor, a wealthy businessman, till he secured its transfer. Instead of winning the mill playing cards, he won the right to purchase it by losing steadily.

To come back to our departure from New York on the *Flandre*, one of my old friends at Stevens, Harold Fee, who now is a secretary there, came to see us off at the boat. Harold returned to Hoboken before we sailed. And as he had agreed to stand on the roof of the old Castle Stevens and wave a red blanket, we climbed on top of the deck to wave back.

I'd heard of Hemingway from Miró and others, and Miró had always told me to present myself to him, as one of his friends, if I ever met him. On the *Flandre*, it so happened that we were right outside the "bridal suite," which was occupied by Hemingway and his wife. He appeared suddenly and I presented myself, but it was not much use. For I had nothing to say to him and he had nothing to say to me. And that went for Louisa too.

Is this what you look like? Sandy

At the end of the voyage, toward Le Havre, we were seated on the deck discussing with some friends how much to tip all and sundry, and we decided Hemingway deserved five dollars for having revived local color, but no more.

It was a pleasant eight days aboard.

Following our arrival in Paris, I picked up a 15 c.v. Citroën which we had bought in New York. They gave me ten liters of gas; that did not last long because I went everywhere in second gear. I parked it in the rue de l'Abbaye, opposite the police station, and some cops conversed with me about the delicate features of the front-end drive—you must not bump a wheel.

We soon set out for Aix, taking our old friend Katherine Dudley with us. Halfway, somewhere near Mâcon, we spent the night in a hotel atop a hill. All the heavy-duty trucks, when nearing the top, shifted gears and drowned out my snoring.

April 10, 1965

11:00 a.m. to 12:45 p.m.

The Mas des Roches turned out to be a charming little house in the midst of the fields, with a big fig tree and three horse chestnuts. Under the roof, there was an amazing array of pigeon roosts, built against the attic walls.

There was no electricity, and the water was made to flow into an all-purpose tank by pumping on a small lever in the carriage shed. One would work for fifteen minutes, hopefully, and rush upstairs, only to hear the *chasse d'eau*—somebody had got there first.

I used the carriage shed as a studio. It was like a big one-car garage with an open door. I put in a little table and did *gouaches* there—many of them. When there was too much water, I would tilt the table and let it flow onto the ground. I would moisten the paper with a flow of water and wait till it dried a bit but not too much; then I would draw on it with a brush full of China ink—this would develop clouds and trees and fungi and things of that nature. In addition to the watery variety, I did some large human heads with crosshatched stripes.

Later, I looked for and found a blacksmith, near Aix, on our road and made four large outdoor mobiles in his shop.

I also had soon built a large wooden table for outdoor meals and we used to sit at this, in the shade of the *maronniers*, and the next-door farmer would go by and say:

214

Aix, 1953. A new "breakthrough" in gouaches

"In addition to the watery variety, I did some large human heads with crosshatched stripes"

"Malvalat, a rather pretentious and very peculiar house"

"Alors, vous êtes bien à l'ombre?" (Well, are you comfortable in the shade?)

We went swimming a few times beyond Martigues, on the way to Marseilles—it was quite an undertaking.

One day, Louisa and I drove to Antibes and had lunch with Marie Cuttoli and Henri Laugier. On our return, the girls told us the proprietor had been around to propose another house, with electricity and hence water. This other house was near by and was called "Malvalat," meaning "foul water" or something of the sort. It was a rather pretentious three-story yellow stucco building with red shutters, and quite handsome in spite of all. There was a beautiful square park in front of it; the earth was held by a low retaining wall, and there were very big trees in this square.

But this was a very peculiar house when you got inside it, because in the rear was a farmhouse, of which our kitchen seemed to be a part. Some of the rooms were very shallow, twelve feet deep, and we never knew what went on behind them. There was also a locked-up chapel.

What with the owls, the cedar tree before the house, and the horses rattling their chains in the stalls of the adjoining farm, the threat of a so-called friend that the house was haunted seemed, more or less, to be true.

I found a very funny room on the third floor, with giddy flowery paper, which I used to continue my *"gouacheries."* I had made *gouaches* before, but here I was practically doing nothing but *gouaches* and concentrating on them. I seemed to develop something new.

We had several parties in that lugubrious dining room, lined with dark wood panels and its cartwheel hanging overhead, with five electric bulbs, of which three were inoperative. But Louisa put a multitude of candles all around. We had a victrola now—electric—and some people brought musical instruments and played for us. We seem to have made a mark with our Aix parties, although they were quite modest.

At Christmas Ritou and André Bac came and André cooked a beastie in the fireplace, on a spit we had made, and we ate the beastie outside. We'd always heard you could eat lunch out of doors most of the winter in Aix; now we were doing it.

In Aix, the Cour Mirabeau was very handsome, with many lines of buttonwood trees and several fountains. At the upper end is the Café des Deux Garcons, which was a wonderful rendezvous in those days. One of the waiters, Léon, had spent several months in Connecticut. We occasionally correspond, and I ran into him in Marseilles just the other day (April 1965).

We took a trip to Sète, to visit Jean Vilar in his native town.

We were much impressed by the canals, staying at the nice Grand Hotel at the junction of the canals. We'd gone to see the *joutes*, but when the time arrived, it started to rain and we ended up dancing in a bistro.

We went several times fifteen miles from Sète toward Agde, to swim at the beach there. In the harbor itself were the remains of what seemed like a lighthouse; it was referred to as *L'Estroun*, meaning "The Turd."

After Sète, we prepared to visit Ritou Bac in Brittany at La Roche Jaune, near Tréguier, Côtes-du-Nord. As we rolled along we took in all the *châteaux*, referring to the less glorious ones as "shiteaux."

On our way, we decided to call on Jean Davidson's brother, Jacques, at the Manoir de Bécheron, Jo's old house in Saché. In Loches, we asked a cop where "Sash" was and he said:

"You mean Saché, probably."

And so we proceeded to Saché and inquired at the post office. As Bécheron was on the other side of the Indre River, we had to cross a narrow iron bridge. What should we see flash in front of us but the old Allard, with Jean and a mass of brats seated on top of one another. He was taking them to his recently purchased mill, near by, in the hope they'd help him clean it up.

April 12, 1965

11:00 a.m. to 12 noon

We followed Jean and found he had a lovely mill in the middle of a wide bend of the Indre River. There was even another house on another little island that did not seem to count.

The mill had three similar stories with one big room each. We had quite a discussion about the fireplace to be. Jean wanted to raise the fireplace over a window fitted in the old axle lodging that gave on the churning waters. His theory was—water underneath and fire above!

Later, I told him that with another arrangement he could have seen the water through the flames, but I was too late.

The following fall, I came down in November for the grand opening of the mill. Jean had built the fireplace ledge three feet from the floor, and as he had planned, you could effectively see the churning waters under a roaring fire.

"We followed Jean and found he had a lovely mill on the middle of a wide bend of the Indre River"

He had invited at least forty people to eat three-inch steaks and a dozen chickens in their skins. He had the meat and the fire, but no implements with which to cook them. So I hunted around the unloved house on the other island and found an old garden chair made completely of iron. I wove some wire across where the back had been, and we cocked it up on the fire and it served very well as a grill. Steak *à la chaise* came to be the *spécialité maison*.

The chickens I throttled each with a piece of wire, the other end of which I attached to a long slender piece of firewood standing on the ledge and leaning against the chimney wall. Thus, the chickens dangled close to the fire.

Afterward, there were fireworks on the river.

Jean immediately said, "You too must buy a mill." And he took me in the Allard around the countryside, to look at water mills and windmills.

But on the first tour of inspection of his new-found property—he did not exactly know that he had in fact acquired four houses, two others across the road as well as the two on the Indre—we discovered he in fact owned a house called "Francois Premier" with a fantastic cellarlike room with a dirt floor and wine press set in a cavity in the hillside rock. At the time one could barely see anything in there, all doors and windows being plugged with loose stones—a typical French custom when a house is abandoned.

I thought to myself: I will make mobiles of cobwebs and propel them with bats.

Calder's home in Saché

"I much prefer this to any mill we've seen," I said to Jean.

And Jean, who had bought a few things from me in the past years and who still owed me a bit, said, "I'll sell it to you for what I owe and you'll make me a few more mobiles."

We got a workbench brought into Jean's mill and I went to work—in front of a large window, wide open on the river Indre. Jean was writing a book upstairs and would occasionally come down impatiently to inspect my proposals.

Jean and I had agreed on what was to be done to Francois Premier—there was not a single door or window in condition, flooring was missing, a part of the attic had been badly burned some time before—and I left him to carry it out with his masons, plumbers, and carpenters. We went on to Brittany and spent a week or so with Ritou at La Roche Jaune, making several forays into the middle of Brittany and along the coast. We discovered a system by which one could go to a bistro for the drinks and bring what he wanted to eat with him. We even went as far as the Pointe

221

du Raz; naturally you could not see anything—there was too much fog.

During all this trip there was a postal strike and finally we got some frantic letters from mother and a neighbor, Mr. Quinn, who did not seem to know there was such a thing as a postal strike in France.

In the fall, I had received a letter from the girl who had written an article on me as her thesis at Vassar. She had had various adventures herself and was now married to an architect who was from and lived in Iraq. She had a young architect friend in Beirut who wanted me to make a mobile for the Middle East Airlines office there.

Beirut was the domicile of our dear friend Henri Seyrig. So I wrote him and said we would, as he had suggested, like to come and visit him. He was doubtful as to the financial arrangements with the architect, but Ellen Jawdat was sure things were O.K.

So early in January, we set out from Marseilles on a Greek steamer, the *Aurelia*. As usual, the girls took to their bunks. While we went through the Straits of Messina, we roused Sandra to come and see Stromboli, which seemed to erupt every seven minutes. When we dug Sandra out, she said:

"Has that earthquake gone by yet?"

We spent a rainy day in Athens and had ourselves photographed on the Acropolis. We spent the evening with Angelo Procopiou in a tavern where the walls were lined with vast casks of wine.

We touched Alexandria and wanted to take a cab there, but the cabbies started haggling over us. Finally, a policeman blew a whistle and selected the cab himself. We went to see ex-King Fuad's palace and a few such things, and you can have them: the worst *goût*—goo!

Then we touched at Limasol, where we bought some wonderful oranges, and finally reached Beirut.

Seyrig was on the dock, looking very much like a cop: he had a raincoat, bowler hat, and umbrella. He took us to his home, which was the Institut Français d'Archéologie.

April 14, 1965

3:00 p.m. to 4:00 p.m.

Arrived at his gate, we walked up a continuous set of steps, then another set, and came to an enormous room painted white. It had a high dome and at one end there was a colored glass window of very bold and strange design—nothing to do with any stained-glass window I had ever seen. It was composed of very large bits of glass, green, yellow, red, blue, perhaps purple. These colored pieces were interspersed with clear glass, so that we got a great deal of light through this window. I believe the room had been an open court which had been roofed in, for along each wall there were smaller rooms. Henri had lived here off and on, working on the ruins of the countryside, for twenty-five years.

We stayed a month or so, with Henri and his wife Miette. We took a week out and hired a car driven by a man named Mansour Mansour.

First Mansour started telling "joke stories" and when we countermanded that, he turned on the radio and we had to squelch him again. But he was pleasant.

Aleppo was our first goal. After leaving the coast, we passed through fields of newly sprouted wheat. We remarked that there were no fences and were told that a man, when his parents die, can inherit something like one single furrow two kilometers long.

As we went along, we saw in the distance a little village with conical domes on the houses. There was one dome over each room. When we got close to this village, we remarked that all façades facing south were painted a sort of powder blue; the other sides were just plain adobe. I am sure this was to reflect the heat.

The Aleppo souks, of course, were remarkable, with odors of spices and here and there a group of six or seven men crouching over a brazier, prodding the ashes with a tweezer, looking for embers so as better to warm their hands. Although the souks were on street level, they were built in such a way, one had the impression of being in a cellar—with the light coming from holes in the ceiling. Once in a while, we would be jostled violently and upon turning around we would discover it was a donkey with a large pack on his back.

From Aleppo we took a side trip to St. Simeon. This was several hours' drive in a Syrian taxi. (As our car was registered in Lebanon, we had to use a Syrian car when taking side trips in Syria. Mansour Mansour went with us as interpreter.) St. Simeon is the fantastic ruin of a Roman temple. We were far out in the country, with no trace of any inhabitants, and not far from the Turkish border.

The next day we drove south to Homs, and en route we passed two vast wooden water wheels eighty feet in diameter. From the racking noise that came out of their axles or hubs, they seemed to be tearing themselves apart. These were for irrigation. As we had been warned not to stay too far away from the car, we did not remain there very long.

223

The next day, we took another side trip to the "Krak des Chevaliers." This too was all by itself. It was a stone fortress, big enough to house four thousand men and their horses. It was complete with its dungeon, which must have been lethal, for there was a cold draft sweeping through it. And in the highest watchtower, where watchmen sat, there were two rows of seven little notches to accommodate some sort of a game with which the men on duty beguiled the long hours.

The following day was devoted to Palmyra.

Then we went to Baalbek. These ruins were in better preservation. What interested me most was one great piece of stone, a sort of obelisk, lying on its side on the incline, much larger than the Paris obelisk; it had been quarried, but never moved. It was a fine shape, with a slight taper.

Finally we went to Damascus. There we saw a tremendous mosque, lined with red rugs of all shades and brilliancies—this was right up my alley. Off to one side, within the vaulted room, was a small temple some fifteen to twenty feet square. Our guide said:

"Here is where the body of Saint John the Baptist is kept. His head is somewhere else."

Within the walls of Damascus were one or two wonderful mosques, with horizontal lines of white, orange, white, black, white, orange, and so on. We went into the caravansary—that was a great-domed building, with black-and-white lines throughout the interior.

While in Syria we often passed a military sentry, who would then blow a whistle and call us back, asking us if we had any arms, then letting us go. When we got back to Beirut, we discovered that Syria was in a state of siege.

In Beirut, I had a bout with the flu. Louisa had a touch of it too, but she recovered quickly. Our Alsatian doctor pulled me through and as recompense asked for a small mobile, such as I had made for Henri. A few days after our arrival in Beirut, I had been allotted a small room by the Middle East Airlines, in their new building. And with two planks across two wooden horses and a few borrowed tools, I set to work on the mobile. I had my pliers with me.

A little later, we flew to Bethlehem on the Arab side and had the Arab side of the case explained to us quite thoroughly by the guide.

We went to the Mount of Olives. There was a man who presented little olive-seed necklaces to the girls. I became rather flustered with the unusual type of currency and give him a tip which, as it later worked out, was worth fifteen dollars.

Immediately after that, the guide said:

"You should not have given anything to that man, but to this other one . . ."

And he was pointing at someone else.

There was a place in a church where Christ was supposed to have been. It was fantastic . . . the feeling of the place. Not exactly eerie, but decorated up to the hilt and—this time—in good taste. There were two stories underground, and they too were decorated up to the hilt with a vast array of bibelots—with a pleasant result.

We had left Lebanon by air for Jordan without a return visa. Twice we had sent somebody to see the Lebanese consul in Bethlehem to get our visa, but he was never on hand. So we flew back without a visa and almost had a bad time, but we managed to talk ourselves out of it.

April 17, 1965

11:00 a.m. to 12 noon

At the end of about a month, we said goodbye to everyone and flew back to Paris.

From Paris, we transshipped to a plane going to Marseilles. There was the mistral behind us and we did some rather funny antics in the air.

The mistral is a strange wind that follows the Rhone River toward the south, gets to the Mediterranean, and turns east toward Provence. It can blow three, six, or nine days and they say the judges have often been lenient with men who strangled their wives on the ninth day.

At the Marseilles airport, we were met by our faithful Citroën garage man. And shortly after our return to Aix, there was the carnaval. We sat on the terrace of the Deux Garçons, indifferently waiting to see what Aix would provide in the way of floats and in the way of a parade. Among us there was a man named Jean Perrier, a ceramist. Personally, I think that it is rather shocking to waste much money buying confetti, which is swept up the next day. But Perrier shocked me by purchasing a whole burlap bag full of confetti. However, we all profited from his gesture and had a very gay time.

There was also a fête foraine in Aix and I almost upset the machine that was supposed to skyrocket me into the air!

It was about at this time that we decided to move to Saché. A

227

"Long Nose"

"Spider"

"Big Spider"

great iron box was brought on a wagon and all our goods—except the mobiles—were put into it. Then we shipped it by rail and it was delivered to Saché by another wagon. It was amazing what came out of that box.

The plumber, Louis Ferry, had not quite finished with the drains and septic tank, and he and his helper would have beautiful *déjeuners* with the tablecloth on an upturned wheelbarrow, with a bottle of wine and everything else necessary. They even warmed their lunch containers on an open fire.

One day, I was fascinated to watch the young mason putting in the ceiling of the lower room. He was standing on a few planks over two wooden horses about five feet high. The horses were so high that he had to crouch. He was attired all in white—white duck suit, white hat, white espadrilles. He held his mortarboard in the left hand, his trowel in the right hand. He would duck even lower, send a trowelful against the ceiling, straighten up, and smear it flat. This went on for some time; it was a beautiful pantomime.

The dirt floor was leveled, covered with sand, and old tiles were carefully laid, each on a pat of cement. The chimney in the main room seemed a bit undistinguished, so I raised the level knee high, with big cut stones, profiting from my experience with the fireplace in Roxbury. Now few people are willing to believe that this is not an original part of the house—that is, several hundred years old.

All the stones had been removed from window holes and door holes. Doors and windows beautifully made were fitted in. The *remise*, or wagon shed, which had two sides open, had a low wall of cement blocks put up on the two open sides and then glass from there up.

In the spring of 1954—by that time we had a new house and studio in Saché—I had a show of thirteen *gouaches*, which I had made in Aix, at Zervos's office, *Cahiers d'Art*, rue du Dragon, Paris VI.

It was about this time that Louisa and Mary took the boat for New York at Le Havre. They were resolved to have a quiet voyage without striking up any acquaintances, but the second or third day they found it a bit dull and said to each other:

"How does Pop do it?"

One day I had a message from Ernesto Rogers, a Milan architect, saying he would be in Paris and would like to see me. I said I would meet him in Paris, with a car. So I drove from Saché.

It was a bright warm day, but I had on a heavy tweed jacket and a wool shirt. As I drove along toward Paris, somewhere after Chartres, I saw a sign indicating a village called "Auneau." I started making conjectures about this and decided:

"Oh! No! They shall not have me."

It seemed to be getting very warm and finally—in spite of my stepping on the gas—the car slowed down and came to a dead stop. I inspected under the hood. It seemed very hot there too. I finally discovered that one of the rubber water hoses, which had no fabric in it, had blown a hole. The motor had been running without its water jacket and it had seized. I was really stuck, and waved at every passing vehicle.

Finally, a little man in a little truck stopped. He had six feet of chain. He tied me right behind him and pulled me toward a friend, "a very good mechanic in the interior," he said. The chain was so short that I did not dare look aside to see where we were going and finally, of all places, we landed in:

"Oh! No!"

April 19, 1965

11:20 a.m. to 12:40 p.m.

Auneau was a very funny little village, with fake wooden Swiss chalets, all decorated and embellished.

I left the car with the mechanic, who seemed nice and who was going to repair it and call me. Then I worked my way to Paris by a system of buses and trains, which I cannot now remember. I finally found my friend Ernesto Rogers and brought him down to Saché by train and was sorry not to be able to show him Chartres, which I certainly would have if we'd come by car.

Ernesto was building labyrinths for the Milan Triennale, in which there were to be drawings by Saul Steinberg. He was also very anxious to have a mobile. I was just finishing one in my shop in the mill, so I confided that one to him. It hung in the middle of the labyrinth all summer and was finally bought by a Mr. Juckers, of Milan.

I followed Louisa and Mary a month later, while Sandra stayed on in France.

Previously, Curt Valentin had come to Aix with Douglas Cooper and Co. and we all had dinner together—it was the last time I saw him. He died in Italy later, in 1954.

In 1954, I received a letter from a young Indian woman who wrote me mentioning Jean Hélion, my good friend. She was Gira Sarabhai, youngest of eight children of a large wealthy family in Ahmedabad, which is somewhere halfway between Bombay and Delhi. She offered Louisa and me a trip to India, if I'd consent to

231

make some objects for her when there. I immediately replied yes. Then she asked when we would like to come and described the weather and a few events of interest.

The weather was propitious during the early months of the year and I had heard from her that on the fourteenth of January there was a national kite-flying festival, in which the participants try to saw off the kite string of the other fellow. It is quite a classic Indian tournament. Weeks before the event, the participants run their kite strings between telegraph poles and glue ground glass to them so that when their string crosses that of the opponent, they can agitate it violently and saw the opponent's kite loose. The day we were there the wind was very strong, so the kites were small and square, about eighteen inches across.

On our way to India we had stopped in Paris and in Rome for an hour. We found Dotty Kidder on the same plane, en route to Saigon. We split a bottle of Chianti, then we all got aboard the plane, Dotty in first and we in tourist. Louisa felt she would not sleep being pinched against me in her tourist seat, so Dotty gave her three pills, apparently telling her to take them all at once. Which done, Louisa began to squirm, more drugged than sleeping.

We stopped two days in Beirut to see the Seyrigs and show the Matter film about me at the American University. I was taking this film to show it to Gira. Louisa was still drugged by the three pills and could barely say goodbye when we left for India.

When we got to Bombay we were met by Kamalini, wife of Gautam, Gira's brother.

The first morning we spent procuring a liquor license for Louisa and me, because Bombay State was dry and visitors were only allowed two quarts a month. These two quarts arrived, sewed up in gunny sack, beautifully labeled, but two or three weeks later, in Ahmedabad. The beauty of the packaging, as well as the contents, made it worth while to have spent a morning getting the license.

Even our host felt a little ill and took some medicinally.

The afternoon of our arrival, we went to see the Elephanta Caves, which are on an island, real caves with the sculpture hacked out of the rock. It was very dark in there and I was very much surprised to hear a shrill voice call, "Calder!"

It was Ylla, the woman photographer, whom we'd known in Paris before. She was killed a year or two later, while photographing elephants from the back of a jeep.

The next day and night we went to Ahmedabad by train—it took some twelve hours. Kamalini brought us a water jug and some accouterments. We were in a first-class compartment, consisting of two lower and two upper berths, opposite each other; there was also a bathroom, at the other end. All the windows were barred, to keep the lower-class people out—a hangover from English days.

The other occupants of the car were an Indian couple, and the lady took the lower berth on one side and Louisa the other one. I expected the gentleman to get in the berth above his wife, but no, he got in the one above Louisa—so that he could eye his wife and I could not.

We arrived at Ahmedabad about seven the next morning, and Gira and a whole row of retainers had come to meet us. So we were off to Shahibag, the nineteen-acre garden of Gira's father, which comprises two palaces and two modern houses, designed by Gira, who had studied with Frank Lloyd Wright. We were assigned one of the modern houses, very simple in structure.

As they did not eat meat, Gira Sarabhai had hired a special cook for us, but I elected, and Louisa agreed, that we should eat what they did and with them instead of being isolated with our meat. This turned out to be the only reasonable solution, for it was very gay with Gira, Kamalini, and Gautam. I succeeded in enjoying their highly spiced food, but Louisa got tired of it.

There was a wall around the nineteen-acre garden of Shahibag and some twenty gardeners working on the garden, and at night there were watchmen every few hundred feet and one would ring a bell, then the next one would ring a bell, and every hour or so a gun would be fired into the air. Madame Sarabhai had worked with Gandhi and gone to prison while he was also imprisoned; Gira had even done six months. Apparently, the English asked her how much time she wanted to serve.

On the other hand, the father, Mr. Sarabhai, was a shrewd businessman, and he had great difficulty but finally succeeded in acknowledging the worth of a mobile.

"Gira and her family come to meet us"

Our little modern house worked very well, except that we demanded toilet paper, which was imported from Canada and finally plugged the small-gauge Indian pipes, which had to be dug out. This is because we did not follow the Indian custom of cleaning ourselves with a bowl of water and the left hand.

The curious thing about the Indians is that they eat with their right hand and do their washing with the left hand, but when they meet a stranger or friend, they advance toward him with their hands joined, as though in prayer.

I had a workbench in the garden, near where the cattle were tied. They milked their own cows; one was a water-buffalo lady and she had a calf, that one. And she would not give any milk to the milker till the calf had had some. She made a very funny noise when she called her calf—a sort of dry rattle.

In all, I produced eleven objects there, either working by myself or working in a blacksmith shop. In the blacksmith's shop, due to

233

some enthusiastic cooperation, I got burned on the base of my right thumb. Somebody smeared it with vaseline and I wrapped a handkerchief around it. When next I appeared at the table, I ate with my left hand and Gautam was horrified.

The Sarabhais were at great pains to entertain us and it was very pleasant.

One evening some shepherds came and danced with sticks on the the tennis court, in a square formation; there must have been sixteen of them.

Gira's aunt, who was a labor organizer, arranged that we should attend a festival of other shepherds, who lived some distance off. We went there about five in the evening and were met by someone who asked us to wait for the "official" greeting. Finally a great troupe of shepherds in brilliant red costumes marched out to meet us, to the rattle of drums. We were led back into a courtyard where there were masses of people, all in red.

We were seated upon a dais. There were various speeches. Then I was induced to make my speech about cattle raising in America —the differences about the use of the barns in the east, where the cattle are confined all winter, and the western system, where the cattle are left in relative liberty till they are taken to the milking room. Also the use of cow dung: in the east one is supposed to spread it right away; in the west they let it accumulate and fertilize the fields in the spring. This was contrary to the Indian system, where cow dung is conserved in patties on the sides of the houses and used as fuel.

As a matter of fact, during some picnic where we went to a pond with our host, we saw a woman and children with a basket, collecting dung. One of the children stood behind a cow with its tail raised in the air. He placed the basket under it and patiently waited to retrieve the dung.

Another use the Indians make of cow dung is for flooring. We saw an old house, belonging to the Sarabhais, which was quite handsome and which had floors of pounded cow dung.

We went several times to the calico factory of the Sarabhais, in the middle of Ahmedabad, over a high bridge, in the heart of the town. Standing on the bridge we could look down at the calico that had been freshly dyed, great varicolored bands, over six feet wide, spread out on the gravel over the dried-out river bed. It made quite a wonderful pattern of stripes.

During the winter, the river bed is very small and there is a great strip of sand on one side or the other. It all depends on luck, on where the river remains at the end of the monsoon. Sometimes they even have to transfer the electric power plant from one side to the other.

As we watched, a herd of water buffalo were led into the water. When they came out, a man with a loincloth came in. First of all, he scrubbed himself. And then he took a drink.

Near by there was a building where holy men lived. In the morning, they seemed to strangle themselves with a stick they introduced into their mouths. I don't know exactly what they were doing, picking at their teeth or prodding their throats, but they were supposed to cough up all the evil.

After three weeks in the guarded garden of Shahibag, and the producing of my eleven objects, we embarked on a tour of India, starting off with Gira, Kamalini, and Gautam. We went to Travancore to stay at a property by a cement mill which belonged to some friend of the Sarabhais. Incidentally, when well-to-do Indians travel, wherever possible they arrange to stay with friends and the friends of friends. The Sarabhais had many friends throughout India, in part on account of the industrial success of Mr. Sarabhai and the former backing of Gandhi by Mrs. Sarabhai.

At Travancore, we took a launch and went through a rustic canal, amid a few little huts and lots of trees. This way we traveled most of the day, and came to a town called Cachin. Here we stayed at a sort of summer hotel and the place was inundated with American tourists, a whole shipload of Americans. Their hats looked very funny—tourist hats.

The next day, we all piled into a big station wagon and went to a place called Pyrmid, which was an ancient hunting reserve of some prince, and we stayed in his hunting lodge.

We had come here to see elephants at liberty. As a matter of fact, the way our whole trip was devised was, Gira would bring out photos of this and that and say, "Do you want to see this or that?" So, in this unliterary manner, we chose our path—we chose it visually instead of through the words of some book. And we did see elephants. We went in a launch over an artificial lake, created some time previously as an irrigation project. It was very dramatic, with blackened trunks of dead trees which had been left standing. It looked as if they had been burned. The trees nevertheless stood erect, emerging from the waters, scattered here and there. One species of tree in particular had great flanges near the roots, so that it looked triangular.

We toured around in the launch and when we saw some elephants bathing at the distant edge of the water, the men shut off the motor and paddled as silently as they could. We must have gotten within a hundred yards of them. There were a dozen of them. Some were bathing, others were dust bathing; they take dust with their trunks and blow it on their backs.

We spent a day here and then Louisa and I took a plane for

Calcutta god

235

Madras, where we stayed with a large family, the Swaminathans, on an estate. We had come here to see a temple with a wonderful façade, and we also saw alongside it a small temple which was being engulfed by the sea. Most of it was out of the water, but the sea was advancing upon it.

In Madras, there is a certain theological seminary that has a banyan tree which must spread some two hundred feet across, because the hanging roots have come down and developed new trunks and this process continues.

Then we went north to see the Indian temple of Karnal. We stayed at another town, where we arrived by plane, and here we were joined by Padmanabhan, from now on called Paddy. He was secretary to Gautam, who kindly lent him to us for the trip. It was rather sad, but he always took the train the night before and met us at the airport with a car, making it very easy for us and difficult for him.

In the village we stopped at, we saw one of the "juggernaut cars" —a great heavy sort of circus float with wood sculptures and a great number of big, very heavy wheels. This is the thing they start rolling and occasionally throw themselves in front of, in a sort of religious frenzy, sometimes getting killed. A great mass of people push it.

From the station wagon, on the way to Karnal, we saw a wedding party traveling. They were afoot and carried all the cooking implements of the new family—pots, and even several large grindstones.

Paddy did not see this, because he was out on the other side of the car, photographing a beggar who was made up to represent the monkey god Hanuman. He had a tail four feet long that supported itself from within. At the end of a pole, he held a sort of leather balloon, covered with tin foil; his head was also plastered with tin foil, which is what we had noticed first in the distance. In the other hand, he held a water pail in which to carry his receipts.

Also on the way to Karnal, we passed through a village—all the houses were covered with rice designs on the outside: a white design on the adobe house.

Then, we went to Assam. The Naga Indians there are supposed to be quite fierce. We had a hell of a time trying to get some water to drink; we wanted boiled water, so whatever we got was always hot—we were afraid of drinking anything else.

In Calcutta, there were starving people sleeping in the streets, covered over with cloths. Cows and bulls were wandering around in the streets in search of fodder.

We were met by Lila Ray, whom I had met on the *Bremen* many years before. She took us off to Santiniketan, where she lived and which had been the town of Rabindranath Tagore, whom the people there kept on referring to as "The Poet."

It was terribly arid and poor. I had felt sympathy with the beggars before that, but upon our arrival at the station in Santiniketan, I saw a beggar who had had his arm hacked twice, as a small kid, I suppose, and whose hand was then turned upward. This disgusted me. But I guess the parents had done this to enable him to beg and that there are, for some, few other opportunities. However, this disgust continued.

After two days with Lila and her family, we returned to Calcutta, where Lila took us to visit the burning ghats by the riverside, where they dispose of the dead. We had already seen in Ahmedabad the funeral processions with five or six men abreast, carrying in their arms the corpse decked with flowers. Now, we saw them actually burning their dead. The oldest son is supposed to crack the skull, so that it will not float when thrown into the river.

In another town, we came near to the tower where the Parsis leave their dead to be devoured by the crows and vultures.

After Calcutta, we flew to Patna, where we stayed with a well-to-do gentleman, a friend of the Sarabhais. On the way to his house we saw them "throwing color," as they say. It is a religious festival where they throw at each other bright dyes, which I hope are not poisonous. And I saw a white horse with pink dots all over him.

At some places, we would come to spots in the road where the local people had brought out their seeds and beans to dry, on half the width of the pavement, and you had to be very careful not to run over these or the people. This was the dusty season and the people would dash across the road as we drove along, to get on the windward side and avoid breathing our dust.

The gentleman at Patna, as soon as he heard Louisa liked the horses' good-luck charms and the beads, rushed out and came back with a dozen necklaces for her.

From there, we flew to Katmandu, Nepal. We went directly north with Annapurna far ahead of us on one side and Everest on the other, in a corridor of snow. Then we turned west and started coming down over beautiful green hills and landed in Katmandu.

We stayed in a converted palace of modern design and were quite disturbed by all the disintegrating palaces surrounding us. There was one in particular, built out of wood, which had a thirty-degree slant over the street and seemed to be splintering.

We were interested to learn that outside the converted palace there are no toilets in Katmandu, and that the dogs alone keep the streets clean. This was impressed on us when we visited another town which had no dogs. We spent two nights in Katmandu, then back to our host in Patna. Thence, to Delhi.

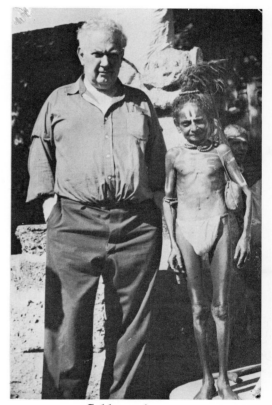

Calder and pygmy

237

I see no difference between New Delhi and Delhi, except that the English wanted to pretend that it was something new. The space consumed between their new buildings of state is idiotically . . . large. Two miles are often consumed going from one building to the other. There is a presumptuous statue in white marble, of I think George the Fifth, that looks like a baby in swaddling clothes. There is a little stream to go with it—they mean a fountain. But the Red Fort, built by the Indians long ago, is handsome from the outside.

We went to a mosque and there there was some stupid marble staircase on the outside and some guide insisted on giving us his services, repeating:

"All one piece. All one piece."

But Louisa said, "It is cracked."

Meaning two pieces.

In Patna, we had received a wire from Miss Paxton Haddow of the United States Information Service, asking me to bring the film on my work. I guess I did. She turned out to be very pleasant and showed us around . . . during these long distances between the Delhi government buildings.

While in Delhi, we took a side trip to Jaipur, which had to be approached by plane. I wanted to go there particularly, because somewhere I'd seen Noguchi's photographs of the astronomical installations of Jaipur. These are almost like large geometrical blocks of different shapes, in a sort of garden with a great staircase leading to the sky—it had been blocked off because of the suicides from the top end. As a matter of fact, the black-and-white of Noguchi's photographs was better than the actual thing.

There were also three palaces in Jaipur, built partly because a rajah thought one palace was haunted or something or other, so he built another. The mountains on one side of Jaipur made one think a dam could have been built and the waters caught from the monsoon. But neither the English nor the Indians seem to ever have thought of it.

There is a story about one rajah, of a few years ago, who was very hard with his people. When his peasants brought a cylindrical jar of grain, he turned it upside down and would only allot to the peasant the grain that could be stacked on the bottom. He was hated by the people and on his deathbed he said to his son, "Do something to make me less hated by the people."

And the son said, "Yes."

And so this new rajah, when the peasant brought his grain in his cylinder, emptied it and turned it on its side—and only the grain that remained on the top surface went to the peasant.

Before we first left Ahmedabad, Louisa and I had made an

Fishing nets of Travancore

overnight trip to Udaipur. That was one of the places I wanted to see. Here also were various palaces, in diminishing order, the oldest being the best. It consisted of a huge whitewashed block of blank walls three stories high, with windows above. In front of it there was a terrace with three circular bays for elephants to lie in. The walls tapered slightly as they went up. Inside, we finally came out into a patio at the top. Two or three old men were sleeping in the sun, and on one side were some strong boxes of wood with iron bands, padlocked. An armed sentry stood guard in front of these, because this was the rajah's treasure.

Off the patio, there were some small rooms with modest-sized windows of colored glass, red, blue, green, in geometrical designs —I liked these very much.

In the next palace, I think the rajah was still living. He had had paralysis as a child and was carried everywhere and remained quite small. His father had a beard that he brushed upward so that he appeared to have sideburns—somewhat like a skunk's tail. The present rajah had remained diminutive, so he covered the walls with tiger skins to cover up this defect.

I think he had just gotten up, because the guide, a tall young man with an orange turban and a bad throat that he cleared all the time, showed us the three bedrooms, with iron cots, blue, yellow, and green. He opened the door to one of the bathrooms beyond and said:

"All the same color."

We did not bother to see the other palace.

The last few days we spent in Bombay with Gira and Kamalini. Gira had transported to Bombay a number of the objects I had made, and about three days before our departure she organized an exhibit in some other person's back yard.

Gira had built the building where we stayed. We were on the top, the eleventh floor, with quite a view of Bombay. One could see a similar building going up near by; they had already arrived at the tenth floor. The cement would come up in a pushcart on an elevator and then be dealt out to a chain of some thirty women workers with baskets; they walked in file with the baskets in their hands and poured the cement out where it was desired, into the form.

I had not felt well during the hanging of the show, and the next morning I had a fever and then I had a row of doctors. The first one came to do a blood test, before I could even take aspirin. Then the most important doctor, the one who prescribes, ordered "three lakhs" of penicillin—about a million units. Then came a very husky man in white shorts and a white shirt with short sleeves, looking terribly athletic, his muscles bulging . . . it was he

The Calders and friendly elephant

239

who was to puncture me.

I had pneumonia.

The penicillin worked and I was able to catch the plane two days later.

However, I had not been able to attend the evening party arranged for the presentation of my film. The USIS man there said to Louisa:

"If he should recover, we'd like to meet him."

Before our trip to India, the same fellow had told Gira, who was inquiring whether they had any data on me:

"We have not, but if you find out anything, please let us know."

From India we flew back to Paris, but this time we went via Cairo and Athens. The view of the desert before we reached Egypt —arid, isolated—was terrific.

While on the ground in Cairo, I said to the stewardess, "Do we fly over any of the pyramids?"

She said, "Ask the pilot." When I saw the pilot, I asked him. In turn, he inquired, "Which side of the plane are you on?"

I told him and he circled three pyramids for us—two big ones and one small one.

Later, when we landed in Athens, I was in the cockpit with the pilot and I was amazed to see him take out a typewritten sheet —check list—with twenty-four items, and read each one and verify it in turn, before landing.

Curt's gallery had scheduled a show for me in the late spring of 1955, and there was a lot of pleading from his people to hold the show as scheduled, in spite of his death the previous year. It was to be a retrospective, but then they wanted things to be for sale. So I finally had the show and nothing came of it.

In the summer of 1955, Carlos Raúl Villanueva, of Caracas, arranged a show for me there. I had met him through Sert in 1951, and he came to Roxbury. I also saw him in 1952 in Paris. He had said then that he was doing an auditorium and wanted me to do something for the lobby, a mobile.

I said, "I'd rather be in the main hall."

And he said, "Oh! No! You can't do that because the ceiling is taken up with ribbons of acoustical reflectors."

I said, "Let us play with these acoustical reflectors." And I made him a sketch.

Carlos had engaged Bolt, Bereneck, and Newman, of Cambridge, Massachusetts, as acoustical engineers. I had to collaborate with them, and had to redraw the whole layout all over, once or twice, for Carlos. Newman kept saying:

"The more of your shapes, the merrier and the louder."

So we drew large round and oval shapes, some of them to be

Caracas: Aula Magna, University of Caracas. "I said: 'Let us play with these acoustical reflectors

thirty feet or so long, painted different colors, and hung from the ceiling on cables from winches. There were also some of these shapes on the side walls.

When John Foster Dulles attended the Tenth International something or other, he was photographed with a big black triangle on the end of his nose.

Apparently the acoustics are very successful.

I flew down to Caracas on the fifteenth of August, 1955, to set up a show that Villanueva had arranged for. I had sent quite a shipload of things ahead of me.

We were two hours late, because we flew around a tornado—that was the fifteenth. On the eighteenth, that very same tornado hit Connecticut. I cabled Louisa on a Saturday to see how things were and got no reply. Monday morning the papers said there were many dead in Connecticut and that Waterbury, twenty miles from Roxbury, had suffered $200,000 worth of damage. So, I was rather perturbed. I went to Carlos' house and we put in a call for Louisa. Then Señora Villanueva suggested that the American Embassy would know about Connecticut. Carlos and I went there, and they didn't know nothin'. So we went back to Carlos's and the call had gone through, carried by radio from Caracas to New York.

Margot Villanueva had given the phone to Francisco, their son, an M.I.T. graduate, but he'd been on a binge that night and did not click. Louisa thought I must be ill, because I did not come to the phone. This roused her so much that she wired the two girls in Saché to tell them that she was all right in Roxbury. And the girls, not having heard about the tornado and floods, wired back, asking why they had been sent a wire in the first place.

Louisa had intended coming down to Venezuela and we were planning to go up the Orinoco and the Gran Savana, but she wrote that the local disaster was too much for her to plan a trip just then, so instead I returned to Roxbury.

During my stay, Carlos had arranged for me to work in the metal shop of the university, and I made, among others, two large mobiles. In my show at the Museo de Bellas Artes, everything was sold, most of it right after the opening, and I even had to send some more objects to Caracas when I got home in Roxbury. It is the only time I witnessed a complete sellout of a whole show, and it was also in complete contrast to my last show at Valentin's gallery, after his death.

One of the larger mobiles I had made in Caracas was bought by some engineers who worked for Jiménez, the president-dictator. He placed this somewhere near his beach house. When he was chased out, the art authorities looked for this object and could not find it anywhere.

Caracas, August 1955. Calder and Carlos Raúl Villanueva

A large mobile hanging in the Universit

"The City": Caracas, Museo de Bella Artes (following spr

Could he have taken it with him into exile?

The other big object I had painted red, yellow, and blue. This caused a certain amount of consternation among my friends—I had painted it unwittingly in their national colors. So I substituted black for the blue, making it either German or Belgian, and everyone was happy.

Upon my return at Idlewild, I was met by Louisa, Sandra, and Mary—the girls had just returned from France. I was wearing a red shirt and had bought two native drums and a *cuarto*—halfway between a ukulele and a guitar—which I had seen played beautifully, down there. The customs agents were very much amused by my burden and the next time I went through Idlewild, they asked me if I had made any progress playing my instruments.

April 21, 1965

5:00 p.m. to 6:30 p.m.

Upon our return to Roxbury, we collected in the kitchen, as usual. Louisa said:

"Sandra wants to marry Jean."

I went over and kissed Sandra. She had not been back to Connecticut for two years and now she wanted to rush right back to France. So we put her on a plane, and Louisa and I arranged to follow within a month, leaving Mary in school at Putney.

In the meantime, one day Sandra received a telephone call from Jean. Nobody could quite recognize his voice and believe it was he. Till I got on and we laughed, and then it sounded like him. He had stuck his front teeth through his lower lip, smacking into a boar (oh! what a boar!) in the Alsfeld forest in Germany, at 100 m.p.h. in full night. Although reduced to a Volkswagen with a Porsche motor, which they had built for him in Stuttgart, he had caught the boar as it wandered from the city side of the forest to the state side.

We arrived in Saché a few days before the ceremony, which was very simple and direct. The proponents were on one side of a large table—in the *mairie* of Saché, on the village *place*, close to the old church—with the witnesses on either side: Louis Catillon and his wife. Opposite were the mayor, in his blue, white, and red scarf, flanked by his secretary and the *garde champêtre*. Louisa and I were at one end of the table; Jacques, Jean's brother, and Zabeth his wife were at the other end.

October 28, 1955. ". . . the ceremony was simple and direct." In front of the Saché Mairie: Sandra Calder and Jean Davidson after the marriage. Calder is behind Sandra and the Mayor is between Sandra and Jean

246

After a few simple questions and positive answers, the ceremony was over and we gathered at Bécheron, at Jacques's, for lunch. Looking at the bridegroom, I reflected:

"Two vague people who got together to lead a vaguer existence!"

And Jean laughed approvingly.

A few days later, we roasted a pig on an open fire at our house in Saché—François Premier. It is called that by the local people, though it probably has little to do with that king.

To prepare the bed for this pig, we went to the local blacksmith and dug out, among other objects, an old iron fence from a grave. Somewhat reluctantly, the blacksmith welded to this four legs and a long handle.

We had invited the mayor, his secretary, the postman, some local people, and a few friends from Paris, and it was rather gay, even though the mayor left when the dancing began.

Shortly afterward, Jean, Sandra, Louisa, and I set out in the 15 c.v. Citroën, first for Frankfurt, where I was to do a stabile for the American consulate. Then Sandra and Jean went on to Hamburg, where he was finishing his book: *L'Allemagne en Cage*— Caged Germany.

In Frankfurt we decided to stay at the Frankfurter Hof. This has an entrance on a strange little street which I cannot at all describe. It was drizzling as we approached the city, and we wandered around in the gloom until we discovered a white rubber policeman on top of a white rubber pedestal, in the middle of a traffic circle. He told us how to get there. We set out, and in twenty minutes we came face to face with the same policeman. He threw up his hands. I don't know how we got to that hotel.

I had gotten an introduction to a local architect, Hermann Mäckler, and he introduced me to Fries et Cie, Bridge Builders. Early one morning I took my stabile model to the plant to enlarge it, and got there before the men arrived. The installation was a long shop which ended out of doors. There were three traveling cranes, all on the same tracks, that went from one end of the building to the other and then continued out of doors. The three cranes had been set in an orderly fashion, side by side at the closed end of the shop. When they were deployed by the men, the artificial lights threw fantastic shadows on the ceiling overhead. This made me feel I could do a wonderful ballet in that shop, if they ever stopped working long enough and let me at it—I think I even suggested it to Mr. Fries.

In two more days my stabile was all cut and ground and ready to be welded. I communicated with the proper authorities at the United States embassy in Bonn, but they did not seem ready to receive the stabile. So, I asked to see Ambassador Conant, whom

Sandra and Jean on the steps of Bécheron, the former house of Jo Davidson

247

"The Hextoped"

I had met upon our arrival in Frankfurt, and that induced the proper authorities to proceed. We managed to obtain electric power of 380 volts to weld the "Hextoped" within a little court in the embassy.

Since, the "Hextoped" has been exhibited in Kassel, and it has now been promoted to the front lawn—I suppose they found it too complicated to get it back to its original setting.

Later on, we all found ourselves again in Saché, and Louisa and I took off shortly for New York and Roxbury. About this time, I was visited in New York and Roxbury by Arnold Rudlinger of the Kunsthalle in Basel. He had shown my things before, in Bern, with Léger. Now he wanted to have quite a show of me alone, in Basel. He selected quite a number of things and I made him some more afterward—so my objects went off to Basel.

Sometime after that, Louisa and I were close to sailing for France when I heard that one of my uncles in Philadelphia was very ill. I decided I'd go and see him.

The same day was the funeral of Patrick Sweeney, the father of James Sweeney. As Jim had come to my father's funeral, I thought it would be nice if I went to his father's funeral. I think the church was up Lexington Avenue.

Being unaccustomed to Catholicism and also to funerals, I arrived well in advance. After a while, two black limousines pulled up, James Sweeney and his family in one and Jack, his brother, and his wife in the other. The two men shook hands with me and then went into the church with their family. I followed at a little distance. They went down the aisle and filled up two front pews, I guess, leaving no room for me.

So I stood in the middle of the aisle, in my overcoat, and listened to proceedings, until a half hour later it was time for me to go. I had to leave in the middle of the service to catch my train. I had been unconscious of anybody behind me, but when I turned to go, I saw the church was almost full.

In the spring of 1956, Jean was the proud possessor of a 2 c.v. Citroën and undertook to drive me down to Basel so we could see the show. With eleven hours of almost airplane flight, but not quite, we got there at an average close to the maximum speed of the small machine. We had adopted little white masons' bags as traveling equipment proportional to a 2 c.v., and we ourselves made some crack about "carpetbaggers" when we got there.

Upon our arrival, Rudlinger was occupied, so we sat in the museum garden, apparently the only one of its kind in Basel. We sipped "Eagle" wine. We heard some strange fluttering coming from one window in the courtyard and went to investigate.

We found a battery of ten or twelve drummers, working on lumps of rubber, in preparation for next year's carnival! They are allowed real drums only the last month before the carnival and they do all their preliminary work on rubber. It must be quite frustrating—you've probably got to be Swiss to take this.

We even had the pleasure of meeting Meret Oppenheim, now married to a Swiss banker. In the old surrealist days she had come forth with a fur-lined teacup—a historical moment.

April 22, 1965

10:00 a.m. to 12:00 noon

On the way back from Basel to Saché, Jean and I stopped near Dijon. Right overhead, crisscrossing the highway at low altitude, four French acrojets were flying in gaily colored planes, almost wing-tip to wing-tip, in a square formation. They were inspired, and gave us a personal recital.

249

Gouaches *inside the Saché studio, 1964 (following pages)*

*Bob Osborn's letter to the Calders
celebrating the birth of Shawn Davidson
arrived in this envelope*

Shawn Davidson was born on the fourth of October, 1956. He is called Willy by preference by his mother, who started calling him "Willy Wee-Bits" right after birth.

As the time for Willy's arrival grew near, Jean and Sandra lined up the clinic in Tours. But Jean had not checked where it was located beforehand. Our friend Kika Nitzschke had come to witness this event.

On the night it did happen, Jean came over from the mill about 3:00 A.M. to say that things were stirring. As the 15 c.v. was balky at times, he next paid attention to that, with his mechanical insight. Then we all piled in, Sandra in front next to Jean, the rest of us in back.

I am afraid Sandra in pain was even saying, "Son of a bitch!"

We got to Tours in about twenty minutes, because Jean knew that road; then fortunately we found two cops who knew where the clinic was and how to get there.

The nurse told Sandra how to breathe, according to the Russian system of allegedly painless birth—it seemed to help a bit, along with the injection. After two or three hours, the doctor arrived and the baby was born shortly. As he was a big boy in rather tight quarters, he'd been compressed, and his arms and legs were blue and his head and sex were scarlet.

To go up to the delivery room to see the baby, we had to take an elevator. It carried the letters MM for *monte-malades,* meaning to take up the sick people. I remarked to Jean that these people were optimists, for there was not any DD for *descend-décédés*— dead people go down.

When we returned to the house next morning, we discovered we had left all the lights on, thus celebrating in advance the happy event.

Also celebrating Shawn's birth, Bob Osborn sent us a fine letter.

Shawn was soon called "The Captain," because Jean used to leap at him and cry:

"Are you Captain Willy Wee-Bits?"

In the summer of 1957, we again went to see Ritou at La Roche Jaune, and we talked about that house at the mouth of the river where it was reputed the lady kept her husband padlocked to the iron bed because he had a ladylove in the area. Her husband was now dead and there were rumors that she wanted to sell the house. So, Jean and I set out to reconnoiter. We came down a very steep narrow gulley in the 2 c.v. and discovered a young man cultivating his potatoes. He turned out to be deaf and dumb. Nothing dismayed, we had a long conversation with him, and he pantomimed for us the descent of the airplanes and bombs that had caved in part of the house prior to the Normandy landing. His pantomime was fantastic: he'd raise his hands out high into the air, then he'd bring them down, gradually crouching to the ground —his mouth remaining open at all times.

This was the son of the house, Yves. We finally got to the door and were told to come in, and found the elderly lady in bed in an alcove, current in Brittany, with a heavy bag of sand on her stomach because there was a pain there.

Well, she finally admitted that she would like to sell and we went to see the notary, Le Carvenec, to settle the transfer.

Upon our first entry into the house, I saw Jean throwing the remains of the iron bed into the river.

In the meantime we had the building, which had been demolished by the aircraft, rebuilt. Its rafters had been burned by the occupants as firewood. We also had the house fixed up with plumbing and electricity. Although the lady did not have electricity, there were eleven cement electric poles leading to the house from the nearest transformer. This had been done as part of the postwar electrification campaign.

In May 1959, before leaving Roxbury for Saché, I had shipped five or six big objects to Rio, for we were invited to go back there in September 1959. I was to have an exhibition at the new Museo de Arte Moderna, built by Alfonso Reidy.

Eventually we flew to Rio, direct from Paris, and spent a wonderful month in the Gloria Hotel on the waterfront, in the middle of Rio. Our visit coincided with the arrival of a group of art critics and museum directors, invited by Mario Pedrosa to come and see the new museum, which was not quite finished, and also to go to Brazilia and see those wonders.

We were there a few days ahead and got the jump on them, so in Brazilia, we had Oscar Niemeyer all to ourselves. He drove us around and some of the architecture was quite fantastic. But the whole project was unequal, because the dwellings were not done with such majesty as the buildings of state, and although we did not visit the insides, I have my doubts. Even the hotel where we stayed had a solid wall of glass bull's-eyes, as I call them, which made the corridor excessively hot.

Niemeyer and I discussed a project for me to do a mobile for a big marble-paved arena between buildings. He wanted to know whether I could do the whole thing in two months and ship it down.

In February 1960, we returned to Rio, to really see what the carnival was like, and I flew out again to Brazilia, this time carrying a little model of what I wanted to do for this city. Niemeyer took the model and was going to show it to the president and get his agreement. I have never heard from Niemeyer, or of the object, since.

Facing the sea, from the mouth of the Tréguier River, Sandy and Louisa's house in Brittany, "Le Palud"

253

All this while, Aimé Maeght, my Paris dealer, was always asking for something new—some *nouveauté*. He asked me:

"Picasso has rooms he keeps locked; why don't you?"

Of course, I did not have quite enough real estate.

But it so happens that Eliot Noyes, the architect, once came to me and wanted a certain stabile—"The Black Beast." It was at the time the biggest thing I'd ever made—eleven feet long by nine feet high, but in fairly light material. Noyes's interest encouraged me to have it done in heavy material, that is, one-quarter-inch iron plate. This, furthermore, encouraged me to do other things as well in heavy material and also supplied some funds with which to do so.

So, I decided to have a show at Klaus Perls's, of fairly large

"The Black Beast"

stabiles, in the winter of 1958. We sold three of these, which made things seem to glisten.

In the winter of 1959, I sent the remainder of the Perls show to Paris with quite a number of other objects. I had a show of about ten large stabiles at Maeght's in February 1959. Madame Maeght, who was a great enthusiast for these objects, was quite surprised and said to me:

"*Tu as du te râcler la cervelle pour trouver ça?*" (You must have picked your brains to find this?)

Maeght must have agreed with Gigitte, because he bought the whole show, outright, before the opening, the first time a dealer had done this to me!

After the show at Maeght's, I had another show in New York, at Perls's, where there was "The City," a large stabile with a little mobile element in its center. Carlos Villanueva saw this and got it for the Museo de Bellas Artes in Caracas.

The following winter, I had still another show at Perls's, little more than two large objects. One of these was a stabile painted red, called "The Crab." Sweeney got this for Houston; he is director of the modern art museum there. The other, "Clouds over the Mountains," eventually went to the Chicago Art Institute.

On its way to Houston, "The Crab" was packed in a truck, between blankets, very carefully, and then nothing was heard of it for some time: it had disappeared. Finally it showed up in Houston, in another truck, piled any old way, as building material; the blankets were neatly folded up in one corner. Sweeney was very angry, and to prove his point took a photograph of the elements on one side and the blankets on the other.

What really had happened was that the original truck driver had heard that someone in his family was ill. While en route to Houston he had detoured for home and parked the truck on his front lawn. Why they transferred the things to another truck, I have never heard.

Upon receipt of some new red paint from New York, Sweeney felt better.

When we proposed to return to Rio for the *Carnaval*, Louisa and I, my mother objected. She said:

"The first time you went to Rio [in 1948], Mrs. James died, and if you go again, I may die."

But we went anyway and actually she died shortly after our return—at the age of ninety-three and a half.

When I embarked on stabiles and heavier objects, following Noyes's purchase of "The Black Beast," I often worked in several metal shops at the same time. In 1958, I had three metal shops

255

Gouache, 1956

"Heads and Tail" at the Biémont factory in Tours

"Lollipops"
Saché, 1964. Calder at work

"The Whirling Ear" at the Brussel's Fair

working for me, two in Waterbury and one, ten miles away, in Watertown. I got a sense of being a big businessman as I drove from one to another.

In one shop, I was making the head of the object for UNESCO, "The Spiral"; in another shop, I was making the forty-five-foot mobile for Idlewild; in Watertown, in the third, I was making "The Whirling Ear" for the Brussels Fair. It is still in Brussels, a gift of the United States.

In the Waterbury Ironworks, I was aided by Chippy Ieronimo, and in the other Waterbury shop, by Carmen Segree. I say I was aided, but actually I took the place of the helper and worked under their direction, keeping my eye open to achieve the desired result.

A helper I was, except for using the sledge. Chippy tried me out once and our hammers met in mid-air—so he kicked me out of that job.

Calder and Chippy Ieronimo

May 4, 1965

9:30 a.m. to 11:00 a.m.

Finally the mobile for Idlewild was painted and ready. It was properly wrapped because it was to be stored in an old wooden shed on the outskirts of the airport, a building dating from World War I.

I rode down with the truck and was present as it was stored away. I don't know the reason for the delay—perhaps the building was not ready to receive it—but I finally urged them to put it up in August 1958. Chippy, my faithful blacksmith, wanted a vacation and I wanted him to be there for the hanging.

The mobile for UNESCO was shipped to Paris in the spring of 1958, and the main S-hook was placed in a shipping crate with two boxes of black paint. When we came to put the object up, the S-hook, which joined the two largest members of the head, was lacking and we had some trouble finding the box, because the paint was called "Japalac" and had been stored with Noguchi's material —he was doing a Japanese garden in the background.

258

"The Spiral in front of UNESCO"

The Kennedy Airport mobile installed

"The Whirling Ear" was installed, without mishap, in a pond next to the U. S. pavilion at the Brussels Fair. During its manufacture, I was talking with a young Scotch engineer. I asked him to cut the original speed of 2 r.p.m. to 1 r.p.m., and he said:

"Then you'll no be calling it 'The Whirling Ear.'"

In the autumn of 1961, on our way to Le Havre in a Citroën that we were taking along with us to Roxbury, we stopped in Normandy to see Pierre Tal Coat, the painter, and his family. He had an old *prieuré*—priory—with a more recent, very large and high barn.

Hundreds of canvases were standing on the floor, leaning one against the other at right angles, giving the impression that if one searched out the key pin and yanked it out, everything would go flat.

But the size of the studio gnawed at me the moment I saw it, and I became very jealous. So, after our arrival in Roxbury, I immediately wrote Jean at the Moulin Vert, in Saché, asking to have a big studio built as soon as possible.

Jean used to go hunting occasionally with Louis Catillon and their ill-assorted dogs—Flet, a little squirt, and Tibby, a retired Labrador. One day they had taken me along, just for the exercise.

On the hillside which had a fine view, we had come to a cabbage patch, and Flet signaled a rabbit. So the gangsters stood, one at each side, and bumped off the poor beastie when it came out. Shortly afterward, it started to rain and I went home.

But this was the spot, approximately, we decided upon for the new studio. So Jean had the hill hollowed out and bulldozed into a promontory, which lies in front of the shop. It dominates the Indre Valley, at Saché. And I kept sending, from Roxbury, little drawings on typewriter paper, describing what it would be nice to achieve.

The next spring when we arrived in Saché, the ground was all prepared, all the parcels of land having been acquired. Some of them were only a few furrows wide. There were fourteen different owners within the building area.

"In eighteen months the building was finished"

*Calder by "The Guillotine for Eight"
in the large Saché studio*

"Tamanoir" in front of the Saché studio

Finally, we had to make a bigger drawing and then get a technician to submit it to the building authorities. However, we did not wait for the authorization to begin.

In eighteen months, the building was finished.

I had already asked the Galerie Maeght the precise height of their ceiling several times before. But just to reassure myself, I did it again in the spring of 1962, while the big studio overlooking Saché was being completed. I was dismayed upon being told that the ceiling was about to be lowered, for before that I had made a large "Spider"—which is now in the Basel Museum—and this object would just clear the gallery as it was, and I wanted to do more objects at least that size. But now, Maeght was going to put in a fancy lighting system that would eat up some of the height.

I said, "The hell with this," and cast around for some place out of doors, where the sky would be my ceiling. I modestly chose the square paved court of the Louvre.

To do things for such a show, I had to have a shop, somewhat similar to those in Waterbury. So Jean and I got in the 2 c.v. and inquired about the biggest ironworks in Tours, some fifteen miles from Saché. It turned out to be an establishment called Royer. We were pleasantly received by a man in an elegant jacket, and as we'd taken a model along, we had something to talk about. But Royer et Cie were not interested and kindly directed us through to the Etablissements Biémont.

Biémont were located in some very old, decrepit buildings, but they had the proper men and equipment and they undertook to enlarge my models. All I had to do was have enough nerve to tell them how big I wanted them.

The Saché studio was soon filled

This can be very dangerous, for in addition to having something that won't fit anywhere, that won't even clear the road, you can easily have an enormous bill to take care of. But you are apt to end up with something worth while.

However, Biémont—their three bosses, some dozen technicians and draftsmen, and their dozens of metalworkers—undertook to produce eight objects for me while I went off to America.

Around December 1962, I heard from Jean that things were ready to be reinforced and braced with ribs and gussets and anything else I could invent. So, in the middle of January 1963, I left Roxbury and flew over to France, during a very cold spell. I had a bad grippe, right off the plane, and had penicillin for breakfast, lunch, and dinner.

As soon as Dr. Révérend, the Azay-le-Rideau doctor, got me on my feet, I was at it again, working in the freezing factory buildings of Biémont. I wore as many as three heavy red wool shirts, one on top of the other, and called them my "tarpaulins," which surprised the Biémont directors and workers, as well.

It is a little difficult at first to get the workmen to understand just what you want. The sympathy seems to be there already, but it takes some repetition to make the hard curves of the silhouette of the objects. When a plate seems flimsy, I put a rib on it, and if the relation between two plates is not rigid, I put a gusset between them—that is, a triangular piece, butting in to both surfaces.

Finally, the men know pretty much what I want and it is a question of a little higher or lower for the reinforcements—that I have to decide.

In a month or so, six of the Biémont objects were transported to Saché and set up in the "big studio." These included "Spiny Top and Curly Bottom," "Thin Ribs," "The Guillotine for Eight," "Cèpe," "Triangles," and "Le Guichet."

But hurray, Maeght did not mess up his ceiling. He realized finally, on his own, that the proposed lighting system would spoil his rooms which are so fine. So in November 1963, I had a show there with two big objects, one of which had been set up outside the Saché studio, on the promontory. These were "Le Tamanoir" —The Anteater—(the outside object), and "Triangles."

We also had "Cèpe" and "Spiny Top" and two other new objects. This would have been a wonderful *vernissage*, except that about 5:00 P.M. Maeght came in and said he heard there had been an assassination attempt on President Kennedy.

As we drove out to Camille Renaud's—Big Boy—to dinner, where we had invited some one hundred people, we heard Kennedy had died. Louisa took it so much to heart that she did not stay and went home to the hotel, but I remained with the guests.

The Biémont factory assembling "Tamanoir"

"Triangles" in the Saché studio

This time, we had intended staying the whole year round in France. And so, when Christmas came, we induced our daughter Mary, the younger one, who was now married to Howard Rower —they have two little boys—to fly over and spend the holiday with us. This was a very hectic period, for we had one set of visitors for Christmas and a relay of visitors for the New Year's— very much like the present system of American football.

About four or five years before this, I had heard from Harvey Arnason, who had just become connected with the Guggenheim Museum, that he'd like to arrange a show for me.

I had made several projects for things to hang in the Guggenheim Museum, when Sweeney was there. But, as I understood, Mr. Harry Guggenheim had said, "There will be nothing hanging from that dome."

I never knew whether it was because the dome was too flimsy, or whether it was because he did not like Sweeney.

However, Arnason raised my expectations, although I had never thought much of the building anyway, and I started thinking in terms of a Guggenheim show again.

For two years there was silence; then Arnason wrote and said they were having people designing coins and would I please do a penny.

I wrote and told him I thought this was somewhat of a comedown.

A year later Tom Messer took up the cry and came to see us in Saché, with Remi, his wife. He came in April 1964, and we chose a lot of things to send from Saché to New York, to the Guggenheim, such as "The Guillotine for Eight," "Bucéphale," and many other objects.

I even undid an old bale of wire I had had in storage since 1929, and took out "Spring," a seven-foot wire lady, and Romulus and Remus and an eleven-foot she-wolf in wire. I'd always thought these particularly humorous, but now they looked like good sculpture—after thirty-five years in the closet.

In all, there were fifteen large and heavy cases, five of which were devoted to the "Guillotine."

To be on the spot while things were brewing, I decided it would be good to go home. So, we left the last of May and immediately set ourselves up in Roxbury.

In spite of the previous trouble with Mr. Guggenheim, I proceeded to make a long trailing mobile to hang in that ice-cream cone of a building, and I managed to keep the weight down to 225 pounds, although "The Ghost"—as we called it—was about thirty by thirty-five feet.

This was later bought by the Museum of Art in Philadelphia,

November 20, 1964. "The Ghost" over "The Guillotine for Eight" at the Guggenheim

where my grandfather had done the William Penn on the top of City Hall and my father had done the Logan Square fountain. So now they say that they have "the Father, the Son, and the Unholy Ghost," or words to that effect.

Five or six years ago, I was called into Wally Harrison's office to meet some Brandeis University people.

Before that, a certain lady had gotten James Sweeney to call me up, saying that she was coming to visit my Roxbury studio—but I never saw hide nor hair of the lady till later on.

I arrived at Harrison's and was introduced to Dr. Sacher and Mrs. Steinberg, the missing lady.

Harrison was designing buildings for Brandeis and he wanted some of my sculpture. Sacher did not seem to know anything of my kind of work. But there happened to be two or three models of my mobiles—good ones—in Wally's own office, under his desk, and I dug them out and presented them. Dr. Sacher looked as though I'd slipped him a bitter pill. So, there was nothing doing.

A year or two later, some jury at Brandeis gave an award, and together with Edgard Varèse and Louise Bogan and a playwright whose name escapes me, we were led upon the carpet to receive awards from Dr. Sacher. As he looked up and saw me, he said:

"I see we have some grade B material."

My reply, which I only hit on next day—usually, mostly by striving, I get there on time—was:

"Better a Busy B than a Horse's A."

During the ensuing year, I had a letter or two from Mrs. Steinberg, asking me to remember this noble award and if ever I were called upon for credentials, to mention it and thus plug Brandeis.

The next fall, I had the opportunity to do so. I had an award from Art in America and I told them these awards are becoming harder to get. Then, I plugged Brandeis and Dr. Sacher—B for Brandeis and A for Sacher.

The Guggenheim show opened in early November 1964, and about the tenth of December the French offspring arrived with their offspring to see the show and see their cousins for Christmas, in Roxbury. Mary and Howie and their two boys came out from New York to spend the holidays, and cousins met cousins again—Holton and Alexander Rower met Shawn and Andrea Davidson.

The first evening Shawn, who is still nicknamed Willy, was very tired from pasting everybody with snowballs. On Christmas Eve, we had the usual party with lots of neighbors coming in. The festivities continued until the fifth of January, 1965, when we of the French department set sail on the *France* for Saché. As usual, I was about six months ahead of my next show, scheduled for July 1 at the Musée d'Art Moderne, Paris.

270

"All in Roxbury for Christmas 1964."
Left to right: Howie Rower with Alexander,
Sandy Calder, Louisa with Holton, Mary
Calder Rower, Andrea Davidson, Sandra
Calder Davidson, Jean Davidson
and son Shawn

At the Guggenheim, there had been few large stabiles and many very small objects suitable for children to bat and crush. To this, I attribute my success. My fan mail is enormous—everybody is under six.

To remedy this situation, this time we hope to have many large stabiles of the dreadnought variety, and mobiles hung out of reach —this may raise the age limit.

To achieve this, I have been constantly running over to Tours to see how my babies are coming along.

Moulin Vert, Saché (Indre-et-Loire), May 22, 1965

271

"…'Deux Disques'—too big to put inside—was erected on the sidewalk by the entrance" Paris, July 1, 1965.

POSTSCRIPT

March 15, 1966

10:30 a.m. to 11:25 a.m.

Finally the first of July, 1965, arrived and I was consecrated one hundred days—somewhat like Napoleon—by the Musée d'Art Moderne in Paris. I was quite touched to see an American flag by the *tricolore* over the avenue du Président Wilson.

Maurice Besset, who assisted Jean Cassou at the time, had done a fine job of the installation. My steel babies from Biémont, weighing from three to five tons, practically touched the ceiling between the light troughs.

The biggest object was "Deux Disques"—too big to put inside, so it was erected on the sidewalk by the entrance. Buses with visitors stopped and people got out to have their pictures taken in groups under the stabile; others took pictures of the object at various angles.

As compared to the previous Guggenheim show, I liked the predominance of the big stabiles in the long hall, although there was no such effect as "The Ghost," hanging from the ice-cream cone, over the "Guillotine."

In January, before leaving New York for Saché and Paris, I had an interview with I. M. Pei. He apparently wanted a large stabile for his building at the Massachusetts Institute of Technology. So, I had that to think about on my return to Saché—as well as my opening at the Musée d'Art Moderne.

I made one model. Feeling it was too dumpy, I made another model, more attenuated, and sent that one to Pei in New York. While they (M.I.T.) were sitting on the model, I was already being bombarded with instructions to get to work. I finally got it back.

And Mr. Brault, the Biémont foreman, built a similar maquette, twice the size of mine, but with all the final elements represented to the last bolt, and also the reinforcing ribs. This was necessary, because the final object was to be forty feet high and had to be dismantled in sections so it could be packed in boxes which could travel on the French railroad. (See Veterans of World War I about 40 and 8.) Before it was shipped to Le Havre and Boston, I had to see it erected to know whether it worked. The erection was achieved in two days with the aid of a fifty-foot crane. Every part fell into place perfectly, bolt for bolt, as on the working model.

273

Show at the Musée d'Art Moderne (following pages)

There was a lot of to-do about the August vacations, which are famous and paralyzing in France. But I urged Biémont along and they put about fifteen men on the job—they went fishing another day.

I also hastened the shipping of "The Big Sail" to Cambridge, hoping to put it up in the fall of 1965. It weighed twenty-five tons, including a ton of bolts. But there were protestations from the powers that be, that the ground would be frozen too hard (to receive a proper base), and from the students too . . . because, of course, I had to play to a gallery and I am still racking my mind for a grandstand play.

Louisa and I followed "The Big Sail" to America, in the middle of October 1965.

In the meantime Gordon Bunshaft, the architect, had picked out an object for Lincoln Center, which was presented by Howard Lippman, my favorite "amateur." Before putting it together, we went out one evening with Klaus Perls to a new restaurant somewhere west of Ninth Avenue, and as we drove across and then south, Louisa saw some big building and she cried out:

"What the hell is that?"

"That" was Lincoln Center.

When we did put "Le Guichet" up in Lincoln Center, I asked for a crane and plenty of men. The crane was hardly as big as the object, so it could not be used. But there were ten men and finally they put it up by hand.

My daughter Mary brought her two boys, Holton and Alexander, on the pretext that they were going to see "Grandpa at work." When we got home, Holton came out with:

"Grandpa was not doing anything!"

Upon our return to Roxbury, I found a prickly-pearish-looking model that I had made the previous year. I took it to Chippy Ieronimo and asked him to blow it up, allowing myself to make it quite large. This was finally delivered to Roxbury from Waterbury just before Christmas, and I decided to leave it coated in red lead.

Louisa calls it "Shiva"—it has so many arms and legs.

We went through the usual struggle of Christmas and the New Year, then the *France* was off to warmer climates—we took the *United States* to return to Saché.

Louisa has a friend, Elizabeth Wolff, who claims she is a reincarnated witch—she lived in 1200 and was very nasty to her slaves. I think they did her in finally. She was very curious about France and asked if she could come. So we brought her along. Sandra and Jean met us at Le Havre with two cars and drove us home to Saché—the weather was balmy. The next day it snowed, and it was very cold till Elizabeth left. Next time, I hope she'll come in the middle of summer.

On February 18, 1966, I had a show of *gouaches* at the Galerie Maeght. To embellish this a bit, I applied the old formula stated by Gigitte Maeght—I scratched my head and came up with some tall black pyramidal shapes with mobile festoons on their heads. They are made out of steel, and their tops of aluminum. For these I took the name

TOTEMS

CHRONOLOGY

1898   (July 22) Born in Lawnton, Pennsylvania.

1902   Poses for "Man Cub" by father, Alexander Stirling Calder.

1905–10 Calder family moves West, first to Arizona, then to Pasadena, California, because of father's health.

1910–12 (Fall) Calder family returns to New York, first to Croton-on-Hudson, then to Spuyten Duyvil.

1913–15 Calder family in California, first in San Francisco, then in Berkeley; father is Acting Chief of Sculpture for San Francisco Fair of 1915.

1915   Calder family returns to New York City.

1915   Enters Stevens Institute of Technology, Hoboken, New Jersey.

1918   (Fall) Joins Students' Army Training Corps, Naval Section (at Stevens).

1919   Graduates with M.E. degree from Stevens Institute of Technology.

1919–22 Holds miscellaneous jobs as draftsman, engineer, insurance company investigator, etc., in New Jersey, New York, Missouri, Ohio, West Virginia.

1922   (June) Signs on *H. F. Alexander* as fireman, from New York to San Francisco. Holds jobs as timekeeper, later draftsman, in West Coast logging camps during following year.

1923   (Fall) Enters Art Students League, New York, where he studies for two years.
Takes first job as artist, making single-line drawings for the *National Police Gazette*.

1925   Receives commission to decorate A. G. Spalding's Fifth Avenue sports equipment store, New York.

1926   Embellishes humpty-dumpty circus made by Philadelphia toy company.

1926   (June) Sails to Hull, England, on freighter *Galileo*, painting ship eight hours a day; continues on to London and Paris.

1926   Studies at Grande Chaumière, Paris.

1926   France–New York–France round trip on Holland-America Line, sketching life on board for advertising brochure.

1926   Studio in rue Daguerre, Paris; creates animals in wood and wire.

1926	Creates objects for Salon des Humoristes, Paris.
1926	Decides to make complete circus of his own; increases output of toys and animated wire sculptures.
1927	(Fall) Returns to United States.
1928	(February) Exhibit of wire sculptures (first show), Weyhe Gallery, New York.
1928	Exhibit of wire sculptures ("Romulus and Remus"), Salon des Indépendants, New York.
1928	(Fall) Commission for wire sculpture received through Batten, Barton, Durstine & Osborn.
1928	(Fall) Returns to Paris; takes studio in rue Cels; meets Pascin.
1928	Participates in group exhibit, Salon de l'Araignée, Paris.
1929	(January 25: opening) Exhibit, Galerie Billet, Paris.
1929	(Spring) Exhibit of wire sculpture ("Romulus and Remus"), French Salon des Indépendants, Paris.
1929	(Spring) Exhibit of wood sculpture, Weyhe Gallery, New York.
1929	(April 1: opening) Exhibit, Gallery Neumann und Nierendorf, Berlin.
1929	Keystone movie short feature on Calder in his studio, Paris.
1929	(June) Returns to United States. Meets Louisa James (future wife) aboard ship *De Grasse*.
1929	(Summer) Presents circus in Elizabeth Hawes's showroom, New York.
1929	(December) Exhibit of wood sculpture, paintings, toys, jewelry, 56th Street Gallery, New York.
1929	Presents circus at home of Mrs. Aline Bernstein, New York.
1930	Exhibit, Contemporary Art Gallery, Harvard University, Cambridge, Massachusetts.
1930	(March) Returns to Paris; takes studio at 7 Villa Brune.
1930	(Summer) Presents circus at Villa Brune apartment.
1930	(Fall) Begins experiments in abstract art, as result of visit to Mondrian's apartment-studio. Meets, through Varèse, Painlévé, Kiesler, Mondrian, Van Doesburg, Léger, Carl Einstein, Le Corbusier.
1930	(Fall) Joins Abstraction-Création group in Paris.
1930	(December) Returns to United States.
1930	Experiments with stone sculpture.

1931	(January 17) Marries Louisa James in Concord, Massachusetts.
	Returns, with wife, to Paris and 7 Villa Brune.
1931	Illustrates Monroe Wheeler's *Les Fables d'Aesope*.
1931	(Spring) Exhibit of stabiles (see below), Galerie Percier, Paris.
1931	Participates in exhibit by Abstraction-Création group, Porte de Versailles, Paris.
1931	Rents house at 14 rue de la Colonie, Paris, while subletting studio at Villa Brune.
1931	(Summer) To Majorca, with Louisa, for vacation.
1932	(April) First exhibit of mobiles—so named by Marcel Duchamp—Galerie Vignon, Paris. Term "stabiles" invented at this time, by Jean Arp.
1932	Presents circus several times at Villa Brune studio during this period.
1932	(May-September) Visits, with wife, in United States.
1932	Exhibit, Julien Levy's Madison Avenue Gallery, New York.
1932	Exhibit, Stockbridge, Massachusetts.
1932	(August-September) Returns, with Louisa, to Paris via Spain, visiting Joan Miró and presenting circus for Mirós and neighbors.
1933	(Spring) Group exhibit (Arp, Calder, Hélion, Miró, Pevsner, Seligmann), Galerie Pierre, Paris.
1933	Exhibit, Pierre Colle Galerie, Paris.
1933	(June) Returns, with wife, to United States.
1933	(Summer) Buys home in Roxbury, Connecticut. Makes studio of old icehouse.
1934	(Spring) Participates in New York City art exposition. Museum of Modern Art, New York, purchases one item.
1934	(Spring) Exhibit, Matisse Gallery, New York. (Exhibits here every year but one until 1943.)
1935	(March) Exhibit, first at Renaissance Art Society, University of Chicago, then at Arts Club, Chicago. Presents circus several times in Chicago.
1935	(April 20) Daughter Sandra born.
1936	Exhibit, Matisse Gallery, New York.
1936	Exhibit, Vassar College, Poughkeepsie, New York.
1937	(May) Returns to Paris, with wife and daughter.
1937	Makes mercury fountain for Spanish pavilion at World's Fair in Paris.

1937–38 (Winter) Rents flat in London, for self and family, and studio in Camden Town. Presents circus in London.

1938 (February) Exhibit, Freddy Mayor's Gallery, London.

1938 (Early spring) Returns, with family, to United States. Time divided between New York apartment and Roxbury home.

1938 (Fall) Retrospective, Smith Museum, Springfield, Massachusetts.

1938 Builds big studio at Roxbury.

1939 (May 25) Daughter Mary born.

1939 Wins plexiglass contest prize.

1939 Commission for water ballet for New York Edison Company exhibit at New York World's Fair. Ballet not constructed.

1941 or Water ballet for General Motors Technical Center
1942 near Detroit, Michigan.

1940 Lecture—only one—at Yale University, New Haven, Connecticut.

1940 Exhibit, Matisse Gallery, New York.

1940 (Fall) Exhibit of jewelry, Marian Willard Gallery, New York.

1941 (December 8: opening) Exhibit of jewelry, Marian Willard Gallery, New York.

1942 on Studies civilian camouflage, occupational therapy, etc., as part of war effort.

1943 Devises "constellations" art form.

1943 (Fall) Exhibit of jewelry, Arts Club, Chicago.

1943 (Fall) Fire at Roxbury home destroys old workshop.

1943 (Fall) Exhibit, Museum of Modern Art, New York (until January 1944). Museum makes film on the exhibit).

1944 (Spring) Gives mobile to Museum of Western Art, Moscow.

1944 (Spring) Presents circus in benefit performance for France Forever, Washington, D. C. Exhibit, offices of France Forever, Washington, D. C.

1944 Illustrates *Three Young Rats,* book of rhymes compiled by James Johnson Sweeney.

1944 (Fall) Exhibit of original drawings for *Three Young Rats* and mobiles cast in bronze, Buchholz Gallery, New York.

1945	(January) Father, Alexander Stirling Calder, dies.
1946	(October 25: opening) Exhibit of large and small mobiles, (Galerie Carré), Paris.
1947	Exhibit (with Léger), Bern, Switzerland.
1948 and later	Film on Calder produced by Burgess Meredith with Herbert Matter as photographer.
1948	(Summer) Travels, with wife, to Brazil. Children left in Berkeley, California, with sister.
1948	(Summer) Exhibit, Ministerio do Educação, Rio de Janeiro.
1948	(Summer) Exhibit, Museo de Arte, São Paulo.
1950	(Spring to September) With wife and daughters, visits France, Finland, Sweden.
1950	(June) Exhibit of mobiles, Galerie Maeght, Paris.
1950	(December) Exhibit, Massachusetts Institute of Technology, Cambridge, Massachusetts.
1950	Exhibit, Gallery of Contemporary Arts, Washington, D. C.
1952	(Spring) Goes to Paris to do sets for Henri Pichette's play *Nucléa*.
1952	(June) Represented in Venice Biennale. Wins prize.
1952	(September) Tours West Germany at invitation of State Department of Germany.
1953	(Spring) With wife and daughter sails to France for year in Aix-en-Provence. Concentrates on *gouache*. Makes four mobiles for outdoors. Buys house in Saché.
1954	(January) With wife and daughters, goes to Lebanon for one month to carry out commission for mobile for Middle East Airlines office in Beirut. Visits Henri Seyrig.
1954	(Spring) Exhibit of *gouaches* at Zervos's office. Cahiers d'Art, Paris.
1954	(Spring) Wife and daughter Mary return to United States. Calder follows one month later.
1954–55	(Winter) With wife, goes to India at invitation of Gira Sarabhai, for whom Calder makes mobiles. Stops at American University en route to show film by Herbert Matter. Has informal exhibit and film showing in Bombay.
1955	(Spring) Retrospective, Curt Valentin Gallery (year after Valentin's death), New York.

1955	(Summer) Exhibit, Museo de Bellas Artes, Caracas, Venezuela. All items in exhibit are sold.
1955	Daughter Sandra marries Jean Davidson in Saché, France.
1955	Creates stabile for American Consulate building in Frankfurt, Germany.
1956	(Spring) Exhibit, Basel, Switzerland.
1956	(October 4) First grandchild, Shawn Davidson, born at Tours, France.
1957	Visits Ritou Bac at La Roche Jaune, Côtes-du-Nord, and buys house.
1958	Creates mobile "The Whirling Ear" for Brussels Fair.
1958	(Spring) Creates mobile "The Spiral" for UNESCO building, Paris.
1958	(August) Creates mobile (".125") for Idlewild International Airport, New York.
1958	(Winter) Exhibit of large stabiles, Klaus Perls Galleries, New York.
1959	(February) Exhibit of large stabiles, Galerie Maeght, Paris. Entire exhibit bought by Calder's Paris dealer (Maeght) before opening of exhibit.
1959	(September) Exhibit, new Museo de Arte Moderna, Rio de Janeiro.
1959	Exhibit, Klaus Perls Galleries, New York.
1960	(March) Mother (Mrs. Alexander Stirling Calder) dies.
1960	Exhibit, Klaus Perls Galleries, New York.
1961	(April 4) Daughter Mary marries Howard Rower.
1962	New studio built at Saché.
1963	(November) Exhibit of large mobiles, Galerie Maeght, Paris.
1964	(November) Exhibit, Guggenheim Museum, New York.
1965	(July 1: opening) Exhibit, Musée d'Art Moderne, Paris.
1965	Creates large stabile for Massachusetts Institute of Technology, Cambridge, Massachusetts.
1965	"Le Guichet" (1963) is purchased for Lincoln Center for the Performing Arts, New York.
1966	(February 8: opening) Exhibit of *gouaches,* Galerie Maeght, Paris.
1966	(March) Exhibit of *gouaches,* Klaus Perls Galleries, New York.

Credits

Thanks are due to the Museum of Modern Art in New York for permission to reproduce *Black Widow* (Collection, Mrs. Simon Guggenheim Fund), and to the following for photographs reproduced on the pages mentioned:

Paolo Gasparini	Pages 241-3
P. E. Guerrero	Pages 65, 88-9, 102, 192 (top and bottom), 271, facing pages 256, 225
Hugo P. Herdig	Page 159
Kurt Hopp	Page 248
Peter A. Juley	Page 81
André Kertesz	Pages 83 (bottom), 104-5
Ubrich Mack	Facing page 161
Herbert Matter	Page 166, facing page 65
Hans Namuth	Frontispiece, pages 260-1, 286-7, facing pages 64, 160, 193
Agnes Varda	Page 210
Marc Vaux	Pages 120, 127

We are also grateful to the Perls Galleries in New York, The Pennsylvania Academy of the Fine Arts in Philadelphia, and Gallerie Maeght in Paris for their assistance in gathering some of the material in this book.